Insights on the Book from Industry Experts and Academicians

This new leadership book, co-authored by one of the leading exponents of value-based leadership education in India and an excellent young researcher in the field of communications, is a must-read for all thoughtful organisational leaders everywhere who dream of bringing about significant transformations in their organisations and societies. This remarkable book offers readers an integrative frame of reference in designing their mindsets as they increasingly face uncertainties and complexities due to unprecedented challenges of technological disruptions, global arbitrages, environmental sustainability, ethical transparency and demographic shifts. It is evident that these uncertainties and complexities can no longer be overcome by techniques and paradigms espoused in popular leadership books. Learning to lead tomorrow's organisations involves broadening of values and competencies with an understanding of a holistic societal context, which this book outlines with wonderful cogency. Leaders of world-class organisations need to make their organisations 'as open as the sky' as well as 'closed as a caring nest'. There lies the secret art of transforming managers into leaders of tomorrow. Each chapter of this book contributes to this transformative theme by integrating age-old elixirs of wisdom with powerful pragmatism by triggering much-needed nuances of self-reflection, self-confidence and balancing of multiple perspectives. This unique and spirited contribution fills a much-needed gap in contemporary leadership literature.

Professor Samir Ranjan Chatterjee
Emeritus Professor,
Curtin Business School, Perth

I am indeed delighted to know that two of my former colleagues at the Indian Institute of Management Calcutta (IIM Calcutta) have written the book titled *The Art of Leading in a Borderless World*. The book is a welcome addition to the literature in the area of leadership. Most books on leadership have been written by researchers with academic training in organisational behaviour or strategy or sociology or psychology. But the authors of this book have had a very different academic background that they have capitalised on to give a very different perspective on the subject. The senior author is an expert in Indology and Sanskrit while the other is a scholar in English and Communications. Together they have come out with a book that has, to my mind, given a new and very valuable dimension to the field of leadership. They have brought ideas from ancient writings that are unlikely to be read by management scholars. Business organisations around the world are increasingly recognising that alignment of their strategic goals with the well-being of current and future social, economic and environmental integrity is no longer an option but an imperative. This book will be of great help in this direction.

Professor Shekhar Chaudhuri
Former Director and Professor of Strategic Management,
Indian Institute of Management Calcutta

In their new and thought-provoking book, *The Art of Leading in a Borderless World*, Professors Bhatta and Rath provide us with a wide-ranging and integrative reflection on the nature of leadership in a diverse and often divided world. Their use of history, literature, religion, philosophy and mythology as sources offer a fresh vantage point that will help readers recognise not only the necessity but the value of inclusive leadership, and to acquire the essential re-framing of our perspectives that allow us to apply this insight. Rather than dry, mechanistic frameworks and axioms, their book provides inspiration, exemplars and a new paradigm for leaders at all levels.

Dr Mary C. Gentile
Creator/Director, Giving Voice to Values
Darden School of Business, University of Virginia,
Charlottesville, Virginia

I believe that leadership knowledge is contextual and not universal, and even if it travels across borders, those who act on it need to be sensitive to local cultural values and social institutions. As a consequence, I have long been an advocate of the need to de-centre leadership knowledge from its Eurocentric (or US) roots. This book re-centres the knowledge it presents by building on the rich knowledge traditions of India and offers contextually relevant advice for leaders who want to achieve excellence in a borderless world by drawing on the leadership qualities displayed by great leaders over different periods in India's history.

Professor Abhoy K. Ojha
Organizational Behavior and Human Resource Management,
Indian Institute of Management Bangalore

The authors have adopted an inspired and thoughtful approach to leadership, which attempts to transcend boundaries of all sorts and re-establishes a focus on the responsibility of those leading to be servant-leaders. Readers will be provided and often confronted with new ways of thinking about the responsibilities of leadership and better appreciating the relationship between those who would lead and those who would willingly follow.

Professor Barry Z. Posner
Co-author, *The Leadership Challenge*
Accolti Professor of Leadership, Department of Management & Entrepreneurship, Leavey School of Business, Santa Clara University

All societies and nations are in need of inspirational leadership. This book is a valuable and in-depth contemplation on what that leadership should be. It emphasises the importance of values in forging such leadership. It also takes into account the diversity inherent in societies, and the need for leadership to be culturally rooted. The book is very useful reading for all those, especially the young, who are aspiring to become leaders in a borderless world where there are common concerns for all humankind.

Pavan K. Varma
Author, *Adi Shankaracharya*

At a time when the world is caught up in identity politics that are deeply conflicting and polarising, this is an important book that emphasises the need for a value-based and inclusive leadership model. A book to read and reflect upon in our troubled times.

Rajdeep Sardesai
Consulting Editor, TV Today Network

To my mind, the compelling attraction of the book is its effort at inclusivity. The combinations of texts, philosophies, events are uncanny and generate food for thought and even debates within the minds of the reader. The authors argue for the responsible awareness of present actions because they have the potential for shaping the future (future of human ethos, environment and business sustenance). The book contains very useful and practical insights for leaders on the concept of living together socially, environmentally and religiously besides equipping them with inclusive communication. The level of expertise in this outstanding book is academically instilled, but the content is expressly designed for general readers as well.

Harsh Vardhan Shringla
Foreign Secretary,
Government of India

The contemporary world is interconnected, borderless and multidimensional in nature. Leadership in such an environment of heterogeneity and plurality is a new challenge. This requires dealing with multivariable dialectical processes and providing new creative solutions to complex problems of society and human development. Further, it also needs a new approach to leadership based on non-violence. Such a leader creates a new vision rooted in higher-order purpose of existence (HOPE) and inspires and motivates others to achieve it. This book, *The Art of Leading in a Borderless World*, is a unique effort in offering us a new perspective on leadership in the contemporary world.

Dr Subhash Sharma
Author, *Management in New Age*
Western Windows Eastern Doors

Panduranga Bhatta and Pragyan Rath have taken an unconventional route to discover 'from-the-excluded' virtues and leadership practices, valuable lessons for sustainable and ethical governance in business and politics. They have drawn leadership values of a humble learner-leader from nearly 2,500 years of history and expanded them through the lives and words of the Dalai Lama, Dr Abdul Kalam and several others. Professor Panduranga Bhatta's passionate research and application from Indology to the business world had brought alive history to the realms of leadership for public sector managers in Leadership Excellence programmes of Indian Institute of Management Calcutta. This book is valuable documentation of the authors' research and teaching and will significantly contribute to leadership dialogues for new age managers and leaders.

Professor Ananta Agasthya
Former Dean,
HAL Management Academy

As change keeps happening, there is always a quest for what constitutes good leadership. This book explores models of such leadership under the interesting title of *The Art of Leading in a Borderless World*, drawing from both the oriental and occidental ethos. I am particularly happy that the book draws from Indian narratives, both from the role models (Ashoka, Swami Vivekananda, Gandhi, Abdul Kalam) and literature (Mahabharata, *Arthashastra*, *Kadambari* and Kalidasa's works). Some of the ideas are very powerful like the 'excluded' being a focus for humanitarian leadership, caring for nature, universal welfare and many more. The book attempts to raise fundamental questions including 'Is there any need for a leader?', reflections which will bring in leadership values not limited by borders.

Professor G. Raghuram
Director and Professor of Public Policy,
Indian Institute of Management Bangalore

This book is an attempt to understand leadership that enables the human race to attain a higher level of good accomplishment. The whole notion of a leader being a value mutation agent, a person who changes the way of thinking of the world, is intriguing. Yet this is what humanity ultimately strives for.

The authors, who are well-known scholars in Indian values and ethics and emerging fields like visual communications, delve deep into the contributions of real and mythical leaders to bring out their point. It is a must-read for a person developing himself/herself into such an ethical transformational leader, and develop others as well on these lines.

Professor S. Manikutty
Business Policy and Strategy Area, Indian Institute of Management Ahmedabad (Retd.)
Co-author, *The Essence of Leadership: Explorations from Literature*

The *Art of Leading in a Borderless World* is a timely and important book of relevance both for South Asia and for the world. Professors C. Panduranga Bhatta and Pragyan Rath put forth a well-documented, cogent call for economic and political leadership based on ancient, but ever more relevant, South Asian ethical values of tolerance, diversity, reverence for life and non-violence. The book shows how these values consistently emerge in Indian traditions and writings dating back more than 3,000 years to the time of the Mahabharata through the transformative polity of Ashoka the Great up through the teachings of Mahatma Gandhi. In a globalised world confronted with growing social, environmental and political challenges, the authors, citing contemporary examples and cases, convincingly argue that in the long run, only leadership inspired by these timeless ethical values will succeed.

Bruce Rich
Author, *To Uphold the World: A Call for a New Global Ethic from Ancient India*

This book views leadership as a social function. Its central argument is that every action of leaders impacts the future. Leaders inherit and create legacies (human ethos, environment and business sustenance) beyond their intentions or conscious knowledge. The authors provide useful practical insights for leaders and organisations to be socially concerned, compassionate, generous, inclusive, ethical and humane. The authors evoke inscriptions, writings, speeches and interviews of great leaders and emphasise three pillars of inclusion—environmental, religious and human. The combinations of texts, philosophies, events and binary confrontations are engaging and thought-provoking for any reader.

Professor Srikant M. Datar
Arthur Lowes Dickinson Professor of
Business Administration, Harvard Business School,
Co-author, *Rethinking the MBA: Business Schools at a Crossroads*

Panduranga Bhatta and Pragyan Rath's book on leadership is very timely and seeks to bring newer perspectives to the issues of leadership. They bring out a central message that 'borderless world requires leaders who are naturally inclined to a borderless (all-inclusive) thinking'. The uniqueness of the book lies in its ability to draw copiously from the ancient Indian wisdom and blend it seamlessly with the thinking and perspectives of some of the greatest contemporary leaders. Serious contemplation of the ideas presented in the book will pave the way for creating new leaders who can take the complex world of business, government and society into the future with confidence and conviction.

Professor B. Mahadevan
Operations Management Area,
Indian Institute of Management Bangalore

This is a must-read book for leaders and will guide them in the right direction in this era of digital disruptions. The highlight of this book is that it covers various aspects of leadership right from the kingship of the ancient Indian literature to the present world of leadership conscientiousness. The book also discusses the importance of caring for nature so that nature can take care of us. It discusses the ancient concept of universal welfare as a guiding principle for leadership, which is the need of the hour. This book will help leaders in adapting creative ways that will increase the understanding among various ethnic, racial, cultural and religious groups but also promote social welfare, economic development and care for the well-being of the planet as a whole.

Nitin Anand
Vice-Chairman and Chair of Executive Council,
Skyline University College, University City of Sharjah

This book goes through various leadership models from the ancient times till recent past and highlights the role of a leader as a value mutation agent, as a guardian and as a custodian of human values. It speaks of leaders who inspire and influence beyond the borders. Authors have discussed

Kautilya, Ashoka, Mahatma Gandhi, Vivekananda, the Dalai Lama and Jackson who have mutated human thinking and have impacted the world. They stress the need for religious pluralism and inclusive approach, '*vasudhaiva kutumbakam*' (the world is a family), and narrate with ample examples that universal welfare is corporate welfare. Both the authors with their profound knowledge in Indian ethos, Indian history and global outlook have stressed the need for positive mutation required in every leader.

Harish, K.
Chairman,
Vagdevi Vilas Institutions

Successful global leaders should have strategies for guiding and empowering a diversified workforce operating in different areas having different culture and distinct local needs. Such leadership essentially involves inclusiveness without which it can never achieve its desired goal. Diversity and inclusiveness have to work hand in hand for the best results. I hope that this book authored by the two celebrated professors of Indian Institute of Management Calcutta, Panduranga Bhatta and Pragyan Rath, will be widely read by not only the students of leadership theories but also by others who practise leadership in their own area of activity.

Gautam Mohan Chakraborti
Kolkata Police Commissioner (Retd.)

This book is set to redefine leadership as a function that will bring about the transformation of human values and virtues to enable individuals of the society to co-exist as a whole rather than following a mundane unidirectional existence. It further looks into the excluded elements in this process. It traces the journey of historical leaders and how their virtues can be mapped onto a modern contemporary day leader. A vignette of the life of Ashoka the Great who was a voracious leader, always in search for more supremacy and triumph, but it took a huge bloody massacre to instil in him what he has lost and whether all of the bloodshed was truly essential? I believe that the true quintessence of humanity should be an amalgamation of compassion, love and forgiveness.

Alokananda Roy
An exponent of Indian classical dance,
a reformer of souls and a mother

This book redefines 'leadership' from a unique and distinct angle of vision, and enlightens present and would-be leaders of the world to focus on interrelated and inclusive humanitarianism. The book contains a series of intelligent case studies along with sumptuous illustrations which reveals the wisdom, prudence, wit and wide networking of knowledge and information of its scholarly authors. What I feel, in unison with the authors, is that today's global leaders are required to evaluate human values, in different work-fields carrying human interests, on the perspective of 'borderless' human welfare, to create an environment of grand harmony among everything for the survival of humankind.

Manish Gourisaria
Managing Director,
Lion India

Firstly, I would like to extend my heartfelt gratitude to Professors Panduranga Bhatta and Pragyan Rath for coming up with this book, which I feel is the need of the hour in today's leadership world. In each and every chapter, the book very elegantly maps the learnings from the bygone days for the modern-day and aspiring leaders. Climate change has already proven the world is borderless, so it is in everyone's well-being that we start prioritising on real value creation for the society and the world. This book is one of your go-to tools to push you in that direction.

Swaminathan Ganesan
Founder and CEO,
Smartail Pvt. Ltd

The inclusions in this book will impress and attract practising and aspirant leaders globally. A true borderless asset.

Aslam Sherieff J.
Chief Growth Officer,
Smartail Pvt. Ltd

This book is a must-read for all middle- and senior-level executives, especially those working in large professional organisations. The authors provide powerful yet easy-to-digest content that compels readers to rethink the leadership theories and propositions so that the essence is quickly internalised. The book also provides enough practical ideas and supplies many important insights for leaders to be successful in spite of challenging circumstances and in bringing changes that transform their organisation, which are the primary tasks of a leader. In sum, this book is a definitive guide for today's potential and growing leaders to gain the right ideas and move in the right path for developing themselves in the quest of taking their organisation to even greater heights.

Dr Kaushik Bhattacharya
General Manager (HR),
Steel Authority of India Limited

THE ART OF LEADING IN A BORDERLESS WORLD

THE ART OF LEADING IN A BORDERLESS WORLD

C. Panduranga Bhatta
Pragyan Rath

BLOOMSBURY
NEW DELHI • LONDON • OXFORD • NEW YORK • SYDNEY

BLOOMSBURY INDIA
Bloomsbury Publishing India Pvt. Ltd
Second Floor, LSC Building No. 4, DDA Complex, Pocket C – 6 & 7,
Vasant Kunj New Delhi 110070

BLOOMSBURY, BLOOMSBURY INDIA and the Diana logo are trademarks of Bloomsbury Publishing Plc

This edition published in 2020

ISBN: HB: 978-9-3898-6719-0; eBook: 978-9-3898-6721-3

2 4 6 8 10 9 7 5 3 1

Typeset in Manipal Technologies Limited
Printed and bound in India by Replika Press Pvt. Ltd.

CONTENTS

LIST OF TABLES AND FIGURES

Tables

Figures

FOREWORD

Leadership has never been more challenging than it is today because human society itself is going through a transformative period when we find ourselves precariously poised between a disappearing past and an indeterminate future. In this context, it is vitally important to formulate an individual and corporate value system that would incorporate the wisdom, both of the East and the West. Professor Bhatta and Professor Rath, both involved with the Indian Institute of Management Calcutta, have made a commendable effort to do this.

The authors have produced a truly interesting book on the whole theory and practice of leadership. They have attempted to integrate a broad spectrum of disciplines—ancient and modern, theoretical and practical, fictional and real life. This illustrates the concept of leadership from various angles and presents new insights into the contemporary challenges of leadership at every level based firmly on widely accepted human values and religious/spiritual insights. Their book *The Art of Leading in a Borderless World* contains many creative ideas and thought-provoking concepts that will, I am sure, be widely appreciated. The chapter on religious pluralism is of special significance for a multireligious country like India.

Dr Karan Singh
Indian Cultural Ambassador

ACKNOWLEDGEMENTS

We started this book project in 2011–2012 during the golden jubilee celebrations of the Indian Institute of Management Calcutta (IIM Calcutta). We owe a lot to many organisations and people for inspiring, encouraging and supporting us during this decade-long book-writing journey.

We express our deep gratitude to all the batches of postgraduate students of IIM Calcutta, both Indian and exchange students, under Student Exchange Programme (STEP) and Confederation of European Management Schools (CEMS), for providing valuable feedback on the course 'Leadership Excellence: Insights from Indian Ethos', which was popularly referred to by them as 'Ethos'.

IIM Calcutta had launched management development programmes under titles such as Responsible Leadership, Leadership Excellence, Organisational Excellence Through Leadership, Educational Leadership Excellence and Leadership Excellence: An Alternate Approach. These programmes were offered not only at IIM Calcutta but also at various locations in India, USA, Europe, Middle East, Japan, Mauritius, Australia, Nepal, Bhutan, Bangladesh, Thailand and Malaysia in the form of workshops, lectures, seminars, symposia, conferences and in-company programmes for more than two decades. We thank all the participants of these programmes who enriched our knowledge through their insightful feedback. We also thank all the CEOs, MDs and heads of public and private sector organisations who frequently organised these programmes for their company executives.

We are grateful to Professor Shekhar Chaudhuri, former director of IIM Calcutta, for extending continuous and unstinted support to our innovative courses and programmes during his directorship of more than a decade. We sincerely thank Professor Saibal Chattopadhyay, former director of IIM Calcutta, for supporting our academic activities.

We profusely thank Dr Karan Singh, Indian cultural ambassador, for taking some time out of his busy schedule to write a foreword to our book with great care, love and enthusiasm.

We sincerely thank all the eminent personalities from different walks of life for sharing their precious time in reading the draft of this book and for providing valuable blurbs.

We express our sincere gratitude to Praveen Tiwari, Publisher, professional and academic, Bloomsbury Publishing India Pvt. Ltd for publishing this book so elegantly with dedication and enthusiasm.

I, Pragyan, personally also thank Dr C. Panduranga Bhatta, who has been the tenacious, never-giving-up force, and who disrupted all disruptions to the production process of the book. He is the spirit behind this book. Thank you for introducing me to this field and for also appreciating and including my European critical theory expertise, corporate communication aptitude and stylisation into this melting pot of inter-sectional, inter-cultural and multi-perspectival endeavour on leadership and what it can be or has been. And above all, thanks to my parents and my sister who helped me imagine a brave world with brave people, brave behaviours and brave thoughts. I owe my imagination to their bravery!

I, Panduranga, sincerely appreciate the rigorous research done by Dr Pragyan Rath in her specialised areas and for applying them into the book wherever needed. But for her tremendous cooperation despite a heavy academic schedule of IIM Calcutta, the book would not have taken the present shape. I remain grateful to her for continuously giving valuable suggestions for improving the content and format of the book. I would like to express my gratitude to Honourable Harsh Vardhan Shringla, Indian ambassador to Thailand (2014–2016), for showing extraordinary concern and helping and encouraging me when I was deputed to ICCR chair professor at Silpakorn University, Bangkok. I would like to thank my older son, Abhijit, for his timely suggestions while writing the book, which helped in fine-tuning certain sections and chapters. I sincerely thank my wife, Shobha, and my younger son, Patanjali, for their immense patience and support throughout the writing of this book.

Dr C. Panduranga Bhatta and Dr Pragyan Rath

I

Is There Any Need for a Leader?

Raja Kalasya Karanam
(The ruler is undoubtedly the maker of the age)
—The Mahabharata

Why Do We Need a Leader?

When Michel Foucault, the celebrated French thinker, wrote 'What Is an Author?', he was redefining the author—it was no more a person but a function of a social system, a system that *needed* such criteria of recognition.[1] Foucault was also establishing 'the manner in which the text points to the author—"figure"'.[2] We do a selective survey of the manner in which various historically relevant Eastern and Western sources have not only pointed to the leader figure but heralded a pattern for the understanding of the function of a leader that manifests itself in contemporary management scenarios—the leader as a social function and leadership as corporate activity today.

The social function evolves with the theory of kingship as elucidated in ancient treatises on polity. The birth of a leader is not shrouded in mystery and it can be very well understood by looking at the origin of kingship: the purpose, the method and the code of conduct for the king, the law that confers power on the king to maintain the rule of law, and the directives for the exercise of power. Particularly, the ancient Indian texts on polity sum up the origin of the ruler (king) through the mythical and also the contractual views. Mythologies *apparently* depicted the ruler as almost god-like with unquestioned authority that can never be taken for granted. This deification of the leader (ruler) perhaps leaves no room for democratic values. On the other hand, the contractual angle traced the origin of the leader (ruler) to a primitive social contract. Here the leader (ruler) is regarded by a social consensus as essential to maintaining law and order in the society. In either case, the king (leader) has been conferred upon with extraordinary power corroborating the social status of kingship (leadership).

We are interested in rediscovering the purpose, reason and necessity of bestowing *this* extraordinary status and power to the function of kingship through either the means of mythology or social agreement for the simple reason that we want to understand the social need for a leader. In sum, we want to re-examine the birth of the need of a leader.

Let us look at one of the *oldest* texts on the need of a king (leader). The *Aitareya Brahmana*, a noted Indian scripture from the pre-Christian era, reveals the indispensability of having a king through an interesting mythological story: once upon a time, the gods and demons were fighting in the world. They battled in the eastern direction; the demons defeated the gods. They then battled in the southern direction; the demons defeated the gods again. Then, they battled in the western direction; the demons defeated the gods again. They battled in the northern direction but still the gods could not win. The gods thought that it was on account of their having no kings that the demons defeated them repeatedly. It was proposed that they should elect a king. Everyone agreed and elected Soma as their king. Led by their king, Soma, the gods were victorious in all directions.[3] The mythological storytelling tradition about the need for a king continued in the popularly quoted Indian epic, the Mahabharata. The epic describes a time known as 'the golden age'—a period when everyone was acting according to the law (dharma) on their own accord. Hence, there was no necessity for anyone to act as a leader to compel obedience to the laws. The Mahabharata gives a vivid account of 'the golden age' that required no ruler to enforce governance.[4] There was neither the kingdom nor the king, neither any punishment nor any guilty to be punished. People were acting according to dharma and thereby protecting one another. There were mutual cooperation and protection. Society was free from the evils arising from selfishness and exploitation by individuals. The sanction that enforced such implicit obedience to dharma was the faith of the people in it as also the fear of incurring divine displeasure if dharma was violated.

The Mahabharata itself also narrates the deterioration of 'the golden age'. The happy state of 'the golden age' did not last long. There arose much confusion among people in their duties of mutual protection. They lost their sense of obligation to each other. Then, greed arrived—people desired to possess what they did not own.

Unrestrained in their appetites and driven only by their greed, people indulged in violence under the misconception that one might flourish at the cost of the other, and there was anarchy. People failed to discriminate between what was right and what was wrong. While the faith in the efficacy and utility of dharma, the belief in god and the god-fearing attitude continued to dominate the society, the actual state of affairs gradually deteriorated.[5]

Based on the epic, we may assume that a situation arose when some people, out of selfish worldly desires, began to violate dharma and became immune to the fear of divine displeasure. They, being infatuated by their desire for pleasure and prompted by their own muscle power, began to exploit and torment the weaker sections of the society for selfish ends. Tyranny of the strong over the weak reigned unabated. Such individuals posed a threat to the peaceful coexistence and consequently perpetuated uncertainty and anxiety about the safety of life and property of the general public. It was the logic of the 'big fish devouring the small fish', popularly known as the *matsya-nyaya* that started to govern the society. This situation forced the law-abiding people to search for a remedy. Since people could no longer successfully govern themselves through self-governance, there arose the need for an external governing force, so that people might not destroy each other by their self-created anarchy and do not stop the human society from flourishing.[6] The 'big fish devouring the small fish' phenomenon prompted people to search for a leader and they selected Manu, the Vaivasvata. He was allotted one-sixth of the grains grown and one-tenth of the merchandise as sovereign dues. Thereupon, he took upon himself the responsibility of assuring and maintaining the safety and security of his people.[7] Thereafter, the ruler began his administration as a representative of the people and used his power for 'bringing about acquisition and preservation of the subjects'.[8]

It is quite evident from these textual sources that the people granted the leader (ruler) political authority and power to be used for their (people's) protection. They gave him economic power by providing him with resources to ensure people's prosperity. The leader was also given a divine status so that he is respected and obeyed by all without any challenge. In return, the leader, bound by duties and responsibilities, was not at all free to act as per his whims and fancies. He had clearly defined political, economic, social and personal responsibilities, and notably, his duty towards the people.

Thus, the social function of a leader (ruler), as depicted in ancient Indian sources, has immense power and rights bestowed upon him. At any rate, it also clearly defines the limitations that are placed upon him in terms of his duties and responsibilities.[9]

These sources also say that the leader (king) was created by divine forces. As stated therein the Lord created the king in order to guard the entire realm, taking elements from various divinities such as Indra, Vayu, Yama, Sun, Fire, the Moon and Kubera.[10] Elsewhere it is stated that '[t]he king has the qualities of all these gods, and therefore, surpasses all living beings in brilliant energy. Even a child king should not be taken lightly; he is God in human form.'[11]

Ancient sources on polity also point out the functional resemblance between the king on one hand and the various divinities on the other. The taxonomy in Table 1.1 illustrates the functional divinity of kingship derived from various noted interpretations.

TABLE 1.1 *The Functional Divinity of Kingship*

Comparison with Gods	*Functional Divinity*	*Interpretations*
Sun	Give back to society	Even when the taxes and tributes are collected, the king's attitude is like the sun, who evaporates the water only to return it thousand-fold in the form of rains.
Moon	Be benevolent always	Like the moon, the king gladdens the people. Generally, the word *raja* (king) is derived from the root *raj* to shine, to appear splendid. But Kalidasa derives it from the root *ranj* to please and suggests that the king must please the people like the moon.[12]
Wind	Demonstrate 24-hour leadership	Just as the wind blows day and night, the king knows no rest.[13]
Death	Establish law and order and discipline	Like the god of death (Yama), the king inflicts punishment on criminals.[14]
Fire	Punish the evildoers	Like the god of fire (Agni), the king burns the wicked and evildoers.[15]
Rain	Be non-discriminative	Like the rain god (Varuna), the king showers wealth on the poor and the deserving.[16]
Earth	Nourish and support	Like the goddess of earth (Prithvi), the king sustains the people.[17]
Wealth	Create wealth	Like the god of wealth (Kubera), the king showers wealth on deserving people.[18]

Source: Author's compilation

It is important to notice that while performing the duties and responsibilities of the king, the divinity aspect did not afford him any immunity or privilege. If he was bad in character and failed in performing his duties, he became demoniac and not divine.[19] A wicked king, by the name Vena, had claimed exemption from punishment on the ground of his divinity, but infuriated sages killed him immediately after he had advanced this impious plea. And then, his son Prithu was elected and consecrated as king by the gods and sages. At the time of coronation, he vowed to rule righteously, to maintain law and order, to not violate the rules of law, to protect the dharma and to sincerely serve the people. He ruled successfully in accordance with law and his undertaking. Thus, we may hypothesise that the concept of divinity was used metaphorically in ancient India to describe the functions of the royal office. Only the king who fulfilled his duties could claim divine stature; the removal of unjust kings was encouraged.[20] It was also argued that the divinity of the king does not confer infallibility on him. As a matter of fact, he is more liable to err and fall than ordinary people as he is exposed to greater temptations.[21]

There are not many examples available to support the metaphor theory of the king's divinity. But examples like the following extracts from Queen Elizabeth I's speech in 1601 (particularly the lines italicised for emphasis) further substantiates the social function of divinity bestowed on kingship:

> And, *though God hath raised me high*, yet this I count the glory of my Crown, that I have reigned with your loves.

This makes me that I do not so much rejoice that God hath made me to be a Queen, as to be a Queen over so thankful a people.

Therefore, I have cause to wish nothing more than to content the subject and that is a duty which I owe. Neither do I desire to live longer days than I may see your prosperity and that is my only desire.

Of myself I must say this: I never was any greedy, scraping grasper, nor a strait fast-holding Prince, nor yet a waster. My heart was never set on any worldly goods. What you bestow on me, I will not hoard it up, but receive it to bestow on you again.

I know the title of a King is a glorious title, but assure yourself that the shining glory of princely authority hath not so dazzled the eyes of our understanding, but that we well know and remember that we also are to yield an account of our actions before the great judge.

To be a king and wear a crown is a thing more glorious to them that see it than it is pleasant to them that bear it. For myself I was never so much enticed with the glorious name of a King or royal authority of a Queen as delighted that God hath made me his instrument to maintain his truth and glory and to defend his kingdom as I said from peril, dishonour, tyranny and oppression.

There will never Queen sit in my seat with more zeal to my country, care to my subjects and that will sooner with willingness venture her life for your good and safety than myself. For it is my desire to live nor reign no longer than my life and reign shall be for your good.

And though you have had, and may have, many princes more mighty and wise sitting in this seat, yet you

> never had nor shall have, any that will be more careful and loving.[22]

Some other ancient civilisations also considered the king to be divine. In ancient Egypt, a ruler, called pharaoh, was regarded as the son of the sun god Ra. The pharaoh intervened at public sacrifices and he only could pray to god for favour or mercy.

In some ancient civilisations, rulers were considered as vice-regents of god and were given great honours. In some civilisations, kings were considered to have descended from a holy person. He was the repository of the knowledge of the godly infallible decrees.[23] In Europe, the theory of the divine origin of the ruler was celebratedly announced when Alexander the Great was treated as a god in his lifetime in 324 BCE. Roman kings were also glorified after their death and shrines were built in their honour. Christianity popularised the divinity of the Pope and it was accepted that he could transfer divinity to the ruler at the time of coronation.[24]

In contrast to the divinity value, the early Buddhist sources held views on the origin of the leader (ruler) similar to the theory of social contract. According to their theory, the authority of sovereignty was not conferred upon rulers by gods, but was given to them by the people through the process of election. A Buddhist scripture contains the following speculation regarding how the election process came about:

> From our evil deeds, sirs, becoming manifest, inasmuch as stealing, censure, lying, punishment, have become

> known, what if we were to select a certain being ... who should censure that which should rightly be censured and should banish him who deserves to be banished? But we will give him in return a proportion of rice. Then those beings went to the being among them who was the handsome, most charming, most attractive and most capable and said to him: Come now, good being, be indignant at that ... who deserves to be banished. And we will contribute thee a proportion of our rice. And he consented, and did so, and they gave him a proportion of their rice.[25]

The phrase 'chosen by the whole people' (*Mahasammata*) was applied to such a ruler because he was elected by the people. It is worth noting in this context the observation made by the Prince Shōtoku of Japan:

> When wise and capable persons are entrusted with high offices, there will arise a unanimous voice of pleased approval; but when wicked persons hold high offices, disasters and disturbances are multiplied. In this world there are few who are endowed with inborn wisdom; sainthood is the goal attained after a long self-discipline. All matters of State, whether great or small, will surely be well ordered, when right persons are in the right positions; in any period, whether critical or peaceful, all affairs will be peacefully, settled when wise men are secured. In this way will the State be lasting and the realm will be free from dangers. Therefore the wise sovereigns of the ancient

> times sought good men for high offices, and not good offices for favoured ones.[26]

Coming back to divinity again, we can say that the doctrine of the divinity of the king's office was intended merely to inspire respect for authority and not to encourage autocracy or irresponsibility in the kingly order. Banabhatta, the biographer of King Harshavardhana (7th century CE), has vehemently criticised the divinity of the king in his famous novel *Kadambari*.[27] He calls it an invention of unscrupulous flatterers of the king. The king is made by the flatterers to consider himself to be the God but while doing so he becomes an object of public ridicule. A few kings, misled by the surrounding flatterers, seem to have claimed infallibility on account of their divinity but that was not acceptable to the people. We produce below an abridged and simplified translation of the satire composed by the poet:

> There are kings who are misled, by means of praises which can only fit superhuman beings, by rogues who are experts in cheating, who are intent on securing their own ends.
>
> Such kings, whose minds are drunk with the pride of wealth, who having lost all discernment, become falsely vain of themselves by believing all that to be true; who although mortal by nature look upon themselves as partial incarnations of heavenly beings, as containing divinity within themselves, and in fact, as superhuman beings; and who accordingly, begin to act and conduct themselves in a manner fit only for celestial beings, and

become the laughing stock of all people... They look upon the advice of old persons as the senseless prattle of senile dotage.

They hardly receive the counsel of a minister, thinking it to be an insult to their own intellect. And they get angry with one who gives them wholesome advice.

In every way him they welcome, him they talk to, him they have by their side, him they advance, with him they stay with pleasure, him they give, him they admit to their friendship, his words they listen to, on him they shower gifts, him they honour, and him they make their trusted confidant, who with all other business set aside, and with folded hands praise them day and night and continuously, as if they were gods, or proclaims their greatness.

Therefore, O Prince, in the administration of the kingdom which is dreadful on account of thousands of extremely crooked and painful practices, and in this youth of yours which generally produces the greatest infatuation, you should strive to conduct yourself in such a way that you will not be laughed at by the people, nor censured by the good, nor condemned by your elders, nor reproached by your friends, nor grieved over by the wise; also that you may not be torn to pieces by the wolves in the form of servants, deceived by rogues, enticed by women, made ridiculous by an improper use of wealth, swayed away by arrogance, maddened by love, attracted by sensual pleasures, drawn away by passion, and carried away (entirely possessed) by luxury.[28]

Similar observation on sycophants is also made by Shōtoku, the prince of Japan:

> Flatterers and deceivers are like the fatal missile which will overthrow the state, or the sharp sword which will destroy the people. Likewise, sycophants are fond of dilating to their superiors on the errors of the inferiors; to their inferiors, they censure the faults of the superiors. Such are the kind of men who are never loyal to the lord, nor benevolent toward the people. All this is the source from which great civil disturbances occur.[29]

Leader's Oath and Its Significance

It is interesting to note here that the oath originated with kingship and it is as old as kingship itself. This reminds us of the oath taken by the kings of ancient India. The oath that the king-elect took in the oath-taking ceremony and the sovereignty the people vested in him at the time of investiture ceremony are of great significance. The king being bound by his coronation oath had to act according to the law established. The oath brought him under the law and did not offer him any scope to be arbitrary. The priest exhorted the king at the coronation—'Strive unceasingly to do good to the people, and above all, protect the country from all calamities.' He was to repeat with faith—'Whatever good I might have done, my heaven, my life and my progeny may I be deprived of, if I oppress people.' He would take the oath 'to follow the scriptural injunctions, to act according to the rule of law, never to violate the rules of law, not to insult the learned, and to serve the people sincerely'.[30]

Leadership purpose is eternal and universal and it does not change according to time or region. Many business schools have started a voluntary oath-taking ceremony for their MBA students, popularly known as the MBA Oath. In this oath, as the students become business leaders, they are asked to recognise their role in society. They are required to promise that they will manage their enterprises with loyalty and care, and will not advance their personal interests at the expense of their enterprise or society. They are also to assure that they will refrain from corruption, unfair competition or business practices harmful to society. This oath emphasises the importance of a myriad of core leadership values such as honesty, equality, selflessness, sincerity, generosity, giving in abundance, and ethical actions, which have been insisted from time immemorial in all countries and cultures. A few lines extracted from the MBA Oath are given below:

Therefore, I promise that:

- I will manage my enterprise with loyalty and care, and will not advance my personal interests at the expense of my enterprise or society.
- I will protect the human rights and dignity of all people affected by my enterprise, and I will oppose discrimination and exploitation.
- I will protect the right of future generations to advance their standard of living and enjoy a healthy planet.

- I will invest in developing myself and others, helping the management profession continue to advance and create sustainable and inclusive prosperity.[31]

What Is Expected from a Leader?

The ancient Indian literature on polity mentions the promotion of wealth creation (*artha*), the fulfilment of people's desires (*kama*) and maintaining law and order through righteousness (dharma) as the purposes for which a leader (ruler) has been created. A leader is urged to promote the creation of wealth by encouraging trade, industry and agriculture, by developing national resources, by bringing fresh land under cultivation and by building dams and canals to make agriculture independent of rain. Kautilya, the ancient Indian authority on the art and science of governance, wrote in his *Arthashastra*, a book on polity, that the leader (ruler) shall be ever active in the management of the economy. The root of wealth is economic activity and the lack of it brings material distress. In the absence of fruitful economic activity, both current prosperity and future growth will be destroyed. A leader can achieve the desired objectives and abundance of riches by undertaking productive economic activity.[32]

A leader's (ruler's) duty is also to promote the fulfilment of desires (*kama*) of his people by ensuring peace and order, so that each individual may enjoy life undisturbed, and by offering encouragement to fine arts such as music, dancing, painting, sculpture and architecture in order to promote aesthetic culture. It is his duty to promote education, religion, arts, agriculture and economic development.[33] The leader is obligated to promote law and order through righteousness by fostering a feeling of piety and religiousness, by encouraging virtue and morality, by extending help to the establishments belonging to all religions and sects and by maintaining free hospitals and feeding houses for the poor and the destitute. These are the supreme duties of a leader (ruler) as he enjoys the rewards in the form of taxes, gifts, etc.[34]

According to the inscriptional sources, even the battles were not merely for conquest, but were said to have been undertaken to protect the people and release them from the sufferings of foreign rule and from their *adharma* or immoral acts. For the protection of the people, the ruler wields the rod of justice and he punishes deviants fairly and deservedly. In ancient Indian literature, the ruler is called *nrupa* or protector of human beings, and *bhupa* and *bhupala*, protector of the earth.[35]

The purpose of creating a leader is given below in terms of functional responsibilities. In brief, a leader (ruler) was created and accepted by the people to perform the following functions:

- Please the people
- Protect them
- Always seek their welfare
- Establish all the subjects in the observance of their duties
- Punish wrongdoers

- Practise the virtues of promptitude, energy, truthfulness, self-restraint, humility, righteousness and compassion

The important question, then, is which precedes the other—the circumstances that need the social function of leadership or the leader as the social function who develops the society. Indian scriptures help us to not get entangled in the chicken and egg dilemma. The profound influence a leader has on the condition of his state and society has been pithily expressed in the following couplet (given in translation):

> Whether it is the leader (king) who is the maker of the age or the age that makes the leader (king) is a question about which there is no room for doubt. The leader (king) is undoubtedly the maker of the age.[36]

Thus, the leader, under whatever system of polity, is largely responsible for the state of the nation or society and whether people, in general, are virtuous or not largely depends upon the character and conduct of the leader and his capacity to enforce dharma, that is the rule of law. In effect, scriptures have even defined times and civilisations depending on the success of the ruling as per dharma or the rule of law by the appointed ruler. There is the familiar division of 'times', or the *yugas*, as in the *krita*, *treata*, *dvapara* and *kali*. On the two ends, there is the *krita yuga*, often called *satya yuga*, which was the 'golden age' of humankind, and the *kali yuga*, or the age that witnesses a collective collapse of all that sustains life and its worth in all its forms.[37] Sometimes, these four *yugas* are compared to a cow standing on four legs. In the golden age (*krita yuga)*, the cow is standing on all four legs. In the next age, the age of three (*treta yuga*), the cow is standing on only three legs and is slightly teetering, which indicates that the world is gradually corrupting. In the next age, the age of two (*dvapara yuga*), the cow is standing on only two legs as there is only half as much righteousness in the world as there used to be. This is followed by the worst age, the age of one (*kali yuga*), where 'the cow is standing on just one leg as there is only one-fourth of the world's original righteousness remaining. The world has become extremely corrupt and utterly unstable'.[38] When the righteous leaders rule the earth, the period *symbolically* or *metaphorically* becomes *krita yuga*: seasons become salubrious, lands yield surplus and men and women live long, healthy and happy lives. Conversely, the reign of an unrighteous leader is *symbolically* or *metaphorically* considered as *kali yuga*: rains become scanty, lands fail to support the crops and men and women live sickly lives.

Code of Conduct (*Rajadharma*) and Sage-like Leaders (*Rajarshi*)

We explore several thinkers and rulers who have theorised and/or lived the code of conduct of good leadership, popularly known as *rajadharma* besides exploring the concept of *rajarshi* (sage-like leaders). In this context, it is interesting to refer to an epic that sets the prototype of an ideal leader in the form of Lord Rama. The following excerpts from the text as well as principles extracted by various researchers provide insights on ideal leadership. The Ramayana by Valmiki (composed between 300 CE and 200 CE) presents an effective leader and according to it, a leader is:

> ...a person of self-possession and of great heroism, firm and of controlled senses; endowed with intellect, tact and power of speech; one who is righteous, true to his vow and intent (always) on what is beneficent to his subjects; rich in fame and knowledge, pure, ease of access, attentive to his duty; one who knows the true import of all the systems of knowledge; dear to the entire universe being absolutely good; never depressed; being adept in duties and acts; a noble person who views everybody equally and looks always in the same pleasing manner.[39]
>
> ...a leader is always calm, talks soft and talks first; though told harsh things, does not retort. Satisfied even with one good turn done to him in some way; and forgets even hundreds of disservice; learned, not addicted to unbeneficial things; has no taste for evil gossip; estimates persons at their worth; efficient and devoid of laziness and carelessness, knows his own foibles and the foibles of others; enjoys pleasure in harmony with righteousness and material welfare but is never indolent; never insults beings.[40]

The Mahabharata (composed 200–500 CE) is one of the great epics of India, traditionally ascribed to Vyasa. It contains many dialogues and anecdotes related to leadership values. The ancient Indian cultural wisdom talks of social welfare as an eternal guiding principle for effective leadership. The Mahabharata says:

> The ideal conduct for the king to follow is that of the pregnant woman, for she rejects what pleases her and only does that which benefits the embryo she is nourishing. Similarly, the king, discarding pursuits and objects dear to him, shall ever be engaged in what is conducive to public welfare.[41]

Through the prominent character Bhishma, who is an exponent of *rajadharma*, the purpose and method of leadership are elucidated in the same text: There is no greater function of the leader (ruler) than to protect the people. Safety of the people is the primary foundation of all civil order. A ruler's first duty is to the people. He/she should take care of them with not thoughts of personal pleasure, subordinating personal desires to the desires of the people. People should be free and happy throughout the kingdom like they would in their parental house. Living a life in fear is humiliating so a ruler must ensure that no one in the kingdom is scared. Therefore, the ruler must make sure that the subjects are not scared of him, of others, of each other and also not of any other, nonhuman elements. Children must be fed delicious food with grace and care. It is a sin to have children go hungry as they watch others enjoy meals. A ruler in whose kingdom crying and helpless women are forcibly abducted in front of their family members who cry and wail in vain, that ruler is as good as dead. Dharma (which means integrity, right action, morality) is the most powerful watchword of a ruler. 'Sacrifice of the self, kindness towards all beings, understanding and protecting all people, redress of the aggrieved and the rescue of the oppressed. These constitute the dharma of the rulers. He should be surrounded with people of like nature, who have qualities that are noble. The only difference between him and his officers is the white umbrella signifying his higher office.'[42]

Kalidasa (4th century CE) is a great poet and dramatist in Sanskrit literature. He has authored two court epics, three dramas and two lyrics. Hailed as the prince among Indian poets, he has absorbed Indian cultural heritage, made it his own, enriched it and given it a wider significance and scope by his well-known works. He speaks of great leaders of Raghu dynasty who ruled India for many centuries. He suggests that the ideal of kingship is complete devotion to the welfare and happiness of the subjects. He adds to the *rajadharma* discourse—Let the ruler strive for the welfare of all his subjects (*pravartatam prakritihitaya parthivah*).[43]

What Kalidasa seeks to impress upon our mind is that true leadership does not lie in self-indulgence at the cost of public welfare, but in the service of the people at the cost of personal enjoyment.

Manimekalai by the poet Chithalai Chathanaar, composed between 890 and 950 CE is a sequel to *Silappathikaram*, one of the oldest Tamil verse epics composed by Ilango Adigal. *Silappathikaram* narrates the story of Kovalan and

Kannaki, a married couple. Kovalan fell in love with the dancer Madhavi and spent all his money on her. Kannaki, however, remained faithful to Kovalan, and penniless, the couple reached the city of Madurai. Kannaki then took off one of her anklets and gave it to Kovalan to sell, but in the market, he was accused as a thief as the queen had lost a similar anklet. The falsely accused Kovalan was put to death, and Kannaki, when she heard of it, stormed through the city in grief. Finally, she was taken to the king and when she showed him her remaining anklet, which was different from that of the queen, the king realised he had falsely condemned an innocent man. 'I am no king,' he said, and in shock, he fell down dead. This book provides guidance for governance based on justice.

If the king fails to practise *rajadharma*, what may happen is graphically described in *Manimekalai*.

> If the king did swerve from his righteous path
> the planets would all change their course;
> if the planets errant turn,
> would dearth of rain surely ensure,
> if dearth of rain there were,
> nothing on earth would then survive.[44]

The concept of *rajadharma*, as discussed in ancient Indian sources, spells a sense of responsible power. But as the well-known saying goes, 'with great power comes great responsibility', we have an interesting output of types of powers as well. The ancient Indian authorities on polity define three types of powers, namely:

- The power of sovereignty (*prabhushakti*)
- The power of knowledge (*mantrashakti*)
- The power of enthusiastic energy (*utsahashakti*)[45]

The possession of a prosperous treasury and a strong army is the strength of sovereignty. The power of knowledge depends upon the intelligence of the rulers and his advisers. The power of enthusiasm depends on the energetic action of the ruler and it is necessary for the success of deliberations. These three powers of a ruler are inter-related and one without the other is of no use. Power by itself is neither good nor evil; there is the divine power (*daivishakti*) and the demonic power (*asurishakti*)—the benign power and the malign power.[46]

To present a picturesque description of power-drunk leaders, we analyse a minster's advice to a young prince found in the Sanskrit work *Kadambari* of Banabhatta. This advice sarcastically showcases some of the bad behaviours of those leaders (rulers) who are swayed by the combination of power derived from being born rich, being young, being beautiful and having extraordinary physical strength.

A few translated lines from this great advice are quoted below:

> ...To be rich from one 's very birth, fresh youth, possession of peerless beauty, and superhuman physical strength-great [disasters] indeed, is this series of evils (undesirable things), anyone of these, by itself, is the abode of all sorts of deeds of insolence; what, then of their combinations?

As a rule, in early youth, the intellect of a person becomes muddy (i.e. clouded)... Extreme attachment to sensual pleasures ruins a person by leading him into wrong paths, just as the confusion about directions makes a person take to the wrong road. ... Persons like you only are the fit receptacles of advice. In a mind freed from its impurities (i.e. wrong notions), easily enter the merits of advice, just as the rays of the moon enter (i.e. are reflected) in a crystal with its dirt removed.

This is just the time to advise you, as you have not yet tasted the pleasures of the objects of senses. For advice trickles away, like water, from a heart which has been shattered with the strokes of Cupid's arrows. The kingly nature is always perturbed, being darkened by the swoon caused by the burning fever of self-conceit; riches produce the delirium in the form of false pride; and regal glory induce a coma brought on by the working of the poison of kingly power.

... And also: some kings come to be miserable-being tempted by riches, being harassed by their senses, which, although only five, appear to number many thousands as it were, in their eagerness to taste the various (sensual) pleasures; and being distracted by their mind, which although but one appears to have been multiplied a hundred thousand times. As persons bitten by deadly black snakes cannot be restored to life even by means of mighty spells, they cannot be roused (into activity) even by means of excellent counsels. ... Even when (merely) thought of, they bring disaster, just like resolves to commit a heinous sin. Being daily filled (with riches), they become puffed up in appearance, as though they

> are inflated with sin. And, being in such a condition, they become the targets of hundreds of vices and never know their own fall (i.e. degradation).[47]

Those leaders who have sufficient self-knowledge to recognise the vicissitudes of power and who will not be tempted away, they will be in the end the most powerful. They will be the ones who are remembered with respect and affection. They will also be the ones truly able to manage the ambiguities of power and lead a creative and productive life. The ultimate judgment of leaders is often not about how they acquire and use power but how they relinquish it.

It is apt to quote Plato and Sri Aurobindo in this context. Plato, the great Greek philosopher of Republic (375 BCE), says:

> The human race would never see the end of trouble until the true lovers of wisdom come to hold political power, or the holder of political power should become a true lover of wisdom. Plato's philosopher-king is without any self-interest, fully knows the statecraft and has the necessary courage.[48]

Sri Aurobindo (1872–1950), a well-known philosophical thinker of modern India, observes:

> Power, wealth and sex are the strongest attractions for the human ego and they are mostly misused by those who retain them. The seekers or keepers of wealth are more often

possessed rather than its possessors; few escape entirely the distorting influence stamped on it by its long seizure.[49]

Concluding Remarks

The message conveyed by the Indian philosophical, spiritual and classical wisdom is that the personal virtues, human qualities, moral, ethical and spiritual values of the leaders in any field should be of the highest order. In addition, they must possess competence in all the different dimensions of leadership skills, including management of human relations. The leaders have to control lust, anger, greed, pride and arrogance.

They have to keep themselves free from all weaknesses and vices as far as possible to achieve success. Haughty and tyrannical leaders have been held to public condemnation throughout the recorded history of India.

Thus, 'what makes a good leader' in the Indological space has a strong ethical and exemplary function, and the social function[50] is such that it inserts the ethical roots into the substratum of a culture, which means it develops an almost centralised ethical governance system. How? Just by practising the governance code yourself (here, the leader). This is typically understood in the popular Gandhi quote—'Be the example you want others to follow'. Hence, what we can derive from this very interesting phenomenon is a governance structure, a systemic structure, a behavioural code. And the face of the code is sustained in an exemplary leader. What makes the Indological function of a leader starkly stand out is that the leader is the first data of systemic governance and not the public. When we talk about Rama Rajya, we talk about Rama, the hero of the epic Ramayana, surrendering to public outcry even at the expense of his wife, Sita. Hence, Rama being a leader had to bear the consequences of being a leader. And he is the first casualty as much as the king, if the code is dishonoured. To understand why should this be an interesting study on leadership and governance, let us go back to the Derridean model of structure, sign and play.[51]

The Algerian-French post-structuralist philosopher, Jacques Derrida, notes that a structure has a centre, let us call that the face, or more in terms of our understanding, the leader. Thus, the rules of the system are played out within the structure, of which the centre is as much within the rules as are the players. So, the centre—the leader—is as much a player governed by the same set of rules, as are the rest of the players within the structure. But, as we move beyond the structure, a point comes where the free-play is reduced to *that* spatial and temporal point, where the free-play is contained. Derrida calls *that* fixed point the 'qua centre'. For us, in the Indological context, the qua centre is the system, the governance code, the leadership module. The central power can be dethroned, but the qua centre, or the governance code, cannot be. This develops a very centralised system of surveillance, where, interestingly, the leader becomes the technology[52] of surveillance, and the technology remarkably is the code of conduct, and hence, is equally under surveillance itself. Hence, Indology shows how a strong centralised governance system is plausible if the leader itself becomes the technology of governance, the symbol of the code. And hence, the leader cannot at any cost tarnish the code. Perhaps, this is one of the most tactical devices in the discourse of centring leadership—make the leader the code bearer! Refer to Figure 1.1 to understand the structural derivation of our Indological leadership governance model.

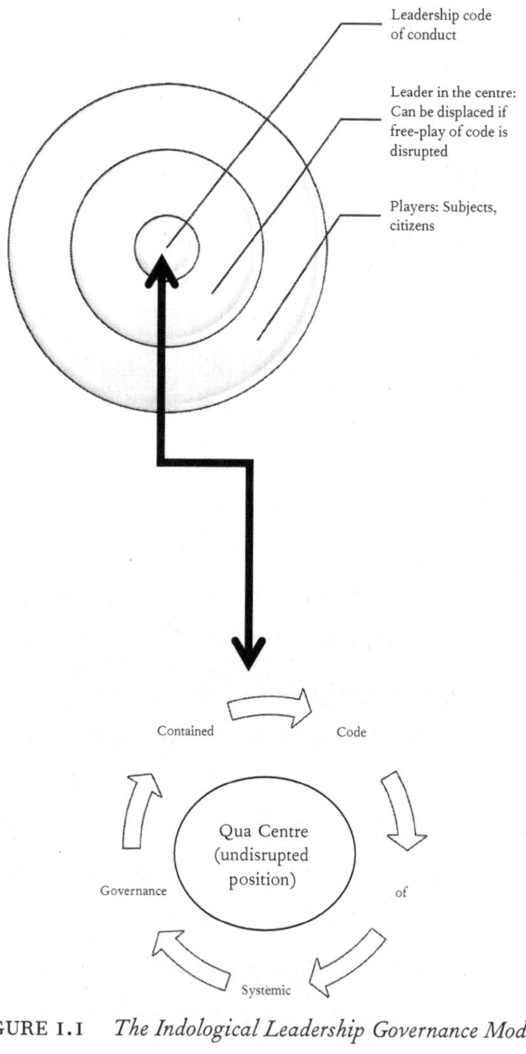

FIGURE 1.1 *The Indological Leadership Governance Model*

2

Exemplary Leadership Illustrated

Pravartatam Prakrutihitaya Parthivah
(May the ruler exert himself for the good of his subjects)
—Kalidasa

Introductory Remarks

Pleasing (*prajaranjana*) and adoring (*lokaradhana*) the people, that is to say, government by the consent and to the satisfaction of the people was always recommended as a worthy ideal for all rulers in ancient India. It was a sort of spiritual curb on the unlimited power of the monarch and a practical test of good and happy government. It is rightly pointed that the authentic Indian model of leadership has always been that of the *rajarshi* (*raja* + *rishi*). *Rajarshi* embodies the keynote of the vedantic ethos—the management of the secular in the light of the sacred. The leadership consciousness should be lifted above the greedy secular path towards the self-fulfilling sacred/spiritual one. The secret of superlative charisma in the successful model of constructive leadership in Indian history has consistently been the high-minded pursuit of self-restraint, self-control, self-sacrifice and renunciation. High-order character, founded on authentic spiritual values, lay at the core of their charisma.[1]

There are many exemplary leaders in the long and rich cultural history of India who may be considered *rajarshi* (sage-like) leaders. In fact, Lord Rama depicted in the great Indian epic Ramayana is an example of *rajarshi*, a royal sage who had a combination of political statesmanship, the practice of kingship and philosophical wisdom. People too had their own views about an exemplary ruler and articulated them at all forums. And their expectations come close to a *rajarshi* leader. As stated in the Ramayana, a ruler must be saintly, always interested in the welfare of the citizens and their families.[2] He or she should choose public interest and the welfare of the subjects over personal considerations. Qualities like charity, kindness, honours to the pious and the deserving, straightforwardness and impartial justice were expected in a ruler. A leader was expected to avoid the vices that spring from lust and anger.[3] The conduct should be exemplary and he or she should not follow their whims and fancies.[4] The subjects would surely follow the leader's example, who is their preceptor in conduct and character.

It is advantageous and necessary to note the sources of influence and the restraints that helped a leader to practise righteousness and other virtues, both in private and public life. A ruler was kept on the path of righteousness by the education and training received when young, and the advice and restraint of ministers, priests and elders.[5] The entire education and training of a prince/princess were directed towards three ends:

- Inculcating in him/her a sense of high respect towards dharma
- Invigorating him/her with a strong urge for public welfare
- Fashioning him/her into an efficient and strong administrator[6]

Moral discipline was of the utmost importance for the prince/princess. Therefore, due attention was given to make them conversant with ancient religious and didactic stories,[7] and to associate them with virtuous persons of mature age and experience.[8] The ultimate aim of education and training was to make them truthful, righteous, virtuous, compassionate, grateful, sacrificing, self-restrained and free from malevolence, grudges, envy and blemish.[9] It is expressly stated that tranquillity, benevolence, compassion, veracity, righteousness, piety and prowess are the qualities of a good leader.[10] Disrespecting the wise, the gratification of the senses, anger, consultation with only a single person concerning the needs of the kingdom and taking counsel from those that are cognisant of evils have been identified as the vices to be avoided by a good ruler.[11] According to ancient sources, the occupational functions of rulers must contain several morally ennobling activities such as the protection of life, the discharge of justice and maintenance of law and order, and the preservation of moral and mental well-being of the population.[12] Such other-centred activities tend, almost automatically, to develop the ruler's moral integrity, sense of justice and social responsibility, compassion, benevolence and unselfishness.

These ennobling occupational works make even heartless and wicked rulers acquire a few important moral virtues. 'One who daily performs this sort of activity for months and years can hardly escape some retroactive ennobling influence.'[13] Whether it was in the days of the Ramayana or in the materialistic world of today, all calamities of individuals and of nations have been caused by the inability of the individuals or the leaders to strike the correct balance between righteousness on the one hand and material advancement and emotional gratification on the other.

Only those governments and ruling activities that have been charitable, friendly and follow moral forces have been really constructive and have contributed towards the establishment of a lasting peace, harmonious order with security, dignity and freedom for all. *Rajarshi* rulers provide practical guidance to administrators all over the world in matters of people-management. But opposite of *rajarshi* leaders also serve as object lessons to leaders, cautioning them against the evil effects of ill-planned and rashly executed low politics.[14]

Let us study the case of an opposite of *rajarshi* leader elaborately described in the epic Ramayana as an illustrative example. In the Ramayana, Ravana who is the antagonist presents the opposite of the *rajarshi* model of leadership demonstrated by Rama. The ruler of the demons had a complex personality, an admixture of strength and learning, and extreme self-denial. At one place he confesses his stubborn nature:

> I may break into two, but I shall not bend to anybody.
> This is my fault, my nature that I cannot overcome.[15]

Ravana's tragic end shows how the greatest may fall if they ignore dharma and take a lopsided view of life, trampling upon the right and ignoring the welfare of the common people. On seeing Ravana seated on his throne, a majestic effulgent personality, shining amidst all pomp, Hanuman, who was Rama's devotee, servant and staunch follower was struck with Ravana's grandeur and might, but remarked:

> Of what avail is this external greatness when there is not that moral purity which alone makes real greatness?[16]

At the death of Ravana, his wife Mandodari remarks:

> Subduing your senses, you became victorious over the three worlds.
> Smarting for vengeance, they have now brought you down.[17]

It is the senses that killed Ravana who believed he was superhuman.

Ravana listened to sycophants as he had them surround him and they blinded his great potential of supreme knowledge that he was internally capable of.

However, it is rather difficult to find persons who speak and hear words unpalatable though beneficial.[18]

Role model rulers, portrayed by Kalidasa, the Sanskrit poet, led a self-sacrificing, noble and ideal life while maintaining a political state where happiness and prosperity ruled, where blazing examples of ideal personal life lifted common life also on to a higher plane. In describing the personalities of his royal heroes, Kalidasa has particularly emphasised their devotion to the good of their people.

About the kings of Raghu dynasty, Kalidasa says:

> They amassed vast fortunes so that they could gift away their treasures to the needy, distressed and the virtuous.[19]

The ruler's (king's) dharma included acts of kingship such as constructing forts, temples and irrigation canals, increasing the welfare of the kingdom and taking precautions in preventing calamities and tragedies.[20] At another instance, he describes a sacrifice performed by one of the kings of Raghu dynasty as:

> He performed the *visvajit* sacrifice in which one's entire wealth is given away; for of the good as of clouds, acquisition is for distribution.[21]

The *yajnas* of the great kings, of course, involve much more than giving free meals. These are occasions for giving away of all kinds of wealth that accumulates in a capital city over a period of time.[22] And such periodical giving away of wealth forms one of the basic principles of the Indian theory and practice of leadership.

King Harshavardhana, who ruled India in 7th century CE, performed a sacrifice and it was witnessed by the Chinese scholar Hiuen-Tsiang who attended it on the personal invitation of Harshavardhana. In this context, King Harshavardhana said to Hiuen-Tsiang:

> ...I have accumulated every kind of treasure and precious substance in the kingdom of Prayaga, and between the banks of the two rivers (that is, the Jamuna and Ganges) I have established a great religious convocation every five years, to attend which all the ascetics and sages of the five Indies are invited, and besides the poor and the orphans and the destitute; on this occasion during seventy-five days the great distribution of alms called the Moksha is attended to; I have completed five of these assemblies and am now about to celebrate the sixth: why does not the Master delay his departure till then, and so, by witnessing the spectacle, rejoice with us?[23]

Another case of a *rajarshi* leader who practised the purpose and method of his leadership (*rajadharma*) in letter and spirit is cited below as recorded by a well-known Sanskrit historian Kalhana in his *Rajatarangini*. The officers of King Chandrapida of Kashmir (680–688 CE) undertook the construction of a temple of Lord Tribhuvanaswami on a certain site. On a portion of that site, there was a hut that belonged to a cobbler. He refused to remove his hut in spite of being asked to do so by the king's officers. Thereupon, the officers complained to the king about the stubbornness of the cobbler. However, to their surprise, the officers were censured by the king for lack of foresight in encroaching upon the site belonging to the cobbler and starting construction without taking his consent. The king ordered thus:

> Stop construction or build (the temple) somewhere else. Who would tarnish such a pious act by illegally depriving a man of his land? If we, who are the judges of what is right and what is not right, act unlawfully, who then would abide by law?

Thereafter, the cobbler got an audience with the king at his own request. He represented before the king thus:

> Just as the palace is to your Majesty, the hut is to me. I could not bear to see its demolition. You can very well appreciate the plight of a man who is deprived of his dwelling.[24]

The lessons from ancient Indian sources for those who manage power is that empires and organisations built and managed mainly by rude force, fraud, bloody strife and violation of the universal moral imperatives are short-lived and disastrous. It has been observed that the empires and organisations built and managed by spiritual and altruistic forces based on the supreme values of god, truth, goodness and beauty are everlasting.[25] The really fruitful and constructive policy of any leader anxious to build a durable organisation is based on the wise realisation of the moral values of love, friendship, mutual help and compassion, and not the policies motivated by unlimited egoism, hate and nihilism and carried by coercion, fraud, hypocrisy and other anti-moral and ugly means.

People's Welfare Is Leader's Welfare

Kautilya recognised that social justice is in the leader's interest.[26] For example, if the people are poor, they will become discontent and either support the enemy or slay the king.[27] According to Kautilya, it is in the king's self-interest to uphold social justice. A king who makes multiple wrongful arrests, seizes property, raises taxes too high, allows hunger and poverty in his country when it is preventable and does not provide for the needy or the jobless is likely to come to ruin either by a revolt from within or attack from outside by an enemy who will find support among those oppressed. This is why Kautilya repeatedly warns that a king must stay in touch with the people and must take care of them just as a father takes care of his children, and that a king must not be distracted by or addicted to wine, women and gambling. He did not recommend slaughters or massacres, but instead recognised the wisdom of acting in a humane and generous manner towards defeated soldiers as these soldiers can become hard-working and loyal subjects.

A very innovative strategy in Kauṭilya's social welfare scheme is the establishment of a department to help and supervise the institution of prostitution, which offers multiple opportunities for both taxation and espionage. The lot of a prostitute in Kauṭilya's society, however, was more desirable and less risky, because the state guaranteed her economic security and that of her children in her old age and applied strict penalties for any violence and abuse on the part of clients. When a prostitute lost her beauty, she could secure the job of 'mother' or 'nurse' in brothels. There were fines for statutory rape. Kautilya wrote:

> If a man robs a courtesan of her ornaments,
> her goods or the payment due to her,
> he shall be fined eight times the amount.[28]

Another significant step with regard to social welfare scheme of Kauṭilya is that the king himself, by means of his administration, should 'maintain children, aged persons, and persons in distress when they are helpless'.[29] His judges throughout the kingdom should concern themselves with the affairs of 'women, minors, old persons, sick persons, who are helpless even when these do not approach the court'.[30] Each judge was, in a sense, an extension of the king who was the final authority in judicial matters.[31]

> Those who are poor and need help to support themselves should be given work. And those women who do not stir out—those living separately, widows, crippled women, or maidens—who wish to earn their living, should be given work.[32]

Even after conquering an enemy, the king should 'render help to the distressed, the helpless, and the diseased'.[33]

As stated earlier, Kautilya's classic statement is 'the welfare of the leader (king) does not lie in the fulfilment of what is dear to him; whatever is dear to the subjects constitutes his welfare'.[34] Leaders flourish more and their rule lasts longer by placing the well-being of all above the well-being of the self.[35]

There are eloquent descriptions of universal welfare-oriented leadership in the recorded history of India.[36] Inspired by the concept of universal welfare (*lokasamgraha*), Ashoka the Great (3rd century BCE) embraced a life of service—as a servant of the subjects. He is remembered as one of the world's earliest and most impactful social innovators. Ashoka dedicated his life to the peaceful promotion of social welfare, economic development and tolerance for all religions. He was rigorously involved in securing the welfare and happiness not only of his subjects, but also of the people of other lands beyond the borders of his empire, as if all people were his children.[37] He provided medical facilities for humans and animals. He would import the required medicinal herbs, roots and fruits and have them grown throughout his empire and also in many other countries beyond its borders. He was responsible for planting shade-giving trees and mango groves along the roads, digging wells throughout the highways at regular intervals and building sheds for supplying drinking water to humans and animals.[38]

Ashoka states that his inspiration for action arises out of his involvement with the welfare of the whole world and helps him discharge his debt to his people, presumably in his role as the emperor. This concept of 'owing a debt to his people' made him devote his entire time to the welfare of his subjects. Ashoka laboured hard at public business and declared that he was always ready for it:

> ...I have given this order, that at any time, whether I am eating, in the women's quarters, the bedchamber, the chariot, the palanquin, in the park or wherever, reporters are to be posted with instructions to report to me the affairs of the people so that I might attend to these affairs wherever I am ... I am never content with exerting myself or with despatching business. Truly, I consider the *welfare of all* [emphasis added] to be my duty, and the root of this is exertion and the prompt despatch of business.[39]

Ashoka worked strenuously in order to establish a welfare state. He, in one of his rock edicts, says:

> I am not satisfied simply with hard work or carrying out the affairs of state, for I consider my work to be the *welfare of the whole world* [emphasis added], of which hard work and the carrying out of affairs are merely the basis. There is no better deed than to work for the *welfare of the whole world* [emphasis added]...[40]

He instructed his officers to create in the mind of the alien subjects the following belief:

> The king (Ashoka) is unto us even as a father; he loves us even as he loves himself; we are to the king even as his children.[41]

This unmistakably shows that Ashoka treated not only his own subjects as his children, but his attitude extended also to the whole humankind. To the many 'unconquered borderers' of his empire, he sent the healing message:

> The king desires that they should not be afraid of him but should trust him, and would receive from him not sorrow but happiness.[42]

Ashoka's ideal was to promote the material and spiritual welfare of the whole world, which he believed included not only humans but also beasts and other creatures, and not only in his own kingdom but all over the world known or accessible to him. This vision of universal welfare stimulated Ashoka to stupendous activity.

In the pre-independent modern India, Mahatma Gandhi demonstrated leadership based on universal welfare. According to him:

> There is no limit to extending our services to our neighbours across State-made frontiers. God never made those frontiers.
>
> ... Just as the cult of patriotism teaches us today that the individual has to die for the family, the family has to die for the village, the village for the district, the district for the province and the province for the country, even so, a country has to be free in order that it may die, if necessary, for the *benefit of the world* [emphasis added].
>
> ... We are all tarred with the same brush; *we are all members of the vast human family* [emphasis added]... Humanity is not divided into watertight compartments,

> so that we cannot go from one to another ... My mission is not merely brotherhood of Indian humanity ... My patriotism is not an exclusive thing ... The conception of my patriotism is nothing if it is not always, in every case without exception, consistent with the broadest good of humanity at large.[43]

In a recent speech, the Dalai Lama, the great Buddhist leader, interpreted 'taking interest in universal welfare' as universal responsibility. He said:

> Each of us must learn to work not for his or her self, family or nation, but *for the benefit of all mankind* [emphasis added]. Universal responsibility is the real key to human survival. It is the best foundation for world peace, the equitable use of natural resources and thorough concern for the future generations, the proper care of environment… We can no longer invoke the national, racial or ideological barriers that separate us without destructive repercussions. In the context of our new interdependence, considering the interests of others is clearly the best form of self-interest.
>
> Interdependence, of course, is a fundamental law of nature … Ignorance of Interdependence has not only harmed the natural environment, but our human society as well.[44]

The implications of discussing and promoting *lokasamgraha* or universal welfare-oriented leadership, as expressed in ancient Indian sources, has far-reaching consequences.

There is a deep relationship between our ethos and contemporary corporate cooperation business models and it may inspire many other corporations to continue the legacy of cooperation. We have a sense of ownership of the tradition. In recent times in India, the universal welfare-oriented leadership model has been translated into a corporate act of benevolence, which also indicates that our acts become sources of inspiration for future actions, even beyond space-time limits. Therefore, we argue for responsible awareness of present actions because they have the potential for shaping the future (future of human, ethos and business sustenance), perhaps without our sensible awareness of even the context, or the person, or the organisation.

What Makes an Excellent Leader?

Researchers have tried to find out universally acceptable essential qualities, values and practices that make an excellent leader. Anthropologists and philosophers have cited fairness, freedom, unity, tolerance, responsibility, respect for life and love as examples of such universals. Great leaders are moralistic—they operate from a deep ethical platform that considers values such as justice and goodness to be the guiding principles for organisational decisions. A leader attains external power due to the position he holds and the authority that is inherent in that position or from technological expertise. Internal power is exclusive to the person. It is the person's leadership qualities, sense of justice and truth, values and ethics that persuade others to look up to him or her for guidance, for leadership and to accept him or her as a role model.

Great stress is laid on the personal character and qualities that a leader, in whom vast power is vested, must possess for the proper and effective discharge of his or her functions. Some of the qualities such as nobility, magnanimity, sagacity, integrity, honesty, generosity, charity, sincerity, truthfulness, gracefulness, forgiveness, intelligence, far-sightedness, steadfastness, kindness, skilfulness, benevolence, political wisdom, statesmanship, courage and bravery are insisted in those who aspire to become leaders. An ideal leader should also possess qualities such as fortitude, retentive memory, knowledge of different branches of learning, ability to uphold law and administer of justice.[45]

Confucius, the old tradition Chinese philosopher, said that a leader (ruler) should have integrity. He said:

> If a man can reform his own heart, what should hinder him from taking part in government? But if he cannot reform his own heart, what has he to do with reforming others?[46]

Kautilya also mentions the qualities that are essential to becoming an effective leader. According to him, a leader should be: 'non-fatalistic, of strong character, taking guidance from elders, truthful in speech and behaviour, grateful, non-procrastinating, intelligent, disciplined, full of shame to do anything evil, free from passion, anger, greed, and capable of self-management'.[47]

He divides the qualities that bring success to a leader into four groups: attractive qualities, qualities of wisdom, qualities of enthusiasm and desirable qualities.

- The attractive qualities are: intelligence, excellence of matured vision, truthful in speech, not inconsistent, graceful, philanthropic, highly enthusiastic, prompt, of firm resolve, keen on training and not seeks lowly council.
- The qualities of wisdom are: a desire to listen, listening, retention, deep understanding and ability to judge a situation and its pros and cons.
- The qualities of enthusiasm are: bravery, impatience, promptitude and proficiency.
- The desirable personal qualities are: eloquent (or wise), energetic, endowed with good memory, thought and strength, good-natured, an expert in art, leader of his forces in calamity, openly responding to a good turn and injury, modest, investing to meet calamity and abnormal situation, very far-sighted, foremost in actions suitable for the place, time and human endeavour, devoid of lust, anger, greed, rigidity, frivolity, oppression, trickery and back-biting, pleasant in speech, talking with a smile and sobriety, acting on the advice of the elders.[48]

According to Kautilya, discipline is of two kinds: inborn and acquired. There must be an innate capacity for self-discipline as instruction and training can promote discipline only in a person capable of benefitting from them, people incapable of natural self-discipline will not benefit. Learning imparts discipline only to those who have the following mental faculties:

- Obedience to a teacher
- Desire and ability to learn
- Capacity to retain what is learnt
- Understanding what is learnt
- Reflecting on learning
- Ability to make inferences by deliberating on the knowledge acquired

Those who are devoid of such mental faculties do not benefit from any amount of training. Kautilya's view on leaders' (rulers') education is summarised below:

> One who is in the process of becoming a leader (ruler) should acquire discipline and follow it strictly in life by learning the sciences from authoritative teachers.
>
> A leader (ruler) should learn philosophy and the scriptures from authoritative teachers, economics from the heads of various government departments, and the science of government from not only theoretical exponents of political science but also from practising politicians.
>
> A leader's education never stops. With a view to improving his self-discipline, he should always associate with learned elders, for in them alone has discipline its firm roots. Only a ruler who is wise, disciplined, devoted to a just governing of the subjects and ever conscious of the *welfare of all beings* [emphasis added] will enjoy the earth unopposed.

> The sole aim of all branches of knowledge is to inculcate restraint over the senses. Self-control, which is the basis of knowledge and discipline, is acquired by giving up lust, anger, greed, conceit, arrogance and foolhardiness. Living in accordance with scriptures means avoiding over-indulgence in all pleasures of (the senses, i.e.) hearing, touch, sight, taste and smell.
>
> A leader who has no self-control and gives himself up to excessive indulgence in pleasures will soon perish, even if he is the ruler of all corners of the earth. When a ruler makes himself inaccessible to his people, and he is seen only by those near him, wrong decisions are bound to be made; the people will become angry and may go over to the enemy. It is only by developing these qualities leaders can utilise their educational attainments and capacities for the benefit of society restricting their own selfish desires and prevent themselves from acting in a manner harmful and detrimental to the common good.[49]

According to the Mahabharata, a leader must adopt a truthful, upright and straightforward style while dealing with people in order to gain their fullest confidence. The leaders who try to discipline the followers without first disciplining themselves become an object of ridicule for not being able to see their own defects.[50]

In short, some of the most desirable qualities of an excellent leader listed in the Mahabharata are:

- Securing wealth without cruelty
- Enjoying the physical senses without excess

- Speaking pleasingly without being pitiable
- Having no alliance with the wicked
- Avoiding confiding in those who are wicked
- Not indulging in self-praise
- Not depending on those who are of low character
- Seeking material prosperity, but not by questionable means
- Never giving false assurance
- Not becoming angry without a strong cause[51]

Kindness and friendship to all beings, sharing and speech that is endearing—there is nothing in the world that can win people better than these three qualities combined. Protection of people is possible only when governance is impartial and the law is not 'held in abeyance'.

A leader who is afraid of dispersing just punishment is impotent as a ruler and is devoid of intelligence and can never protect the people. Because governance is a complex affair, and a burden too, the ruler who is not skilful in the art of governing can never protect the people. Freeing themselves from likes and dislikes and keeping their personal preferences, anger, greed and vanity far away, a leader must *treat all beings with a sense of equality*.[52]

Some of the bad qualities of a leader outlined in the Mahabharata are:

- Lack of faith
- Untruth and lies
- Anger, carelessness
- The habit of delaying

- Laziness
- Taking decisions wholly on one's own
- In matters of importance, consulting those who have little knowledge of them[53]

The Mahabharata also says:

> Anger must be controlled by forgiveness; fear by vigilance; inclination and aversion by patience; confusion and doubt and laziness by practice; greed by contentment; *adharma* by generosity; dharma with careful thought; attachment to objects by meditation on their passing nature; the tendency to talk too much by periods of silence; pride by compassion; all ill-effects of material prosperity and wealth by sharing.[54]

Mere knowledge of what is a virtue and what is not does not enable a leader to be virtuous. This aspect is forcefully brought forth by the character of Duryodhana in the epic Mahabharata. He says:

> I know what righteous conduct is, but I have no inclination to act accordingly.
> I know what unrighteous conduct is, but I cannot abstain from doing it.[55]

Buddhism also throws significant light on the methods of developing these virtues. The good ruler vanquishes ill-will with loving kindness, wickedness with virtue, parsimony with liberality and falsehood with truth. Lord Buddha, who was moved by the inhumanities of rulers who governed their countries unjustly, had directed his attention to the problem of good leadership and governance. According to him, for a country to be happy it must have a good leader (ruler). He has provided a list of ten important attributes of a good leader in his teaching of the 'Ten Duties of the King'.[56] They are:

- *Dana*—liberality, charity and generosity
- *Sila*—morality
- *Pariccaga*—self-sacrifice for the good of the people
- *Ajjava*—integrity, honesty and sincerity
- *Maddava*—kindness and gentleness
- *Tapa*—austerity, self-control and simple life
- *Akkoda*—non-anger, freedom from hatred and ill will
- *Avihimsa*—non-violence and promotion of peace
- *Khanti*—forbearance, patience, tolerance and understanding
- *Avirodha*—non-opposition, i.e. ruling in harmony with his people

The 'Ten Duties of the King' is widely accepted as a yardstick that could be applied to modern government as well. As listed earlier, the duties are liberality, morality, self-sacrifice, integrity, kindness, austerity, non-anger, non-violence, forbearance and non-opposition (to the will of the people).

The first duty of liberality (*dana*) demands that a leader (ruler) should contribute generously towards the welfare of the people. It is assumed that a leader has the competence to provide adequately for the people. One of the prime duties of responsible leadership would be to ensure the economic security of the people.

Morality (*sila*) in traditional Buddhist terms is based on the observance of the five precepts, which entails refraining from the destruction of life, theft, adultery, falsehood and indulgence in intoxicants. The leader must bear a high moral character to win the respect and trust of the people and to ensure their happiness and prosperity, and must be a role model. When the leader does not observe the Dhamma, the associates become corrupt, and when they are corrupt, the people have to suffer. It is further believed that an unrighteous leader brings down calamity on land. The root of an organisation's misfortunes has to be sought in the moral failings of the leader.

The third duty, *paricagga,* is self-sacrifice. The good ruler sublimates his or her needs as an individual to the service of the nation.

Integrity (*ajjava*) implies incorruptibility in the discharge of public duties as well as honesty and sincerity in personal relations. Leaders should strictly practise the truth in thought, word and deed. To deceive or to mislead the people in any way would be an occupational failing as well as a moral offence.

Kindness (*maddava*) in a leader is, in a sense, the courage to feel concern for the people. It is undeniably easier to ignore the hardships of those who are too weak to demand their rights than to respond sensitively to their needs.

In the matter of love, leaders should not make any distinction between citizen and their own children, and should be equally loving and kind towards all.

The duty of austerity (*tapa*) means a leader must adopt good habits, develop self-control and practise discipline. The self-indulgent leader who enjoys an extravagant lifestyle and ignores the need for austerity brings down the organisation to doom along with his or her own downfall.

The seventh, eighth and ninth duties—non-anger (*akkodha*), non-violence (*avihamsa*) and forbearance (*khanti*)—are all related. Because the displeasure of the powerful leaders could have unhappy and far-reaching consequences, leaders must not allow personal feelings of enmity and ill will to erupt into destructive anger and violence. It is necessary for a leader to develop the true forbearance that moves them to deal wisely and generously.

The tenth duty of a ruler, non-opposition to the will of the people (*avirodha*), is a reminder that the legitimacy of government is founded on the consent of the people, who may withdraw their mandate at any time if they lose confidence in the ability of the ruler to serve their best interests.

Ashoka the Great who ruled his realm in accordance with the principles of non-violence and compassion is considered as an ideal Buddhist king.[57]

Finally, Indian classical wisdom has developed the concept of an effective leader who:

- has self-control, having conquered the inimical temptations of the senses,
- cultivates the intellect in association with elders,

- is ever active in promoting the security and welfare of the people,
- ensures the observance by the people of their duties and responsibilities by authority and example,
- improves his own discipline by continuing learning in all branches of knowledge and
- endears himself to his people by enriching them and doing good to them.[58]

Inclusive Communication for Leadership Effectiveness

In a globalised world, where people of many faiths (and no professed faith) are invited to participate in all spheres of society, only a leader practising inclusive communication can contribute to a harmonious and peaceful world.

The history of ancient, medieval and modern India provides many inspirational political leaders who demonstrated inclusive communication. We try to showcase here such leaders, through their own words and actions, in order to guide leaders in all areas who are interested in developing inclusive communication.

Even though a lot of works are available on these leaders, not much is researched on their inclusive leadership styles, especially their communications and actions. Hence, we propose to fill this gap.

Inclusive communication adopted by the leaders prepares the ground where people following different religions and cultures can live together with mutual respect and tolerance, rather than in suspicion and animosity. Today, many nations suffer from crises due to growing hatred, exclusion, discrimination of various types and hence, they search for a philosophy that addresses these issues and helps leaders and people in developing inclusive communication in all matters so that peace may prevail in the world.

Ashoka the Great attached a lot of importance in achieving successful and good governance through communication. Ashoka realised that the progress among the people through *Dhamma* can be encouraged by persuasion and not by strict regulations. According to him, persuasion had a greater effect. In order to persuade his subjects, Ashoka got his message of *Dhamma* inscribed on stone pillars and stone slabs throughout his kingdom so that it may remain forever. Ashoka is a remarkable champion of religious pluralism and he promoted global religiosity even then (3rd century BCE) as is evident in his Rock Edict XII in which he has communicated his intention of allowing all religions to grow in his kingdom without any special favour for any one religion or any discrimination against other religions of his time.[59]

King Bukkaraya-I (reign 1356–1377 CE), one of the founders of Vijayanagar kingdom of Karnataka in India, brought about reconciliation in 1368 CE between the Jainas and Vaishnavas, two different religious communities that existed in his kingdom, through inclusive communication.

The Shravanabelgola inscription, which records this incident, is one of the most beautiful pieces among the epigraphic records of Karnataka and highlights inclusive communication and action. The original inscription is in

Kannada language, translation of relevant portion is given below:

> Dispute having arisen between the Jainas and Bhaktas (Sri-Vaishnavas), the *bhavyajanas* (the Jainas) of all the *nadus*... having made a petition to Vira Bukkaraya (1368 CE), about the injustice done by the *bhaktas*, the king taking the hand of the Jainas and placing it in the hand of the Sri-Vaishnavas of the eighteen *nadus*, including all the *acharyas* of the places... and declaring (at the same time) that there was no difference between the *Vaishnava Darshana* (Vaishavism) and the *Jaina Darshana* (Jainism).
>
> If loss or advancement should be caused to the *Jaina Darshana* through the Sri-Vaishnavas, the Sri-Vaishnavas will kindly deem it as loss or advancement caused to their own (*Darshana*). The Sri-Vaishnavas will to this effect kindly set up a *shasana* (inscription) in all the *bastis* (Jain worshipping places) of the kingdom.
>
> For as long as the sun and the moon endure, the Sri-Vaishnava creed will continue to protect the *Jaina Darshana*. The Sri-Vaishnavas and the Jainas are one (body); they must not be viewed as different.[60]

This exemplary epigraph will remain eternally as a monument of a very significant and large-hearted religious tolerance as preached and practised in Karnataka and as a piece of one of the best examples of inclusive communication. The successor of Bukkaraya was his son, Harihara II, who too maintained the glorious traditions of his father.

One of his inscriptions found at Belur in Karnataka contains a remarkable inclusive statement in the Sanskrit language. Its English translation is as follows:

> May Hari, the ruler of the Universe,
> worshipped by the Saivas as Shiva,
> by the Vedantins as Brahma,
> by the Buddhists as Buddha,
> by the Mimamsakas as Karma,
> by the Naiyayikas as Karta,
> by the Jainas as the Arhat,
> grant our prayers.[61]

Akbar the great Mughal emperor of India (1543–1605 CE), being a firm proponent of universal tolerance and religious freedom for all, welcomed to his court, representatives of all religions known to him: Muslims, Hindus, Jains, Parsis, Jews and even Jesuit priests from the Portuguese settlements in Goa. Credit goes to him for unifying the various creeds of Hindustan under his victorious banners, and for creating a strong Mughal Empire. He not only appointed Hindus to high posts, but also tried to remove all distinctions between the Muslims and non-Muslims. He abolished the pilgrim tax in the eighth year and the jizya in the ninth year of his reign. Akbar built a building called the *IbādatKhāna* (House of Worship), where he encouraged religious debate, inviting Hindus, Roman Catholics and even atheists to participate. He tried to reconcile the religious differences by creating a new faith called the *Din-i-Ilahi* (Faith of the Divine), which incorporated both 'pantheistic' versions of Islamic Sufism (most notably the

Ibn Arabi's doctrine of *Wahdat ul Wajood*, or unity of existence) and bhakti or devotional cults of Hinduism. Even some elements of Christianity—like crosses, fire worship of Zoroastrianism—were amalgamated besides Jainism in the new religion. Akbar the Great was particularly famous for creating this new pluralistic and synthetic faith.[62]

A universality of outlook is visible in him as he patronised the painting, literature and architecture. It is of great significance to note that paintings were totally devoid of religious symbolism. He patronised artists without being concerned with their religious affiliations. It was in his time that the form of Indo-Islamic architecture became part of the landscape that was a synthesis of Islamic as well as Hindu traditions. Akbar left a deep impact not only on the Mughal Empire, but also on the strengthening of a liberal Indian tradition that has led to continuity of the Indian civilisation over centuries.[63]

Akbar was a great military leader and builder of the imperial empire. He was also was a man of deep compassion for all living beings. As an inclusive leader, he respected women, firmly rejected religious formalism and intolerance, disapproved inhuman practices such as slavery, *sati* and polygamy. He was deeply involved with his people and helped them in solving their problems. The inclusive and humane facets of Akbar's personality are often overshadowed in historical records and other narratives by his military exploits and administrative measures.[64]

Akbar's writings provide valuable insights on fundamental issues that preoccupy the world: power, justice and fundamentalism against diversity and tolerance. Akbar's first letter to the Jesuits of Goa is worth reproducing here:

In the name of Jalal-ud-din Muhammad Akbar, King placed in the Seat of God. To the Chief Priests of the Order of Saint Paul:

Be it known to them that I am a great friend of theirs. I have sent thither Adbullah my ambassador, and [the translator] Domenico Perez, in order to invite you to send back to me with them two of your learned men, who should bring books of the law, and above all the Gospels, because I truly and earnestly desire to understand their perfection; and with great urgency, I again demand that they should come with my ambassador aforesaid, and bring their books. For, from their coming I shall obtain the utmost consolation; they will be dear to me, and I shall receive them with every possible honour.

As soon as I shall have become well instructed in the law, and shall have comprehended its perfection, they will be able, if willing, to return at their pleasure, and I shall send them back with great honours, and appropriate rewards. Let them not fear me in the least, for I receive them under my pledge of good faith and assure them concerning myself.[65]

Akbar's 'all-inclusive' views are best summarised in the following verses that he wrote towards the end of his life:

O god, in every temple I see people that are seeking You, and in every language I hear, people are praising You! Polytheism and Islam feel after You[,]
each religion says, 'You are One, without equal!'
If it be a mosque, people murmur the holy prayer,

> and if it be a Christian Church, people ring the bell out of love to You.
> Sometimes I frequent the Christian cloister, and sometimes the mosque,
> but it is You whom I search, from temple to temple.[66]

Akbar and Ashoka and Buddha may be reflected in Gandhi who aimed to establish communal and religious harmony and peace through non-violence (ahimsa). He encouraged tolerance and respect for every religion in order to establish peace amongst various religious communities in India. He believed in *advaita* philosophy (non-dualism), one of the Indian philosophical systems. According to Gandhi, *advaita* teaches the essential unity of man and in his view if one man gains spiritually, the whole world gains with him and if one man falls, the whole world falls.[67]

The doctrine of *anekanta-vada* developed in Jainism, an ancient Indian philosophical system, captures the spirit of tolerating plural truth-claims in all walks of life. The comprehension of a thing from different points of view develops an inclusive outlook necessary for peaceful co-existence. Gandhi says:

> It is this doctrine that has taught me to judge a Mussalman from his own standpoint and a Christian from his. Formerly I used to resent the ignorance of my opponents. Today I can love them because I am gifted with the eye to see myself as others see me and vice versa.[68]

Gandhi adds:

> ...if people of different religions grasp the real significance of their own religion, they will never hate the people of any other than their own... there may be many religions, but the true aim of all is the same.[69]
>
> If a man reaches the heart of his own religion, he has reached the heart of the others too.[70]

In his own ashram, or wherever he attended a prayer, Gandhi made it a point to have hymns read out from the sacred scriptures of all major religions: Islam, Hinduism, Buddhism, Christianity, Sikhism. It may be noted here that during India's pre-partition and post-partition days, when some members of the audience objected to the recitation of the Quran, Gandhi refused to have hymns read out from any of the scriptures. He stuck to his point until every objector eventually withdrew his objection. He honoured all religions and asked his followers to do so because they all voiced truths that were part of humankind's total precious heritage. He said:

> Cleanse your hearts of all narrowness
> and make them as broad as the Ocean.
> That is the teaching of the Quran and the Gita.[71]

It is necessary to illustrate Gandhi's inclusive communication strategies. He always used the appropriate words to communicate his ideas to his listeners and readers. He used words or symbols that could be easily understood by his listeners and readers. One such example is Gandhi's famous concept of an ideal order which was called *ramarajya*. This ideal order promotes prosperity, peace, inclusion, virtue and discipline.[72] Millions of Hindu listeners and even listeners of other religions who were Indians understood what *ramarajya* stood for. In places where the majority of his listeners were Muslims, he was using the word *khuda*, or Allah, while to a Christian audience he would describe it as the Kingdom of God.[73] This clearly indicates Gandhi's strategy of convincing the masses by using analogy and metaphors with which they are familiar, so that his message is well understood without any confusion or misunderstanding. He practised inter-cultural codes.

Dr A.P.J. Abdual Kalam (President of India, 2002–2007) was a great follower of Gandhi. He is an exemplar of an inclusive leader. He once mentioned an incident from his life. He was invited by the bishop of Rajkot, Rev. Father Gregory to inaugurate the Christ College in Ajmer, India. Before the inauguration, on invitation from the nearby Swaminarayana Temple, they entered the inner sanctum of the temple and they were all received with the offering of tilak (auspicious mark) on their foreheads. Dr Kalam wrote:

> It was a great sight with Rev. Father Gregory, Abdul Kalam and Y.S. Rajan all having the shining tilak on our foreheads. This incident demonstrated the strength of connectivity of several religions in our country leading to a unique spiritual experience.

> ...every religion has two components: religious preaching and spiritual insights. The spiritual focus influenced by compassion and love must be merged in integrated mission and this alone is capable of developing inclusive leaders for the betterment of the world.[74]

An eye-opening example worth discussing here is the Iftar dinner during the holy month of Ramadan organised by Swami Vishvesha Teertha (1931–2019), a well-known Hindu seer of Pejawara Mutt at Krishna Temple in Udupi, Karnataka, India. It was a positive step towards achieving communal harmony. More than 150 members of Muslim community attended the '*Souharda Upahara Koota*' (meal to promote harmony). When several people criticised and opposed this move, Swami stood his ground and clarified his position in an interview. He said that during his *paryaya* (religious ritual held every alternate year), he had noticed hundreds of people including Christians and Muslims coming to the public dining hall of the Krishna Temple for food. But this time, he especially invited Muslims during Ramadan. He justified his invitation to Muslims by saying that the Muslim community had offered their service through donations in kind and cash and Muslims have always supported the mutt during crisis. At many instances, Muslims had invited him to their homes as well as to inaugurate mosques. He was honoured by them and their extended support and cooperated in his activities. The mutt honoured them since they have shown respect towards it. He also told people that the harmony among two religions did not begin with him. His teacher Madhvacharya had propagated the same. He recalled that several Hindu religious heads shared a good bond with Muslims. He observed:

> God is one to all mankind. Hindus and Muslims should live together in harmony. When there was an attempt to gherao the Krishna Temple, Muslims came forward to defend the temple. There is a history where both communities have co-existed peacefully in Udupi. It should become the model for people in Karnataka.[75]

Concluding Remarks

In the 21st century, it is very common for people to have encounters with people of diverse religious perspectives. Insightful learning from Indian history of different periods can help in preparing a framework and provide adequate guidance to leaders to practise inclusive communication while respecting the diverse religious, political and cultural identities of their people. It may also be pointed out here that the leaders who practised inclusive communication and established peace and harmony, invariably practised a galaxy of virtues such as equality, respect, reverence, sympathy, tolerance, gratitude, compassion, charity, humility, forgiveness and sincerity. Self-control, patience, sacrifice, unselfishness, self-negation, discipline and courtesy are also found in these leaders. Therefore, it may be said that in order to develop and practise inclusive communication, it becomes necessary to develop these eternal virtues for any leader in any field.

3

Violent Leaders to Non-violent Leaders

Ahimsa Paramo Dharmah
(Non-violence is the supreme virtue)
—The Mahabharata

Ashokan Victory: Rewriting Violence

It is interesting to imagine how polished stones or rocks and pillars with texts inscribed on them in vernacular languages (such as Prakrit, Greek and Aramic)[1] can inspire an entire generation of historians, linguists, philosophers, leaders, intellectuals and people all over the world to re-think about humanism and its relevance, with even greater resonance today. We are talking about the now famous edicts of the Indian Mauryan king fondly revered as Ashoka the Great, also known as King Piyadasi or 'Beloved-of-the-Gods', that date back to the Mauryan period of Indian history, somewhere around 300 BCE and 200 BCE (Rich puts it at 268 or 269 to 232 BCE).[2] The edicts have been identified by historians and other academicians as reforms and moral principles instituted and recommended by the king to establish a *humane* society in his kingdom. In other words, the use of rock edicts suggests a certain mode of communication that he preferred. And the preference suggests a certain ideology attached to the mode of communication chosen.

Why a king should choose to locate, fix, sculpt pillars and inscribe on them the principles he wants his citizens to follow? It is an interesting visual display of the king's intentions, values, ambitions and, more significantly, foresight, for himself and his people, both as a leader as well as a communicator. We say *interesting* because the laws appear in a visual format and are made available in *strategic* locations in a manner similar to milestones that are found on contemporary highways. Imagine driving for a long haul. After every five miles, there is a visual inscription. Say at the first five miles, you see:

> Here (in my domain) no living beings are to be slaughtered or offered in sacrifice.[3]

After the next five miles:

> Formerly, in the kitchen of Beloved-of-the-Gods, King Piyadasi, hundreds of thousands of animals were killed every day to make curry. But now with the writing of this Dhamma edict only three creatures, two peacocks and a deer are killed, and the deer not always. And in time, not even these three creatures will be killed.

Then there is a fork and on either side is a different inscription. On the left, it may read:

> Everywhere within Beloved-of-the-Gods King Piyadasi's domain, and among the people beyond the borders, the Cholas, the Pandyas, the Satiyaputras, the Keralaputras, as far as Tamraparni and where the Greek king Antiochos rules, and among the kings who are neighbours of Antiochos, everywhere has Beloved-of-the-Gods, King Piyadasi, made provision for two types of medical treatment: medical treatment for humans and medical treatment for animals. Wherever medical herbs suitable for humans or animals are not available, I have had them imported and grown. Along roads, I have had wells dug and trees planted for the benefit of humans and animals.

On the right, it may read:

> These and many other kinds of Dhamma practices have been encouraged by Beloved-of-the-Gods, King Piyadasi, and he will continue to promote Dhamma practice. And the sons, grandsons and great-grandsons of Beloved-of-the-Gods, King Piyadasi, too will continue to promote Dhamma practice until the end of time; living by Dhamma and virtue, they will instruct in Dhamma.

And many such inscriptions appear throughout the journey. The visibility (written script), the enduring capacity (material) and the doctrine (Dhamma) that spread all over his enormously growing kingdom, definitely accentuate the impact of the king's reforms in the most durable manner, so much that they survive till today.

Yet, a closer introspection of the content of the reforms reveal the desire of durability contained in the meaning of the words—a desire of a legacy in making at *that* time and a legacy bequeathed to us *over* time. In other words, we interpret two basic characteristics that describe the Ashokan edicts for us:

- A legacy *openly* bequeathed to his future generations and through this world and the next.
- The doctrine of non-violence as not a constant but as experienced through the horrors of violence.

Many great kings have had great edicts. And many great writers have extensively interpreted edicts. One such great interpretation comes from the 19th-century English poet Percy Bysshe Shelley in 'Ozymandias', where he writes about the irony of such edicts:

I met a traveller from an antique land
Who said—'Two vast and trunkless legs of stone
Stand in the desert. Near them on the sand,
Half sunk, a shattered visage lies, whose frown
And wrinkled lip and sneer of cold command
Tell that its sculptor well those passions read
Which yet survive, stamped on these lifeless things,
The hand that mocked them and the heart that fed.
And on the pedestal these words appear:
'My name is Ozymandias, King of Kings:
Look on my works, ye mighty, and despair!'
Nothing beside remains. Round the decay

Of that colossal wreck, boundless and bare,
The lone and level sands stretch far away.[4]

Shelley thinks about the plight of edicts that had been ordered to advertise the ancient king's, and by extension, a leader's glory. Ozymandias was the king of kings. His edicts declare his supremacy as looking at his works (his colossal statue, for instance), one is expected to despair in awe and terror.

Yet, as Shelley describes, there is decay and wreck, with only the words still visible. The meaning established by the words and the wreck of the statue of Ozymandias have an ironical relation. Power and greatness bow before time.

King Ashoka enacts a similar feat—sculpting edicts to let the world know of his conquests and his ideologies. But what makes his edicts memorable is the *unique* advertisement of not only his doctrines and conquests but an *open* self-introspection on those ideologies and conquests.

In a peculiar manner, here is a leader thinking aloud while advertising his glory; here is a leader announcing to the world not merely his doctrines, but how he arrived there; here is a leader declaring to the world not merely what needs to be followed, but also the benefits of the rules that need to be followed; here is a leader not merely validating the rules he has inscribed, but dreaming of the eternity of these rules and their good consequences for this world and the next till the world ends. In other words, here is a king who is not merely glorifying *himself* in *his* times but looking for the glory of the *world* at *all* times. Here is a king who describes the pain caused by war (the Kalinga

War) and how non-violence establishes a better kingdom, thus highlighting the need to practise such virtues by his children, grandchildren and generations to come. The movement from war to peace makes his analysis of peace stronger, and the desire for the practice of peace by future generations makes his doctrine of peace relevant.

In short, King Ashoka thinks beyond himself, though he encrypts his personal advertisement as the Beloved-of-the-Gods, King Piyadasi, the harbinger of peace and justice. Yet, in his personal advertisement as well, he admits remorsefully to the horror of the Kalinga War.

It is from his introspection, change from war to peace and foresight for eternity, that our great theory of mutation evolves—a theory that validates the genesis of this book. Though Charles Darwin, the English naturalist, in the 19th century, had already established the theory of evolution and transformation of human species, the very same species is also responsible for the evolution and transformation of human values.

King Ashoka's self-introspecting edicts stand out in the process of evolution and transformation of human values more than in their declaration of virtues, and it is here that we pitch the evolution of global leadership—a form of leadership that is continuously handling differences in all social forms: geographical, political, economical, cultural and the rest. Ashoka lived at a time when 'global' as a word was not a contemporary and inevitable phenomenon as it is today. We do not claim that the world was *not* global then; we say the world was not *termed* global then.

However, the edict on the Kalinga War requires more in-depth introspection to understand how Ashoka can be *global* even then, and definitely even today.

The edict describes the king's remorse: a large number of people were dying, deported, injured, killed or separated from their loved ones due to the war. Thus, the edict accepts the tragedy that befalls any victory in war (here, it actually documents the casualty list):

> ...that Brahmans, ascetics, and householders of different religions who live in those countries, and who are respectful to superiors, to mother and father, to elders, and who behave properly and have strong loyalty towards friends, acquaintances, companions, relatives, servants and employees—that they are injured, killed or separated from their loved ones. Even those who are not affected [by all this] suffer when they see friends, acquaintances, companions and relatives affected.

On the other, the edict also dates the Kalinga War as *that* significant event that changed Ashoka from a warring to a peace-loving king who followed the Dhamma, or 'the secular ethic of non-violence...'[5]:

> After the Kalingas had been conquered, Beloved-of-the-Gods came to feel a strong inclination towards the Dhamma, a love for the Dhamma and for instruction in Dhamma. Now Beloved-of-the-Gods feels deep remorse for having conquered the Kalingas.

Why is it so very important to record the remorse of the king, and *by the king himself*? Is not warfare a natural feature of a king's duty? Is not every king who wishes to increase his geographical boundaries or conquer other enemy territories is a great king? Great leaders like Alexander, Augustus and Napoleon have been celebrated for warfare and victory. King Ashoka by annexing Kalinga to his already huge territory must have become the emperor of emperors. Kalinga was a very important territory in terms of natural and labour resources, not just for Ashoka but for any king who wished greatness and power. So, where does remorse feature in a victory that actually had been a great victory, as many other great remorseless victories have been without the romanticism of remorse?

Ashoka has been popularised in history as a great king *precisely* because he renounced violence in war. And in his own edict, he puts in great effort to narrate the tale of change. For most great emperors, winning wars was essential. Ashoka, too, was focused on winning the Kalinga battle, which he eventually did. His victory cannot demean his greatness as per the socially defined laws of victory for a king on the battlefield. But, in the process of winning the battle, he gradually became aware of what he was *excluding* or *losing* (human life and by extension, human resource), even if they were the enemies. The greatness of the emperor was accentuated multifold when he *integrated* his *loss* (or what he excluded) into his strategy.

We contend that Ashoka did not merely change the *function* of victory and emperorship (and hence, leadership), but also created a space for further replication and/or emulation of the changed *function* of victory. That is where the legacy part comes in. In other words, he expects his children, grandchildren and the rest of the world for eternity to mutate the *function* of victory in a manner similar to his own efforts at value mutation. Thus, he ignites a chain reaction of value mutation from the moment he depicts how he transformed from a violent king to a king who followed the Dhamma.

Ashoka's mutating efforts are vital to our understanding of values, and it is in this context that Ashoka's self-introspecting style of documentation of values is very relevant.

Let us *first* understand the mutation theory in the context of value mutation. Say, there is a constant value, which has a fixed definition for universal time and space, such as violence. Such a value would have its consistent evaluation against the social radar that would judge it. But if we consider violence as a bad habit, such an evaluation can only happen when violence is pitched against something else that is set up as a parameter of evaluation by the social radar itself; a parameter that is itself not violent or must be different from violence. Violence is bad *only* when compared to non-violence; or else it has no value. In this context, let us consider the works of two famous path-breaking thinkers, an early 20th-century scientist and a late 20th-century philosopher: Albert Einstein, the German theoretical physicist, and Jacques Derrida, the French philosopher.

Einstein is important because of his contribution to our understanding of constants and relatives. In the light of

Einstein's theory of relativity, meaning is always relative to a position of interpretation, such that if that position is changed, the meaning also changes. Amidst the Einsteinian relativism, let us situate the Derridean pluralities. We are using plural oppositions to construct meanings and values. For instance, violence is determined as a powerful value, even if negative, when interpreted against its opposing value, non-violence.

We propose that violence or non-violence are not stand-alone entities but may be seen as a molecule/gene consisting actions of violence and non-violence *simultaneously*. Depending upon the dominance of the action, the quality gets pronounced. But the important point for consideration is the existence of the not-so-dominant action as well. See Figure 3.1 to understand the point being made.

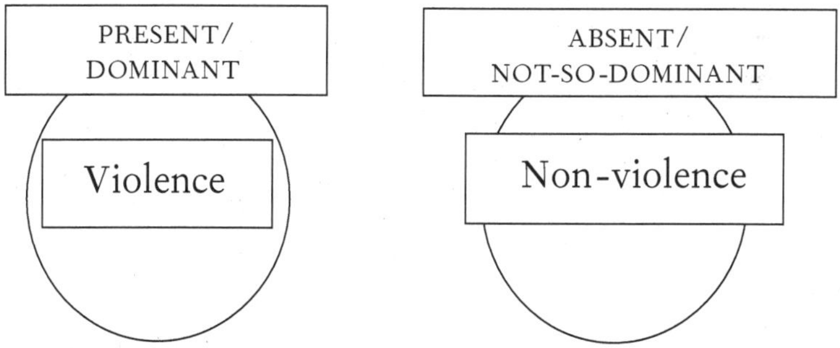

FIGURE 3.1 *Genetic Modelling of Violence as a Molecular Quality*

The emphasis is on the *silent* presence of non-violence in a dominant value of violence. A comparison between the Indian classical yogic tradition and the Western modern tradition of psychoanalysis would support our contention. We are reminded of a significant concept called *pratipaksha bhavana*, or contrary meditation, that features in the famous *Yoga Sutras* of ancient Indian sage Patanjali. According to him, when a person is obsessed by a strong desire or hatred to cause injury to others, one must reflect on the contrary thoughts. If, for instance, one feels a strong desire to tell a lie, one must reflect upon the virtues of truthfulness and the consequences of falsehood. If one thinks of hating a person and desires to hurt him/her, then one must think of virtues of mercy or about the good qualities of that person.

In short, one should cogitate upon the motives that impel one towards an evil thought or deed and the consequences of endless pain and delusion that are bound to flow therefrom. Hence, *pratipaksha bhavana*, or contrary meditation, is the strategy recommended by yoga in the moral struggle against evil thoughts or tendencies.[6]

Geraldine Coster in *Yoga and Western Psychology* (1968) has brought out very clearly the common features between the yogic method of contrary meditation and the psychoanalyst's use of suggestion.[7] The yogic technique is essentially a process of self-treatment in which a person suffering from an affliction or a bad habit identifies it through introspection and then practises meditation on its opposite. Coster points out that this opposite one is advised to meditate upon must be the psychological and not merely the verbal opposite of the form of affliction or the habit that has to be overcome. If, for instance, a person takes to drinking as an antidote against insecurity or depression, the opposite, which he/she should meditate upon, is self-confidence and courage. The awareness of pain and misery out of vindictive action would make him/her more conscious of the streak of vindictiveness in his/her nature and reinforce his/her resolve to restrain it.

At the same time, he/she should deliberate upon the qualities of gentleness and lose no opportunity to practise it in one form or another. In the course of time, the latent impressions of vindictive acts will get inhibited by those of gentleness and he/she will find that his/her tendency for vindictive acts does not recur as frequently as before, even under the gravest provocations. This profound change, however, is not possible unless contrary meditation is practised over a long period with faith and without interruption, and a sort of inner resistance is built against the habit.

Here, one of the authors of this book is reminded of an incident narrated by an executive of a multinational corporation (MNC) in one of his management development programmes on leadership excellence conducted in 2005 at IIM Calcutta. The executive, who narrated the incident, disliked a person in his organisation because of certain negative qualities in the said person. But during the restructuring of his organisation, the said person became his boss. The executive pondered over the options available to him in such a situation. He could not think of resigning from his job as he wanted to continue to stay in the place where he was posted because of some compelling personal reasons. Also, he was promoted to a higher grade beyond his expectation and he really liked his job. After spending one week on leave, he thought he should meet the new boss and invite him for tea.

Fortunately, the new boss was not aware that he was disliked by this executive. He readily went with him for tea. This cordial gesture was repeated many times and over a period of time, they became very good friends. What worked here is the *pratipaksha bhavana* (contrary meditation). The concerned executive concentrated on the good/positive qualities of his boss instead of concentrating on his bad/negative qualities.

What makes Ashoka's transformation enlightening is his actualisation of the absent or the *silent* presence of non-violence in his dominant violent act, such that he transforms violence into non-violence from *within*, thus mutating the internal constituents of the larger value. That the edict highlights loss and remorse and not merely preaches non-violence as a constant and reinforces the internal mutation interpretation. See Figure 3.2 to understand the Ashokan mutation of violence into non-violence.

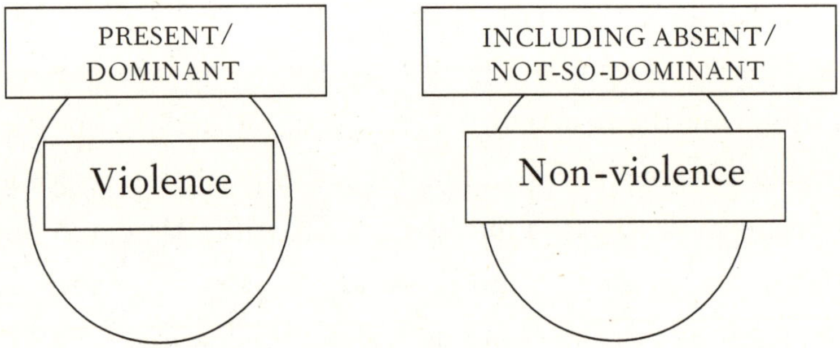

FIGURE 3.2 *Mutation of Violence to Non-violence*

We thus propose that the leader becomes a value-mutation-change-agent, where the mutation happens to molecules of values in a manner similar to that of biological genes. The process of biological mutation is depicted wonderfully in the music video created by Hammer & Tongs[8] for the 1999 UK singles chartbuster 'Right Here, Right Now', a song by the British big beat[9] musician Fatboy Slim, featured in the album *You've Come a Long Way, Baby*. The music video depicts the process of the evolution of life. From '350 billion years ago' as a single cell organism in the ocean, the evolution is mapped across varying stages of human-form development: from a jelly-fish, a putter-fish, a predatory fish to a land-fish (movement from ocean to land), then transforming into a creeping alligator to a tree-climbing ape-like creature, after that, in an icy landscape and through a blizzard, the human form evolves from early *homo sapiens* to the civilised citizen.[10]

Here, the environmental change in the forms of the ocean, the land, the forest, the blizzard and the hamburger-dominated metropolis plays the mutation agent. Post the Kalinga War, Ashoka played the role of a value-mutation-change-agent.

The leader as a value-mutation-change-agent alters the ingredients of a virtue. For instance, the dominant ingredient of victory as a virtue is 'owning' or 'possessing by winning'. However, while owning through victory, we are ousting or excluding or losing other elements as well. Victory as a *function*, thus, simultaneously works on winning (and hence, owning) while losing (and hence, excluding). Ashoka's enlightened awareness of the simultaneous presence of ingredients of loss or exclusion in victory makes him a change agent with a *difference*—he pays attention to what he loses when he wins. In the process, the molecular module of victory as a value-laden *function* mutates by displacement of its hierarchical constitution; the *exclusion* becomes ever more present and even more integrated into the language of victory—I wonder what I lost when I won; and does that matter to me?

So, there are two points to think about:

- Why is a mutation agent important for global leadership?
- Why is there an emphasis on ownership?

To answer these questions, we must first understand the essence of the word 'global' in its contemporary sense. A Google search would show the following phrases for 'global' from various sites and online dictionaries: 'of or referring to a globe'; 'pertaining to the whole world'; 'worldwide'; 'universal, covering, influencing, or relating to the whole world'. The essence we get is that *global* is *that* which takes in everything. The study material for the University of Illinois's Principles of Microeconomics gives a *metaphorical* definition of globalisation—'ongoing process by which regional economies, societies, and cultures have become integrated'. In its economic sense, globalisation is the:

> ...process enabling financial and investment markets to operate internationally, largely as a result of deregulation and improved communications; the emergence since the 1980s of a single world market dominated by multinational companies, leading to a diminishing

> capacity for national governments to control their economies; the process by which a company, etc, expands to operate internationally.[11]

The words/phrases 'deregulation' or 'diminishing capacity of national governments controlling their economies' resound with possibilities of freedom of expression in economic and social categories for *smaller* players with greater force. Thus, from a bird's-eye view, global is all about pertaining to everything; more specifically, it is about including or integrating the lesser-known or regional economies, societies and cultures in a world dominated by the dominant economies. The thrust on world reputation as against the national is, therefore, fascinating.

Along with the word 'global' comes another word, 'cosmopolitan'. If we look for the qualitative meaning of the word (again from several Google results), we get the following dimensions: 'free from local, provincial, or national ideas, prejudices, or attachments'; 'at home all over the world'; 'ideology that all kinds of human race belong to a single community, based on a shared morality'; 'belonging to all the world'; 'not limited to just one part of the world'. The contrasting positions of the *regional* or the *provincial* in both the global and the cosmopolitan sense of the world are well witnessed in the randomly selected protocols documented above.

For the global, the *provincial* has the chance to make meaning for itself in the whole wide world; for the cosmopolitan, meaning-making is not bound to any provincial agenda. And yet, in both, the provincial is the point of contention so as to realise the utopian humanitarian agenda—to be at home with the world. Thus, the same provincial is set to maintain its identity on one hand and lose on the other. It is in this contrasting contention that springs the biggest problem of all—how to prepare and teach the humanitarian agenda of being at home with the world.

Thus, the problem is not so much that the world is global and cosmopolitan. The problem is the new role that the representatives of the agenda-making-and-distributing factories or industries need to play; the new role of leaders of any capacity, individual or organisational, to be more particular.

Today, global insights are not surprising, nor are they enlightening. They are a reality; they are inevitable. That various resources can be used so as to survive in a rapidly changing (by extension mutating) environment is *not* an insightful discussion; it *is* inevitable that diasporas of resources, connectivities and knowledge are available; there is no escape from such heterogeneity. We have to *integrate* differences in the technical sense of the word, when there is no other possibility but to; we survive through integration. Thus, integration is also not a virtue propagated; we cannot escape it (integration) if we have to survive in this system. So, in what capacity, does our value-mutation-change-agent contribute to global conditions of human understanding? We contend dual perspectives on global integration:

- Perspective One: The value-mutation-change-agent creates in us the ability to accept heterogeneity as our own and not just as any inevitable responsibility, which it is anyway.

The complexity then is how to show respect to the inevitable and worry for it the way we would for what we consciously think is our own, or like to call our own. And to do that we must understand what it is that we exclude when we integrate. In other words, the idea is to evolve an agenda to 'not exclude' by sensitising ourselves to 'what is excluded in any process' in order to understand how integration happens, if at all. Ashoka stands tall here.

- Perspective Two: We feel very responsible for our own. We cannot avoid the desire to own, how about owning what we do not desire?

  The idea of ownership of knowledge, resources and stakes that are not ours is an important point of departure for the value-mutation-change-agent.

Thus, ownership may be understood as a binary gene consisting actions of owning and ousting, as shown in Figure 3.3. We cannot own without ousting. So, for every action that we own, we are simultaneously ousting something. Events or characters that have learned to synthesise the binary elements by assimilating the ousted into their agenda of ownership have consciously and/or unconsciously led to a gene mutation that has augured well for the contemporary cosmopolitan and global ideology—the ideology of willful cooperation. It is in this context that the Ashokan Victory is path-breaking (see Figure 3.4).

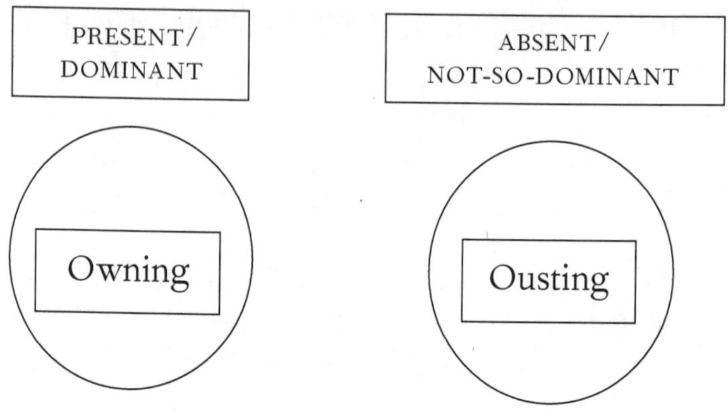

FIGURE 3.3 *The Model of Ownership Had It Been a Gene*

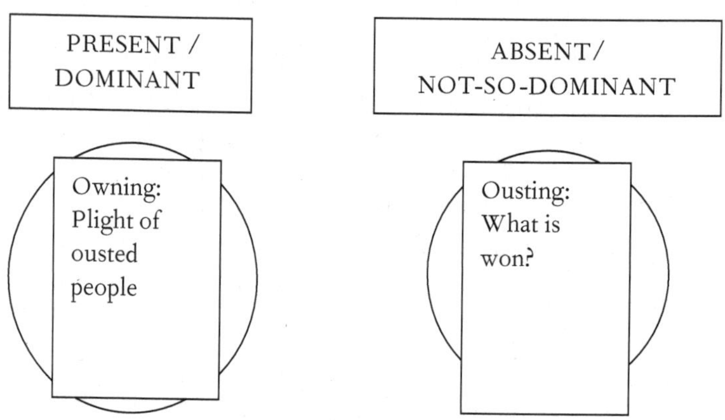

FIGURE 3.4 *The Model of Ashokan Victory*

The moment a mutation happens, the consequences of that very mutation resonate through time and space beyond the moment of mutation.

The next striking characteristic of the Ashokan edicts is his open display of the knowledge of the consequences of his value-mutation-change—his desire for legacy through eternity:

> These and many other kinds of Dhamma practices have been encouraged by Beloved-of-the-Gods, King

> Piyadasi, and he will continue to promote Dhamma practice. And the sons, grandsons and great-grandsons of Beloved-of-the-Gods, King Piyadasi, too will continue to promote Dhamma practice until the end of time; living by Dhamma and virtue, they will instruct in Dhamma. (quoted again)

In other words, Ashoka establishes that consciously or unconsciously, what we do will continue to mutate future histories, with or without our knowledge. This chain of legacy has been depicted in Figure 3.5. So, the bottom line is—why not be conscious about it, if we want better futures for our own generations, and in that capacity for all generations?

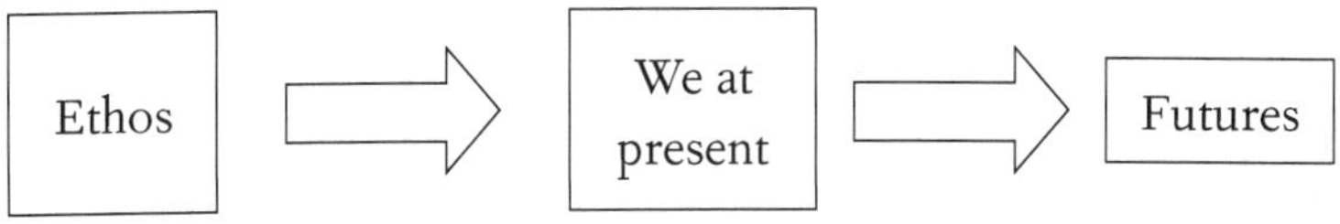

FIGURE 3.5 *Interpretation of the Chain of Legacy*

The Dalai Lama's Compassion: The Inevitable Interconnectedness

In one such endeavour of the value-mutation-chain-reaction, we connect the edicts of Ashoka with the lecture delivered by the contemporary Tibetan Buddhist monk, the Dalai Lama, in 1993, centuries after the Ashokan edicts. Tibet House, New Delhi, had organised an International Conference on 'Ecological Responsibility: A Dialogue with Buddhism' in

1993, where the Dalai Lama spoke about 'A Human Approach to World Peace'. If Ashoka described the severity of loss that the Kalinga War victory brought onto him in his time, the Dalai Lama interestingly and similarly began his address with his lament on the power of violence today:

> No former generation has had to experience so much bad news as we face today; this constant awareness of fear and tension should make any sensitive and compassionate person question seriously the progress of our modern world.[12]

The 'bad news' includes 'violence, crime, wars, and disasters', notwithstanding advanced industry, technology, universal education, material progress and their united contributions to modern society.

The Dalai Lama openly claims that 'the age-old spiritual and humanitarian values that have largely shaped world civilization' cannot be replaced by science and technology. Almost a century back in 1939, the British poet W.H. Auden conveyed a similar message in his poem 'Musée des Beaux Arts':

> About suffering they were never wrong,
> The Old Masters: how well, they understood[13]

So, what are the 'age-old spiritual and humanitarian values' for the Dalai Lama? He lists them as follows:

- Universal humanitarianism, which is essential to solving global problems
- Compassion, which is the pillar of world peace

- All world religions, which are already for world peace
- Individual responsibility that has a universal responsibility to shape institutions to serve human needs

In this chapter, we will discuss the first two pillars of world peace: a) universal humanitarianism and b) compassion. We suggest that universal humanitarianism is not very different in its genetic modelling from that of Ashoka's transforming victory model. Let us re-look at Ashoka's edict on Kalinga in this regard: 'Indeed, Beloved-of-the-Gods is deeply pained by the killing, dying and deportation that take place when an unconquered country is conquered' and 'These misfortunes befall all (as a result of war), and this pains Beloved-of-the-Gods.'

We discover the existence of the lowest common factor/ denominator (LCD) in Ashoka's consideration of the Kalinga victory through war. Look at the edict again. It discusses the pain caused by killing when 'an' unconquered country is conquered, and not merely Kalinga.[14] Thus, the pain of war is universal to any matrix of war, and not particular to just the Kalinga episode.

Now let us relook at the Dalai Lama's speech in the light of the Ashokan LCD: '...people fight each other for petty ends, losing sight of the basic humanity that binds us all together as a single human family'.

Both Ashoka and the Dalai Lama go for the method of arriving at an LCD. Ashoka talks about the loss of natural and human resources in *any* war as the *basic* premise of war. The Dalai Lama talks about the need for *basic* humanity for universal bonding. What is the basic humanity that 'binds us all together as a single human family?' or, what is that common point of interest or the LCD that exists in all human desires? The Dalai Lama asserts: '...all others' desires are the same as mine. Every being wants happiness and does not want suffering. So why should it matter to me that my neighbour is unhappy?'

The Dalai Lama illustrates the point with nuclear war as one possible example.[15] He claims that nuclear war is the worst danger facing humankind today. If the Kalinga War had been a nuclear war, we do not think Ashoka would have survived to order edicts or there would have been anyone living on planet Earth to read them. In the Dalai Lama's words: 'We know that in the event of a nuclear war there will be no victors because there will be no survivors!'

Thus, victory in a war with contemporary technology would kill everyone: the winner, the loser and more significantly, unconnected people like us—the indifferent. So, even if we are not concerned about world wars, we would still be affected by it and suffer for the subsequent ill-consequences of wars with nuclear weapons. We need not remind our readers of the consequences of the international financial depression (2008) or even the oil price crisis during the Bush–Hussein/US–Iraq war in the 2000s or the casualty of COVID-19.

One of the authors, here, was contemplating, like many others of the generation, on the permanent escape from her 1995 ICSE Board Exams due to the possible end of the world attributed to the effects post the US–Iraq War.

The important logic, then, is that indifference does not work in today's times; even if it might have in Ashoka's times. This observation makes Ashoka so much more significant as a mutation agent; more so because he could see the present in a way, most of us still cannot; he is like Auden's Old Masters. Auden in 'Musée' was lamenting over the indifference of the ploughman ploughing the field when wars were happening around him:

> ...how everything turns away
> Quite leisurely from the disaster; the ploughman may
> Have heard the splash, the forsaken cry,
> But for him it was not an important failure...[16]

The Dalai Lama portends that Auden's ploughman (us?) will not be able to even indulge in indifference if a nuclear war happens! Auden was lamenting during the Spanish Civil War in 1939, the Dalai Lama expressed worry in 1993, while Ashoka was concerned in 300–200 BCE. Certain things have not changed through time.

Though the Dalai Lama was worried about nuclear wars in the 1990s, he is still important today, not because he attempts to spiritualise humanism, he rather contends that spiritual outlook is a required practicality now. He admits that 'it is difficult to achieve a spirit of genuine cooperation', particularly when we are forcibly required to feel for things that we do not consider our immediate own. In this context of alienation, he also goes on to show the interconnectedness of the contemporary world, where indifference will not work, not simply because indifference is not a virtue but more because there is no space for indifference. The interconnected premise perhaps makes his logic of basic humanity so commendable to our understanding of the global dream of 'being one with the world', as discussed in our analysis of the *global-cosmopolitan* dilemma in the Ashokan section. In his words:

> One nation's problems can no longer be satisfactorily solved by itself alone; too much depends on the interest, attitude, and cooperation of other nations.

Thus, if financial depression in a far-off city in the Northern Hemisphere might cause a town in the Southern to go bankrupt, can we afford to be indifferent about anything or not feel responsible for anything?

Moreover, like Ashoka, the Dalai Lama does not preach universal consideration for humanity as a constant. Rather, he contemplates about the *transformation* from the personal and the self-centred to the rational and the universal; the utilitarian to the absolute. As a first approximation, he proposes a practical personal condition: 'The premise behind this idea of universal responsibility is the simple fact that, in general terms, all others' desires are the same as mine. Every being wants happiness and does not want suffering.'

Thus, if each of us has to be happy, then everyone is required to be happy as well. It is better *for my personal happiness that people around me also live happy*. Then, from the personal the Dalai Lama moves to the collaboration effort: 'The wiser course is to think of others also when pursuing our own happiness.'

The logic of collaboration is also arrived at through the LCD method—that we all desire the same thing, which is happiness. On a similar note, Oprah Winfrey, the famous American talk show host and philanthropist, on receiving the first Bob Hope Humanitarian Award in the 54th Annual Emmy Awards on 22 September 2002, described how she learned to *transform* her personal desires to universal concerns.

For Ashoka, the LCD was freedom from loss of life in war; for the Dalai Lama, it is happiness and avoidance of suffering; and for Oprah, it is hunger and recognition:

> And I would often say to my father afterwards, 'Dad, why can't we just have regular people at our Christmas dinner?'—because I was looking for the Currier & Ives version. And my father said to me, 'They are regular people. They're just like you. They want the same thing you want.' And I would say, 'What?' And he'd say, 'To be fed'. And at the time, I just thought he was talking about dinner. But I have since learned how profound he really was because we all are just regular people seeking the same thing.
>
> The guy on the street, the woman in the classroom, the Israeli, the Afghani, the Zuni, the Apache, the Irish, the Protestant, the Catholic, the gay, the straight, you, me—we all just want to know that we matter. We want

> validation. We want the same things. We want safety and we want to live a long life. We want to find somebody to love. Stedman, thank you. We want to find somebody to laugh with and have the power and the place to cry with when necessary.[17]

The Dalai Lama coins the phrase 'wise self-interest' to define any practical act that involves *thinking for others when pursuing personal happiness*. And from the premise of a 'wise self-interest', he *hopes* to move towards a better level of human bonding, which he terms as 'compromised self-interest'. Notwithstanding the utilitarian agenda of human interdependence, the conscious effort at *integration* of others' problems when pursuing own interests, for the Dalai Lama, accentuates the *hope* of actual 'mutual interest'. In his words:

> Today we are so interdependent, so closely interconnected with each other, that without a sense of universal responsibility, a feeling of universal brotherhood and sisterhood, and an understanding and belief that *we really are part of one big human family*, we cannot hope to overcome the dangers to our very existence—let alone bring about peace and happiness.

Thus, from the common desire in all to interconnectedness as the necessary means of contemporary existence to the ultimate realisation of 'mutual interest', the Dalai Lama charts the course of *transformation* of humanitarian responsibility as an accountability we owe to each other for our *own* survival so that we can lead towards a world based on *mutual* survival as well.

Thus, like the Darwinian evolution or the Fatboy representation, the Dalai Lama also charts an evolutionary graph for humanitarian responsibility; a responsibility that is starkly evident in Ashoka's edicts. The king exemplarily is concerned about the outsiders beyond his conquered borders; a concern that predicts the Dalai Lama's 'mutual welfare':

> The people of the unconquered territories beyond the borders might think: 'What is the king's intention towards us?' My only intention is that they live without fear of me, that they may trust me and that I may give them happiness, not sorrow.
>
> Therefore, acting in this way, you should perform your duties and assure them (the people beyond the borders) that: 'The king is like a father. He feels towards us as he feels towards himself. We are to him like his own children.'

The Dalai Lama's next important pillar for world peace is compassion; a pillar he arrives at in his attempt to understand the *reason* for the existence of violence. Following the LCD pattern again, he posits the root problem of every human being—attachment to things deemed important for our survival. In his words, 'The pursuit of the objects of our desire and attachment involves the use of aggression and competitiveness as supposedly efficacious instruments. These mental processes easily translate into actions, breeding belligerence as an obvious effect.'

He, thus, proposes compassion in place of attachment and that too using the LCD formula: 'The rationale for compassion is that every one of us wants to avoid suffering and gain happiness.' Thus, compassion arises from somebody suffering.

In this case, your compassion will remain as a humane response to suffering as long as beings continue to suffer. And, the longevity of compassion is *directly proportional* to the condition of suffering. Compassion is different from attachment. Attachment remains as long as the object of our attachment manages to keep us attached. So, attachment is more 'I' oriented. But compassion is altruistic. I feel compassion for anybody suffering because that is my *natural* response as a human being to a condition of suffering. Thus, the Dalai Lama establishes that as human beings we are *naturally* compassionate. Even when attachment is over, we can still be compassionate to the same object/person in their suffering.

The Dalai Lama, therefore, nullifies the 'I' effect further, when he contends that if every 'I' wants to avoid suffering, then by just looking around, we would find ourselves insignificant compared to the enormity of the 'I's surrounding us—we are *all* suffering. Our personal insignificance and our realisation of the unaccountable suffering around us makes the Dalai Lama wonder at the possibility of arousing true compassion within us for the whole world, including our enemies. In his words, 'The kind of love we should advocate is this wider love that you can have even for someone who has done harm to you: your enemy.'

For the Dalai Lama then, compassion is for any condition of human suffering, even if that be our enemy. The moment we have compassion for the suffering of our enemy, the enemy ceases to exist. The moment the enemy ceases to exist, violence ceases to exist. Thus, the *excluded* or *ousted* element of our attachment gets *integrated* into our feelings of compassion. From the amazingly compiled writings of Gandhi by Krishna Kripalini in *All Men are Brothers* (1960), the text titled 'Ahimsa or the Way of Non-Violence' is significant here—it voices similar opinions. Gandhi foresees the Dalai Lama when he states:

> In its positive form, ahimsa means the largest love, greatest charity. If I am a follower of ahimsa, I must love my enemy. I must apply the same rules to the wrong-doer who is my enemy or a stranger to me, as I would to my wrong-doing father or son.[18]

The manner in which we would forgive our own children is similar to the Dalai Lama's compassion for the enemy. Gandhi states that we must forgive the *other* as we would forgive our own. In this capacity, the whole universe becomes our own, and in turn, we become universally responsible to it, and to every sentient living in it. Even Ashoka voiced similar sentiments in his edicts, centuries before Gandhi or the Dalai Lama: 'All men are my children. What I desire for my own children, and I desire their welfare and happiness both in this world and the next, that

I desire for all men.' Figure 3.6 shows the mutation model for compassion.

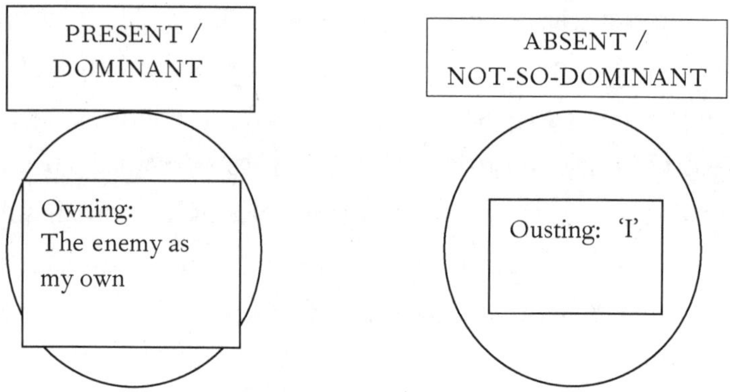

FIGURE 3.6 *The Mutation Model of Compassion*

Inclusive Growth

We produce here excerpts from the speech of Aamir Khan, the famous Indian actor. His speech on inclusive growth during Economic Times Awards in January 2010 is worth quoting in this context. This is our direct transcript from the YouTube version.[19]

> Inclusive growth, I have heard that word being used a number of times today, and I am very happy to hear that word and really I am, and this is a thought that I have and I had this thought for some time since I was researching for my film *Taare Zameen Par* and then *3 Idiots*, both about education and this is something I have felt, and which I have felt I must share with

all of you because you are all very important people, people who can really make a difference to our society and to our lives, to our country.

He thus comments on the selfishness in human beings and how the seed of competition is sowed into children. He continues:

> What I am hoping to see is that the parents of our country, of our nation, instead of asking our children, have you come first, did you score high marks ... instead of all that if we ask our children whom did you help today? Is there any child who needed your help and you came forward and you helped that child. Whose face did you bring a smile on today?
>
> If these are the questions, we asked our children, from that young tender age, I think that when those children reach the age of 20/21, we will have a society which is caring. I think it will be a completely altered society. This is what I actually wanted to say. I feel so strongly about this.
>
> This whole concept of inclusion is so wonderful. I think it should be inculcated in our children right from the time they were born.
>
> I think this is the only way we can really, practically bring about a change, because I am sure all of us wanted to do something good, but what is it that stops us from taking that extra step, what is it that really stops us.

He also adds a personal narrative about his childhood describing how when he won a lot of matches, his mother would be very happy. She would always ask whether he lost or won:

> And then invariably after 5/10 minutes she would come to me and say, you know that the boy who lost, he must have reached home by now and his mother must have asked him did you win or lose and he must have told his mother that he lost.

The above quote is perhaps the representative quote for us and what we would understand and want and request the human kind to endorse!

4

The Politicisation of Non-violence

Now the option before us is non-violence or non-existence.
—Mahatma Gandhi

Mahatma Gandhi

What makes Mahatma Gandhi commendable is his argument for ahimsa as not merely the highest form of spiritual awakening, but something that evolves from our *basic* consciousness—another LCD pattern, and, in fact, an evolutionary pattern. He illustrates the stages of awareness of ahimsa in human beings through the gradual evolution of *Homo sapiens* bonding through history. Thus, even Gandhi, like Darwin, Fatboy Slim and the Dalai Lama, charts an evolutionary growth. First, our primitive ancestors were cannibals and violent. Then, fed up with cannibalism, they started living on the chase. Ashamed of living a wandering hunter's life, s/he started collaborating with Mother Earth for agriculture and sustenance.

Collaboration led to a more civilised life, with the establishment of villages, families, communities and nations. In Gandhi's words: 'Had it been otherwise, the human species should have been extinct by now, even as many of the lower species have disappeared.'[1]

Thus, the evolution and transformation of the human condition is thanks to the quality of ahimsa, which is inherent in us. Darwin, the Dalai Lama and Gandhi present an evolution of value-system for human sustenance. See Figure 4.1 for a graphic representation of the same.

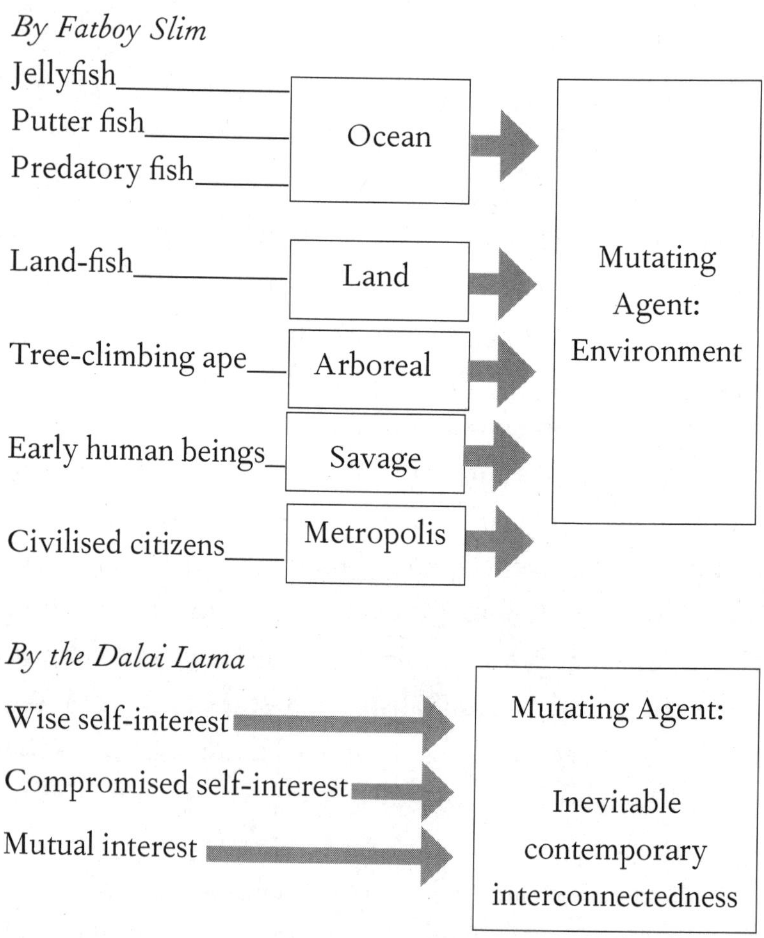

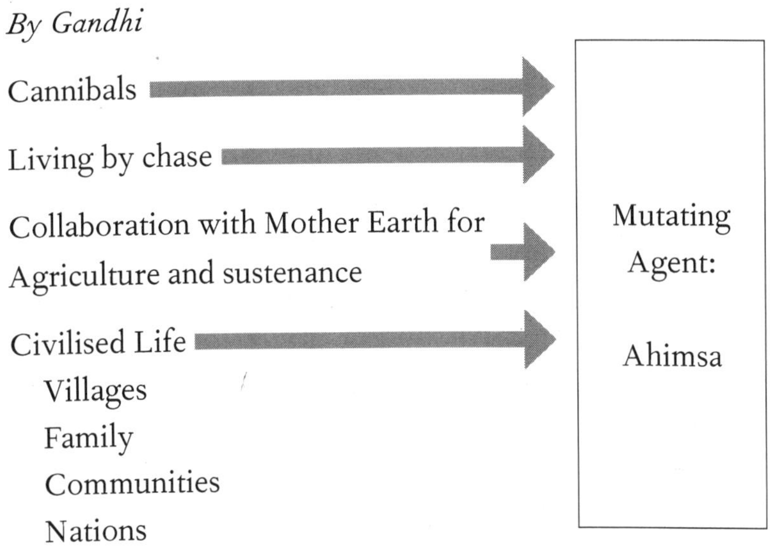

Figure 4.1 *The Process of Evolution*

Gandhi's valorisation of ahimsa as the important factor of human civilisation is reminiscent of contrasting contentions by Jean-Jacques Rousseau, the Genevan philosopher who wrote the seminal work of modern Western philosophy, *Discourse on the Origin and Basis of Inequality among Men*, in 1754. The founding philosophy is echoed loud and clear in the opening passage of the second part of the treatise:

> The first man who, having enclosed a piece of ground, bethought himself of saying *This is mine*, and found people simple enough to believe him, was the real founder of civil society. From how many crimes, wars and murders, from how many horrors and misfortunes might not any one have saved mankind, by pulling up the stakes, or filling up the ditch, and crying to his fellows,

> 'Beware of listening to this impostor; you are undone if you once forget that the fruits of the earth belong to us all, and the earth itself to nobody.'[2]

Similar sentiments have been voiced by Purandara Dasa, a great Kannada saint-poet (1484–1564):

> *yaru hitavaru ninage ii moovarolage*
> *naariyo, dhariniyo, balu dhanada siriyo*
> *munna shatakoti rayarugalalida nelava*
> *tanndennuta shasanava baresi*
> *binnanada mane katti kote kottalavikki*
> *chennigana asuvaliye horage hakuvaru*

> Whom would you prefer of the three, woman, wealth or land? A human being builds fanciful houses and fortifies it, on the land, which has been ruled by millions of kings earlier, and claims as his own by writing inscriptions. But he is thrown out of the house as soon as he dies.[3]

For Rousseau then, it was the primitive population without the idea of civilised and, hence, legitimate ownership, and the civil human unconsciously 'shared the fruits of the world'. A more muscular and agile man might have earned the prize (hunting) faster, but no society or government decided the ownership of the prize, and any impeachment of that would not have led to a consciously decided war.

Hunger and other appetites made him, at various times, experience various modes of existence, and among these was one that urged him to propagate his species—a blind propensity that, having nothing to do with the heart, produced a merely animal act.

With an improvement in the standard of living as per civility and ownership laws, Rousseau contends, we lost our innate sense of being part of the world (let us remind our readers of the global-cosmopolitan dilemma and the basic premise for both—'to be at home with the world'). We became more and more the type who claimed, patented, copyrighted. Gandhi is marvellous here because Rousseau's dissatisfaction with the development of civil society from the barbarian to the civilised does not coerce Gandhi to disdain civil society completely. The Dalai Lama showed how we are *inherently* compassionate; Gandhi shows how we are *inherently* non-violent. We must remember the value Gandhi discovers in human species—we, as a species, have survived this long because we have ahimsa inbuilt in us.

Some lower species have become extinct due to the lack of the quality of ahimsa. In other words, if 'inequality' is the product of progressive civilisation for Rousseau, ahimsa for Gandhi is the reason for the same progression as well—'If they had not done so, only the fewest and the most ferocious would have survived.'

That we are naturally and biologically non-violent becomes an even more motivating factor when we contrast Gandhi with Hobbes! The latter published a treatise in 1651 on human nature in his celebrated discourse on the same called *Leviathan*. Let us look at a few comments from *Leviathan*, more closely from 'Chapter XIII: Of the Natural Condition of Mankind as Concerning Their Felicity and Misery':

> For such is the nature of men that howsoever they may acknowledge many others to be more witty or more eloquent or more learned, yet they will hardly believe there be many so wise as themselves; for they see their own wit at hand, and other men's at a distance. But this proveth rather that men are in that point equal, than unequal.[4]

From equality, Hobbes charts the path towards competition:

> And therefore, if any two men desire the same thing, which nevertheless they cannot both enjoy, they become enemies; and in the way to their end (which is principally their own conservation, and sometimes their delectation only) endeavour to destroy or subdue one another. The competition element keeps us diffident of each other. And from this diffidence of one another, there is no way for any man to secure himself so reasonable as anticipation; that is, by force, or wiles, to master the persons of all men he can so long till he see no other power great enough to endanger him: and this is no more than his own conservation requireth, and is generally allowed.

And, notwithstanding success:

> Again, men have no pleasure (but on the contrary a great deal of grief) in keeping company where there is no power able to overawe them all. For every man

> looketh that his companion should value him at the same rate he sets upon himself, and upon all signs of contempt or undervaluing naturally endeavours, as far as he dares (which amongst them that have no common power to keep them in quiet is far enough to make them destroy each other), to extort a greater value from his contemners, by damage; and from others, by the example.
>
> So that in the nature of man, we find three principal causes of quarrel. First, competition; secondly, diffidence; thirdly, glory.
>
> The first maketh men invade for gain; the second, for safety; and the third, for reputation. The first use violence, to make themselves masters of other men's persons, wives, children, and cattle; the second, to defend them; the third, for trifles, as a word, a smile, a different opinion, and any other sign of undervalue, either direct in their persons or by reflection in their kindred, their friends, their nation, their profession, or their name.

Thus, Hobbes contends that if there is no power to keep us super awed (by *that* power), we will continuously be in a state of war, and in such a state: '...the life of man ... [is] solitary, poor, nasty, brutish, and short'.

Hobbes and Gandhi are both writing in the times of civil unrest, though in different centuries and different geographies. Hobbes writes during the English Civil War between 1642 and 1651; Gandhi writes during India's fight against the British in the first half of the 20th century. What makes Gandhi different from Hobbes is not that Gandhi discounts the evil in human nature—he does acknowledge the existence of 'animal-force' as against 'soul-force' in all of us. But Gandhi, like the Dalai Lama, is attractive because (we contend), he has found a further common denominator in even Hobbes's LCD (human beings are brutish in a state of war)—Gandhi invests in the human value of ahimsa notwithstanding war, greed and tragedy documented by history. In the recent movie, *The Dark Knight* (2008), the penultimate scene of the imprisoned passengers of two ferries captured by the famous villain, the Joker (played fabulously by Heath Ledger), perhaps explains, and very explicitly so, Gandhi's philosophy of our inherent nature of ahimsa. The scene is a high drama situation where the iconic villain, the Joker, captures two ferries with a different set of passengers (harmless citizens in one and prisoners in the other) and rigs them (the ferries). Let us look at the plot structure in the screenplay:[5]

> The Joker (O.S.)
> Tonight, you're all going to be part of a social experiment. Through the magic of diesel fuel and ammonium nitrate, I'm ready right now to blow you all sky high. Anyone attempts to get off their boat, you all die... But we're going to make things a little more interesting than that. Tonight, we're going to learn a little about ourselves... There's no need for all of you to die. That would be a waste. So, I've left you both a little present... Each of you has a remote to blow up the other boat... At midnight, I blow you all up [in case you fail to blow up

> the other]. If, however, one of you presses the button, I'll let that boat live. You choose. So, who's it going to be: Harvey Dent's most wanted scumbag collection... or the sweet innocent civilians?

This movie becomes important for us in understanding the simultaneous presence of mutually contradicting emotions such as good and evil. As discussed earlier, in such situations as per Patanjali's *pratipaksha bhavana* or the Western psychoanalysis technique, 'evil' may be controlled by concentrating on the 'good'. Gandhi goes one step further. According to him, human beings are basically 'good'; they need to be aware of their inherent goodness. Through the Joker's ill-meant 'social experiment', the villain ironically authenticates Gandhi's view, as is evident in the documented scenes of provocation and self-realisation below. For instance, in the ferry with the citizens, we find a mother with two kids voicing her typical anxiety: 'We don't all have to die. Why should my babies die? Those men [convicts] had their chances.'

Similarly, on the other ferry, the prisoners get angry. On the one side (ferry with citizens), the voting is on, and the obvious result is a green signal for blowing the other ferry. Passengers shout, do it now! In this kind of tension, the Joker's social experiment is working very well. The Hobbsian nature in human species (that the Joker wishes the world to see) is well developed. Yet there is a catch—the pilot of the passenger ferry says something interesting: 'I didn't say I'd do it. Don't forget. We're still here. Which means they haven't killed us, yet, either.'

He places the remote on a bench in front of all of them, as they keep staring at it. The scene quickly shifts to the other ferry, with the warden facing the music from so many angry prisoners: 'You don't wanna die. But you don't know how to take a life. Give it to me.'

In contrast, the businessman in the first ferry says: 'No one wants to get their hands dirty. Fine. I'll do it. Those men on that boat made their choices. They chose to murder and steal. It makes no sense for us to die, too.'

The utilitarian desire for life is well evident in all kinds of human species, whether a citizen or even a prisoner. Yet, the hesitancy to kill and the paradoxical desire to survive is strong. And with great anguish slowly portrayed on screen, the story progresses to a great height of human expression; an expression coming from the prisoners! As the warden hands the remote reluctantly to the prisoner, the latter looks the warden in the eye and then tosses the remote out of the window.

The social experiment failed for the Joker—neither of the passengers blows the other. They simply could not, notwithstanding the knowledge that their only way of escape was killing the other! The 2008 movie reiterates Gandhi—had there been no ahimsa in us, we would have long been extinguished. But we must also add, the movie could have been Hobbsian as well, and yet been a classic! In a similar vein, even Rousseau finds compassion as the essential character that distinguishes the savage from the civil. He contends that civilised politics spoilt the natural quality of compassion in the native. This is contextual because Gandhi also considers the absence of ahimsa in politics:

> Some friends have told me that truth and non-violence have no place in politics and worldly affairs. I do not agree. I have no use for them as a means of individual salvation. Their introduction and application in everyday life has been my experiment all along.

In an even more compelling manner, Gandhi echoes Rousseau's filial bonding as well as the Dalai Lama's theory of compassion and suffering. He proposes that the 'expansions of the human heart' hold each other stronger when suffering. In other words, many mutual groups have developed through each other's compassion for sufferings. On 26 November 2009, The Taj Mahal Palace hotel in Mumbai, which had been housing international officials as well, was attacked and residents held hostage by terrorists. The hue and cry was tremendous, more so because of the bottom line—terrorism could happen to anyone, the common person on the road, the official in the most classy and luxurious hotels, the indifferent middle class like one of the authors of this book who was planning to travel to Kurla station, Mumbai, on the very fateful day that witnessed simultaneous firing in The Taj Mahal Palace hotel as well as the CST railway station, Mumbai. On seeing heavy security force, she realised for the first time in her life that she could have been a part of the entire tragedy, which, till now, was always an abstract intellectual concept that *happened to other people*. The realisation that 'it could happen to me as well' is a realisation of bonding of sufferance, as per Gandhi, and interconnectedness, as per the Dalai Lama. All we need to do is have a wider acceptance of members in our groups; *involve the whole world as our family*. And the question is how? Do we have to wait to suffer together? Today, COVID-19 has made us realise this universal suffering.

Ashoka felt the suffering when he won. This is not strange, since he won more sufferings, and he realised that. The Dalai Lama talks about the interconnected nature of the world today; any nuclear threat would be a threat to the most indifferent person on planet Earth. Gandhi wrote at a time when the world was not considered global the way it is today; the world was fighting for equality, nationalism, individualism. The interconnectedness for the Gandhian India was more about the bonding of people in a colonised nation. It is fascinating that Gandhi considered ahimsa the best tool for fighting the colonisers.

He felt that war would generate more war because there would be some party who felt wronged. I kill him, his son avenges me; my daughter avenges the killer's son's son, and the *Gangs of Wasseypur* chain continues. Hatred would generate more hatred because there would be some party who *still* hated. The genetic component of war would still be the chromosomes of war, violence and hatred. This almost reminds us of Hobbes, when he says that in a state of war 'the life of man… [is] solitary, poor, nasty, brutish, and short'.

But then Gandhi also opines, 'If they had not done so, only the fewest and the most ferocious would have survived.'

So, there must be some space that must not have done so. There must have been a space for remorse (Ashoka), some space for compassion (the Dalai Lama), some space for ahimsa (Gandhi). Otherwise, how do we justify that the '*not the fewest*' and the '*not the most ferocious*' have survived? If Gandhi says, there *is* ahimsa already within us, the famous singer, Michael Jackson, states there is love in our hearts. 'Heal the World' is a song from Jackson's chartbuster *Dangerous* released in 1991, where Jackson's love reminds us of the Dalai Lama's compassion. The song goes:

> There's a place in your heart
> And I know that it is love
> And this place could be much
> Brighter than tomorrow
> And if you really try
> You'll find there's no need to cry
> In this place you'll feel
> There's no hurt or sorrow.
> There are ways to get there
> If you care enough for the living
> Make a little space, make a better place.

And then the chorus follows:

> Heal the world
> Make it a better place
> For you and for me and the entire human race
> There are people dying
> If you care enough for the living
> Make a better place for
> You and for me.[6]

Even Jackson establishes the single most significant fact of human anatomy:

> There's a place in your heart
> And I know that it is love

And yet, he also insists that we need to get *there*; a very remarkable insight from Jackson since we need to *work* to get to a place that actually exists in our hearts. In other words, though we *own* the space for love of the living in our *own* hearts, we are still not *there*, because we have yet not discovered that space. The greatest human contradiction is thus brilliantly spelled out by Jackson—we have love in our heart, but more often than not, we do not know that we have it.

In a similar instance, when writing for world peace, two decades before Jackson's 'Heal the World', the English musician and the founding member of the famous band *The Beatles*, John Lennon, released his album *Imagine,* whose title track went on to become perhaps a signature song for world peace. For Gandhi, we all have ahimsa within us; for Jackson, we all have space for love of the living within us; for Lennon, the dream of a single, borderless and undivided world is also a common dream for all of us:

> Imagine there's no countries
> It isn't hard to do
> Nothing to kill or die for
> And no religion too
> Imagine all the people living life in peace

You, you may say
I'm a dreamer, but I'm not the only one
I hope someday you'll join us
And the world will be as one.[7]

Thus, Ashoka, the Dalai Lama, Winfrey, Gandhi, Jackson and even Lennon have been able to identify the basic need for change in our approach towards human society through the lowest common denominator (LCD) method. The same is represented in Table 4.1.

TABLE 4.1 *The LCDs so Far*

Value-Mutation-Change-Agent	*LCD*	*Inference*
Ashoka	Misfortunes in all wars	Advocation of Dhamma
The Dalai Lama	Need for Happiness Suffering Compassion	Interconnected Compassion Mutual interest
Winfrey	Hunger	Acceptance, recognition, validation
Gandhi	Ahimsa	Political consciousness of civil society
Jackson	Love	Make a better place
Lennon	Dream	World as borderless

Source: Author's compilation

Yet, in each of their approaches, a similar contradiction continues. Like Jackson, Lennon has to invite all of us to join him in his dream, which he claims is not only his, since 'I'm not the only one'. The paradox in all these writings is the need to discover the bottom line of our existence when the bottom line actually exists within us.

In other words, in the works of all these great writers, lyricists, thinkers and practitioners, we need to interpret the bottom line of our existence, which is itself a process of contradiction—contradiction because it is there and yet we do not know. In this context, let us look at the Ashokan edicts again:

> Beloved-of-the-Gods, King Piyadasi, does not consider glory and fame to be of great account unless they are achieved through having my subjects respect Dhamma and practise Dhamma, both now and in the future. For this alone does Beloved-of-the-Gods, King Piyadasi, desire glory and fame. And whatever efforts Beloved-of-the-Gods, King Piyadasi, is making, all of that is only for the welfare of the people in the next world, and that they will have little evil. And being without merit is evil. This is difficult for either a humble person or a great person to do except with great effort, and by giving up other interests. In fact, it may be even more difficult for a great person to do.

It is in the effort highlighted by Ashoka that a certain line of thought evolves. The remarkable confession (and we would like to call this a confession) from such a great king comes from his public acceptance of the difficulty of practising Dhamma. Such difficulty for Ashoka is no different from the difficulty of practising ahimsa for Gandhi, as admitted by Gandhi himself:

> It is not non-violence if we merely love those that love us. It is non-violence only when we love those that hate

> us. I know how difficult it is to follow this grand law of love. But are not all great and good things difficult to do? Love of the hater is the most difficult of all.

The embracement of the suffering of others, and to work towards annihilating sufferings of all kinds, becomes the Dhamma for Ashoka. And yet, Ashoka admits that Dhamma is not easy to follow. It is not easy to seek the annihilation of others' suffering and Gandhi elaborates that further—it is not easy to strive towards annihilation of others' suffering *at your cost*.

Hence, Jackson says, we need to *find* that place full of love; Lennon says, we need to *join* him in the united dream; the Dalai Lama says, we need to *evolve* from 'wise self-interest' to 'mutual interest'. That it is difficult, both Gandhi and Ashoka have admitted. But that world welfare is dependent on the achievement of such self-sacrifice or Dhamma is also well established. Dhamma, compassion, ahimsa, love, dream—these are all metaphors for the 'effort' that Ashoka urges for in all people, yet an effort that Ashoka establishes as a *must* for a better world.

Arun Gandhi: We are Responsible for World Terrorism?

Perhaps the finest global understanding of Gandhi's propositions on non-violence is well exemplified by Arun Gandhi, his grandson, in his lecture entitled 'Non Violence in the Age of Terrorism', a lecture delivered on 20 April 2005, at Lehigh University, Bethlehem, Pennsylvania.

He discusses the effect of the 9/11 in the contemporary, interconnected world:

> I have been asked to speak to you today about nonviolence in the age of terrorism and I think what happened to us on 9/11 makes nonviolence all the more important for us to understand, because what happened on 9/11 has taken violence to a new level, to a level that is unimaginable. It has brought war to our doorsteps and nothing is sacrosanct about it anymore.[8]

Apart from the fact that the quote above reminds us quite starkly of the Dalai Lama's interconnectedness of destruction and suffering through nuclear war, and one of the authors' (of this book) realisation of 'this can happen to me as well', it is also important to highlight Arun Gandhi's worry about the 9/11 incident as a 'cumulative effect of our greed'. He says that his grandfather had similar fears when in 1945 the Hiroshima and Nagasaki happened. The world peace committees like the League of Nations could not stop the Second World War. The fear that both the Gandhis are referring to is the reaction of the victims and the world against the attackers or the opponent; the fear of war being fought with greater intensity; the fear of revenge that does not merely eradicate the opponent, but actually kills more, and breeds more similar acts of violence that once evolved because of the opponent's attack. The *return* war is another war all over again and no amount of justification can alter the brutality of war, as made obvious by Ashoka. In Arun Gandhi's words:

> We will have to throw all the conventions, the Geneva Conventions and all the rules of engagement and all that overboard, and now it's going to be free for all kind of war there, and that is what my grandfather was afraid of, when in 1945 ... the bomb was thrown on Hiroshima and Nagasaki...

What Arun Gandhi tries to explain is in sync with what Ashoka depicted in his edicts, centuries before. Let us juxtapose the Kalinga Edict with Arun Gandhi's significant line from his lecture.

Ashoka's edict states:

> Indeed, Beloved-of-the-Gods is deeply pained by the killing, dying and deportation that take place when an unconquered country is conquered ... These misfortunes befall all (as a result of war), and this pains Beloved-of-the-Gods.

Now look at Arun Gandhi:

> [A] correspondent asked grandfather what do you think the future of the world is going to be. And his response was that we no longer have the luxury of choosing between violence and nonviolence. Now the option before us is nonviolence or nonexistence. And I think we are coming to that stage of nonexistence

> very quickly, may be not in the terms of annihilation, but certainly in terms of annihilating our humanity. We are destroying our humanity, we are becoming inhuman because of the culture of violence that dominates us to this great extent, dominates every aspect of our life.

And look at the Dalai Lama, again:

> We know that in the event of a nuclear war there will be no victors because there will be no survivors! Is it not frightening just to contemplate such inhuman and heartless destruction?

Ashoka *felt* the suffering of the victims, not just because people died in the Kalinga War. Yes, Ashoka was pained by the suffering lying around him in the visual depiction of death. But what strikes us is his admittance in his edict of the totality of suffering in *any* war; when 'any unconquered country is conquered'. It is the same sentiment voiced by Gandhi, and also emphasised by his grandson.

Whether we fight for our rights, for a right cause, for greed, or even for terror, the bottom line again is that any war or any act of violence, despite its seemingly legitimate target, would result in the same pain, suffering, and sorrow that you were subjected to by your opponent. The *return* violence does not eliminate violence at the end. And if violence is not annihilated, who would remain to enjoy the victory and what kind of victory; a question already posed by the Dalai Lama when considering nuclear war;

or a laughable choice posed by Gandhi—choose between non-violence and non-existence. With every form of war, today, we are *all* going to suffer, and for the greatest practical reason possible, as stated by the Dalai Lama—the contemporary world is tremendously interconnected. Hence, Arun Gandhi attempts the best of logical reasoning when he wonders at the cause of terrorism, rather than merely accusing the terrorists forthright. Interestingly, similar logical reasoning has been witnessed in the discourses of Gandhi as well as the Dalai Lama.

For Gandhi:

> Violence does not mean emancipation from fear, but discovering the means of combating the cause of fear.

For the Dalai Lama:

> And, is it not logical that we should remove the cause for our own destruction when we know the cause and have both the time and the means to do so? Often, we cannot overcome our problems because we either do not know the cause or, if we understand it, do not have the means to remove it.[9]

And for Arun Gandhi:

> Now we have to ask ourselves, what caused terrorism against us, what was it that happened. It wasn't just that one 9/11 morning these people got up and decided that they were going to hijack some planes and crash the tower. It was planned for a long time, and we need to

> find out what were these issues that involved and made these people do such things.
>
> Just as we have to ask ourselves what caused Hitler to emerge and do what he did in World War II. Hitler didn't drop from the sky and he didn't perform this atrocious act of holocaust just because he thought about it one day.

The astonishing revelation from all these interactions is that *we* are responsible for events like the Holocaust or even 9/11; *we*, when we actually sit and condemn these acts of violence so vehemently! Even after the First World War, with all the unaccountable loss suffered by almost the entire European continent, the development of a worse form of war—the Second World War—was a development that was impossible to drink in, but drink in, we must, and we had to. Arun Gandhi states that it was the 'cumulative effect of our greed' that led to the Second World War as well as the 9/11 terrorist attack:

> But it was a cumulative effect of our greed after the First World War that caused Hitler to emerge and lead the world into the Second World War and all the atrocities that we experienced. And in the same way, it is again our greed and our thoughtlessness that has given rise to terrorism against us. We were so keen on finishing off communism that we got the Islamic jihadis trained in Afghanistan; internationalised the conflict and told the Muslim nations that communism is a threat to Islam all over the world and you've got to fight it and destroy it. We gave them the weapons to do this and then when

> they were able to destroy communism in Afghanistan, we just walked away leaving them high and dry with all the weapons that we gave them. And these people, coming from poor backgrounds, illiterate backgrounds, fundamentalists, were left there with nothing at all, no future for them. And they realised that if communism has been a threat to us, so is the United States; so, let's attack the United States. That's what they have been trained to do and that's how this whole question of terrorism against us has emerged and we are today faced with the challenge of dealing with this.

The 'our' here happen to be the people living in the US. But it is also a well-known fact that many nationals, who have migrated to the US or have even been working in the country for some time, have had to face the wrath of terrorism. In other words, the 'us' now is a whole lot of people from all over the world who were there in the World Trade Centre on the fated day, and experienced the worst moments of their lives. It is no different from the experiences of the international officials, along with their Indian counterparts, lying huddled in The Taj Mahal Palace hotel, Mumbai, when the terrorists attacked on, the now infamous, 26/11. The inevitable logic has been to blame the *other*, the *opponent*. And yet, we are also responsible for constructing the opponent out of the other, and that leads to violence. Arun Gandhi makes an interesting statement about the US ('our') foreign policy, and interestingly relates a similar pattern to the environmental cause; both these interpretations reflect the Dalai Lama's inevitability of the interconnectedness of contemporary existence. Arun Gandhi wonders:

> [W]hy are our relations with the rest of the world so bad that these people were motivated to attack us and cause such distress and harm to innocent people.

And it is in his answer that we find the reflection of the Dalai Lama:

> It's obvious that our relationship has not been ideal because our relationships, like all foreign policy relationships everywhere else, have been based on what is good for the United States and what is good for us.
>
> Each country thinks only about themselves and what is good for themselves. And that is a very selfish way of looking at things. And such selfish attitudes can only lead to conflict.
>
> And I think that we have reached the stage of the United States when we no longer need to look at what is good for us, but we can look at what is good for the world and do the right thing for the world.

Arun Gandhi, hence, establishes the crux of a non-violent relationship in two important political contexts: a) in drawing up foreign policies and b) in environmental sustainability. For the foreign policy, he interprets:

> So, our foreign policy needs to be based on a philosophy of what's good for the world and let's do that which is good for the world.[10]

If other nations will suffer, then however developed we may be, we cannot escape terrorism, since we cannot escape the bitterness of suffering, and this is evident in the universality of terrorism today. If we would have taken care of the Dalai Lama's universal humanitarianism and compassion in our foreign policies itself, the Gandhian fear of hatred giving rise to hatred would have become a distant myth:

> We would have been able to deal with terrorism much better than what we are doing now with the war that we have declared on terrorism because in this war we are killing more innocent people than terrorists and for every innocent person that is killed in war, in violence, we are giving rise to at least a hundred other terrorists against us. So, we are not putting an end to terrorism.[11]

The same also applies to environmental sustainability. Even the Dalai Lama had claimed:

> [I]f humankind continues to approach its problems considering only temporary expediency, future generations will have to face tremendous difficulties. The global population is increasing, and our resources are being rapidly depleted. Look at the trees, for example. No one knows exactly what adverse effects massive deforestation will have on the climate, the soil, and global ecology as a whole. We are facing problems because people are concentrating only on their short-term, selfish interests, not thinking of the entire human family. They are not thinking of Earth

> and the long-term effects on universal life as a whole. If we of the present generation do not think about these now, future generations may not be able to cope with them.[12]

And now look at Arun Gandhi. He interprets from his experience with his grandfather. He threw his pencil (3 inches long only) because he thought he deserved a better one. He asked his grandfather for an improved one. On the contrary, his grandfather subjected him to a number of questions, one being, why throw the pencil at all, and finally, go and search for the pencil. Arun spent two hours trying to find his pencil, which he eventually did. Arun Ghandhi recounts Mahatma's answer here that further mutates the value of non-violence itself:

> Now I want you to sit here and learn two very important lessons. The first lesson is that even in the making of a simple thing like a pencil, we use a lot of the world's natural resources and when we throw them away, we are throwing away world's natural resources and that is violence against nature. And the second lesson is that because in an affluent society we can buy all these things in bulk, we overconsume the resources of the world and because we overconsume them, we are depriving people elsewhere of these resources and they have to live in poverty and that is violence against humanity and that was the first time I realised that all of these little things that we

> do every day, consciously or unconsciously, add to the violence that we are experiencing in the world today.[13]

So, Gandhi redefines non-violence for us—passive violence or non-physical violence, which is far more rampant in our daily activities. Are we concerned about the other nations, other geographies, their poverty, their problems? This is also passive violence. Are we concerned if our neighbour is doing fine or not when we are doing fine? This is also passive violence. And wars evolve from these apparently insignificant negligence from affluent societies, nations and economies. See Figure 4.2 for a diagrammatic understanding of the role of passive violence in violence.

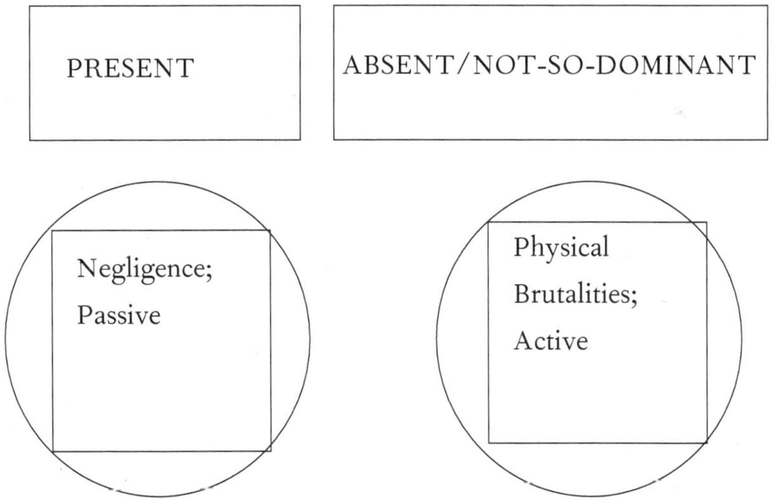

FIGURE 4.2 *The Gandhian Molecular Module of Violence*

Promotion of Non-violence for Business by Business

The human relationships depicted in the famous Indian epic, the Mahabharata, get so disrupted due to the destruction of lives and property in the civil war. The heart-rending scenes depicted at the end of the war show the sufferings of the women who lost their husbands and sons, which reduce into insignificance the gains of the so-called just war. The virtuous king, who won the war, is unable to derive any pleasure in victory and he hankers after quietude and final emancipation. Virtually, all his kinsmen have been slaughtered and the kingdom he has won been desolated. Pained by remorse, he wants to renounce the kingship and retire as a hermit. He says:

> Fie on the usages of the warring class, fie on might and valour, fie on wrath, since these have caused such a calamity on us.[14]
>
> We who had won have now been defeated, and the others, who have been defeated have now won. Having killed our brothers and companions, fathers, sons, lots of our friends, kinsmen, counsellors, and grandsons: having conquered them all, we have now been defeated... I, someone is victorious but then grieves like a poor blockhead, how can I think of it as victory? In fact, my enemies have defeated me worse than I did them.[15]
>
> The heroes are dead. The evil is done. Our kingdom has been laid waste. Having killed them, our rage is gone. Now this grief holds me in check.[16]

He raves about the consequences of war and seeks the life of a recluse in order to get peace of mind. He realises towards the end that 'peace of mind' cannot be attained through just knowledge of different kinds of tranquillity. For real peace, the peace-seeker himself must become the means of attaining it.[17]

In fact, the most effective, the most equitable and the most economical way of meeting violence is to use non-violence. If violence is answered by violence, the result is the physical struggle, which inevitably arouses hatred, fear, rage and resentment. In the heat of passion, decent norms are thrown to the winds, all the habits of forbearance and humaneness acquired during years of civilised living are forgotten. In brief, violence leads to the moral degradation of the victor and the vanquished, both. To use nonviolent means is often extraordinarily hard, but history shows that it can be done and not only by exceptional individuals, but by large groups of ordinary men and women and even by governments.[18]

Peace is notoriously difficult to define and even more difficult to measure. However, the Institute of Economics and Peace (IEP), particularly in its work related to the Global Peace Index, has made substantial headway. IEP has developed a framework for measuring peace, understanding the factors that create peace. This enables a business to place an economic value on peace and understand its impact on their markets, costs and profits. Research undertaken using data from the Global Peace Index has shown that societies with well-functioning governments, low levels of corruption, high participation rates in primary education, respect for human rights and good relations with their neighbouring states are more likely to experience low levels of violence. The benefits brought about by peace can also be measured in economic terms since peace also has a monetary value independent of the human values associated with it.

It can be expressed in terms of the additional value to global GDP that would ensue from creating a peaceful world. IEP has released an insightful study that assesses the economic effect of the cessation of violence on the world economy. According to it, the cost of reducing levels of violence in society was significantly lower than economic activity lost due to violence. This would certainly encourage business leaders to engage with government and civil society to create peace in the markets in which they operate.[19]

There has been a school of thought (Kant, Montesquieu, Hayek and others) which argues that trade promotes peace. This reciprocal relationship—that business needs peace to thrive and thriving business promotes peace—suggests a particular role for business in fostering peaceful societies. It is a proved factor that business needs relatively stable conditions in order to survive. The vast majority of commercial firms benefit from stability and is significantly harmed by violence and unrest. It is also true that only 4 per cent of the world's GNP is related to military expenditures and the vast majority of business thrives on peace and stability. Stability brings with it, better investment opportunities, reduced operations costs.[20]

We may refer to an interesting and lengthy report released by International Alert in 2006 which advocates the concept of 'peace entrepreneurship'. It groups the actions business houses could take in response to conflict into three major categories viz. conflict sustaining, coping strategy and conflict reducing/peace-building. As stated in this report, business houses have already contributed to peace-building by engaging in formal peace negotiations, addressing economic contributions, building relationships that reach beyond borders, helping to protect their own security and encouraging women entrepreneurs. It is pertinent to point out in this context that the World Bank and the United Nations have each produced studies demonstrating that poverty-stricken countries tend to be more violent than prosperous ones. According to these studies, one reason for this relationship seems to be that the productive engagement of individuals in work prevents leaving them idly occupied and, therefore, ripe for charismatic leadership to inspire them into violent acts. Another reason may be that the competition for resources is so severe in poverty-stricken societies that violence may be the preferred means to secure them.[21]

Business can contribute to sustainable peace in many ways. It can contribute to economic development through employment which is likely to contribute to less violence, particularly if jobs provide 'value-added' work.[22]

Business leaders can also contribute to the non-violent aspects of a country if they do business without corruption. This is proved by Transparency International's Corruption Perception Index reports.

According to these reports, those countries in the highly corrupt list settled their disputes by violence 60 per cent of the time. Those countries featured in next most corrupt countries settled their disputes by violence 44 per cent of the time, the moderate corrupt countries settled disputes by violence 26 per cent of the time and least corrupt countries settled their disputes by violence 14 per cent of the time.[23]

As violence and instability persist in much of the world and spending trillions of dollars on military activity each year is unsustainable, alternative methods of fostering peace are called for. One valuable yet underutilised asset is the business community. Business and peace are often understood as opposing concepts, but growing evidence of their association suggests that firms should not be excluded from the broad array of stakeholders working towards peace.[24]

Firms vary in size, ownership and industry, each influencing a company's impact on peace differently. Micro and small enterprises have the closest links to local communities, providing subsistence and a specialised understanding of local context. Small- and medium-sized enterprises (SMEs) contribute substantially to gross domestic product (GDP) and can influence stability through employment and attraction of foreign direct investment. Large multinational corporations (MNCs) can add value through resources, influence and scale.[25] Conflict sensitivity and ethical business behaviour remain good practice regardless of context and can contribute to broader peace-building efforts.

Interest in corporate houses to promote peace is growing worldwide. International alert's report viz. 'Local Business, Local Peace' presents many examples as well as case studies showing corporations from many countries engaging in peacemaking. These actions are the hope of peace through commerce. There are examples of many companies which partner with UNICEF and NGOs to promote training women entrepreneurs for engaging in microfinance besides promoting interethnic dialogues in Nigeria, Somalia, Northern Ireland, Sri Lanka, etc.[26] These examples suggest that there are models of the firm that can contribute to peace through commerce. The possibility of such business houses' success indicates that there is a choice business houses can make between being instruments of domination and instruments of peace.[27] Media, internet and NGOs are playing a big role in making corporate reputation increasingly noted and this would influence corporate houses to get into activities that contribute to their reputation, such as promoting peace. We provide below executive summaries of three examples of business houses' involvement in peace creation.

Example 1

Astra Technologies Limited's primary vehicle for reducing conflict is its Peace Camp programme, which operates in various conflict-affected countries including but not limited to Kosovo and Uganda. Through these peace camps, Astra hopes that the children who attend these camps can use the skills, relationships and attitudes they developed in the peace camps to contribute to their countries' progress towards peace and development. The firm does not see any direct linkages to its business. While it acknowledges and welcomes the possibility of its charitable activities positively affecting its bottom line, perhaps by increasing consumer goodwill towards the Astra brand, the company views the peace camp programme as a worthy goal in its own right.[28]

Example 2

In 2008, the United Nations launched a global peace campaign to raise greater awareness of the International Day of Peace (21 September). Safaricom Limited, Kenya's leading mobile phone service provider partnered with the United Nations Office in Nairobi to implement Text for Peace Campaign in Kenya. During the campaign, which lasted four days between 18 September to 21 September, Kenyans were invited to send a message of peace to the number 222, provided by Safaricom. These messages were collated and presented as the messages of peace from Kenyans at the 63rd United Nations General Assembly in New York on 21 September 2008, the International Day of Peace. Safaricom used its core business skills to mobilise thousands of Kenyan citizens to participate in a large global campaign for peace organised by the United Nations.

Through the nationwide campaign, the company provided its consumers with an opportunity to join forces in uniting the country divided by a serious crisis which caused suffering to many fellow Kenyans. Through this campaign, the company showed how mobile technology can contribute to promoting peace and healing communities.[29]

Example 3

Newmont operates the Batu Hijau copper/gold mine in Sumbawa, Indonesia. Its multi-ethnic mix-employee population has introduced many challenges, both to the company and the employees. To address these challenges, Newmont revived and improved its cross-cultural understanding by conducting mandatory and elective training programmes for expatriates and national employees. Over the years, several conflicts took place among employees in the mine. Most of these incidents were rooted in religious, cultural and ethnic differences. The conflicts highlighted the need to improve employees' understanding of cultural and religious diversity. Newmont believed that, unless these issues were properly managed, conflict would persist, creating unnecessary losses in Newmont's operations through a substantial decrease in productivity. Initially, Newmont encountered difficulty convincing its employees to participate. Employees stayed within their respective cultural, ethnic and religious groups and resisted management's attempts at fostering collaboration with others. Newmont's management embarked on various initiatives to address these challenges including:

- Encouraging cross-cultural understanding through interaction and cultural events, such as 'Cross-Cultural Quiz Nite' and 'Indonesian Cultural Nite'.
- Establishing a non-segregated housing complex.
- Creating a cross-cultural understanding training for expatriate employees and dependents.
- Holding local language courses for national employees. The language course is a key component of the initiative as it is intended to promote discussion among participants.
- Providing mosques for Muslims and a community hall for Christians.
- Improving host community understanding about the mine and its diverse workforce by organising mine tours.

Newmont had made it mandatory for all new expatriate employees to attend cross-cultural training before commencing their employment. Newmont's management considers cultural and religious sensitivity before making any decision that impacts its employees.[30]

Concluding Remarks

For all those who disbelieve in the efficacy of non-violence in creating a new world order, we quote a small episode from Mahatma Gandhi's life.[31] Gandhi once said:

> Do not resort to violence even if it seems at first to promise success; it can only contradict your purpose. Use the means of love and respect even if the result seems far off or uncertain... Violence can never bring an end to violence; all it can do is provoke more violence. But if we can adhere to complete non-violence in thought, word and deed, India's freedom is assured.

The historian J.B. Kripalani, one of Gandhi's closest co-workers, who heard for the first time Gandhi talk this way, was so shocked that he went up to him and told him point-blank:

> Mr Gandhi, you may know all about the Bible or the Bhagavad Gita, but you know nothing at all about history. Never has a nation been able to free itself without violence.
>
> Gandhi smiled:
>
> You know nothing about history... first thing you have to learn about history is that because something has not taken place in the past that does not mean, it cannot take place in the future. In this age of wonders, no one will say that a thing or an idea is worthless because it is new. To say it is impossible because it is difficult is again not in consonance with the spirit of the age. Things undreamt of are daily being seen, the impossible is ever becoming possible.
>
> He also added:
>
> We are constantly being astonished these days at the amazing discoveries in the field of violence. But we must

> all maintain that far more undreamt of and seemingly impossible discoveries will be made in the field of non-violence.

It is then perhaps time to reiterate Gandhi through the British 19th-century dramatist Bernard Shaw, who was famously quoted by the Kennedy brothers in their individual capacities:

> You see things; and you say, 'Why?' But I dream things that never were; and I say, 'Why not?'[32]

So, can the corporate see themselves in peace-keeping activities? We say they can, are and have to. It is not merely inevitable; it is also desirable.

5

If We Care for Nature, She Cares for Us

Sarvah Sarvatra Nandatu
(May everyone everywhere be happy)
—Kalidasa[1]

Introductory Remarks

In his message 'A Human Approach to World Peace',[2] the Dalai Lama revisited a discourse that has consistently influenced the human experience of political existence and continues to do so—world peace cannot be understood without world politics, and world politics has primarily been approached by humankind to work towards world peace. Greatest of wars have been fought due to political necessitation, but the need for peace has always haunted world politics—both world wars had a league of nations. Hence, political peace has always been negotiating with a world of wars, successfully or otherwise. In other words, peace is not merely personal but also political; it needs legitimisation and a leader's job has been to legitimate peace as an essential criterion to be met with in his/her organisational vision, mission and work norms, the corporate included.

That is what made Ashoka enchanting for us—he made Dhamma legitimate within his political discourse. But that was possible because he *included* the need to think about those who suffer when in war. That is also what makes Gandhi essential for us—he proposed non-violence as a political tool and lived by it. Again, that was possible because he included the suffering of the 'enemy' and decided that 'self-suffering' is the best tool for resistance. Arun Gandhi, the grandson of Mahatma Gandhi, insisted that international foreign policies should include what is good for the world, so that other nations do not suffer, and if other nations do not suffer, we do not as well. Terrorism would then lose its pronounced impact. The same goes for environmental sustainability. If we make it a legitimate mandate to protect the environment *now* by including concerns of nature in our daily activities, the environment will protect our future generations *later*. Astra Technologies Limited included a Peace Camp programme in its corporate agenda; Safaricom Limited included the Text for Peace Campaign in its marketing mandate; Newmont included multi-ethnic employee mix in its organisational goals. In short, His Holiness also says that we need to legitimise the following factors, or pillars of world peace, in any human sphere:

- Universal humanitarianism
- Compassion
- World peace through world religions
- Individual responsibility to shape institutions to serve human needs

In Chapter 3, 'Violent Leaders to Non-violent Leaders', we concentrated on the first two pillars of world peace: basic humanitarianism, which also meant including the concerns of the world, when concentrating on a person or a nation; and compassion, which included concerns of the 'enemy' as well. It is in such concerns that we evolved the binary model of violence and non-violence. Ashoka mutated the value of violence when he consciously recognised and legitimised the *silent* presence of non-violence in acts of violence. Thus, as mentioned earlier, for every act of inclusion, there is a simultaneous action of exclusion, and the mutation-change-agent becomes momentous for us when he/she attempts to include what gets *excluded* in any act of possession, victory, ownership and profit.

The ability to think about the 'other' when thinking of the 'self' is now a practical inevitability, as per the Dalai Lama, when hitherto, it had been spiritual. In other words, spiritual considerations ask for political legitimisation in contemporary society; an effort for such legitimisation has been evident from time immemorial and in various fields of human endeavour. In this chapter, we attempt to historicise such efforts. And for such historicisation, we need to quote the Dalai Lama again, when he talks about *exclusion* in two episodes of political civilisation—wars (in the 1990s, the threat of nuclear wars was rampant) and environment (the current world concern):

> By far the greatest single danger facing humankind—in fact, all living beings on our planet—is the threat of nuclear destruction. I need not elaborate on this danger, but I would like to appeal to all the leaders of the nuclear

> powers who literally hold the future of the world in their hands, to the scientists and technicians who continue to create these awesome weapons of destruction, and to all the people at large who are in a position to influence their leaders: I appeal to them to exercise their sanity and begin to work at dismantling and destroying all nuclear weapons. We know that in the event of a nuclear war there will be no victors because there will be no survivors!

And:

> The global population is increasing, and our resources are being rapidly depleted. Look at the trees, for example. No one knows exactly what adverse effects massive deforestation will have on the climate, the soil, and global ecology as a whole.
>
> We are facing problems because people are concentrating only on their short-term, selfish interests, not thinking of the entire human family. They are not thinking of the earth and the long-term effects on universal life as a whole. If we of the present generation do not think about these now, future generations may not be able to cope with them.

In a similar tone, but in 2005, Arun Gandhi voiced the same—more *inclusive* international foreign policies and environmental sustainability:

> And then repair our relationships with foreign countries. It is obvious that our relationship has not been ideal because our relationships, like all foreign

> policy relationships everywhere else, have been based on what is good for the United States and what is good for us. [Countries] think only about themselves and what is good for themselves. And that is a very selfish way of looking at things. And such selfish attitudes can only lead to conflict. And I think that we have reached the stage of the United States when we no longer need to look at what is good for us, but we can look at what is good for the world and do the right thing for the world.[3]

And (in Mahatma Gandhi's words to Arun Gandhi):

> Now I want you to sit here and learn two very important lessons. The first lesson is that even in the making of a simple thing like a pencil we use a lot of the world's natural resources and when we throw them away, we are throwing away the world's natural resources and that is violence against nature.
>
> And the second lesson is that because in an affluent society, we can buy all these things in bulk, we overconsume the resources of the world and because we overconsume them, we are depriving people elsewhere of these resources and they have to live in poverty and that is violence against humanity...[4]

Till now, we have been considering violence from the point of view of wars. Let us now concentrate on violence from the point of view of:

- Environment
- Religion

- Individual responsibility to shape *inclusive* organisations to foster world peace

Environmental Sustainability: From Divinities and Legalities to Narratives

We knew we would go through the beaten path when we decided to project ancient Indian scriptures and their concern for nature. Yet, the beaten path is necessary when we correlate Ashoka's concerns for nature, and similar concerns by contemporary ecologists, with those documented in the ancient Indian scriptures. The interesting debate, then, is—contemporary ecologists start with the assumption that we have to take care of the environment as it affects our living.[5] On the other hand, the ancient Indians' concern started with the assumption that they were a part of a larger existence.[6] It is to be noted here that the Norwegian philosopher Arne Naess first coined the phrase 'deep ecology' to describe deep ecological awareness. Deep ecology is rooted in a perception of reality that extends beyond the scientific framework to an intuitive awareness of the oneness of all life, the interdependence of its multiple manifestations. Arne Naess says:

> Care flows naturally if the 'self' is widened and deepened so that protection of free Nature is felt and conceived as protection of ourselves. ... Just as we need no morals to make us breathe... [so] if your 'self' in the wide sense embraces another being, you need no moral exhortation to show care. ...

> You care for yourself without feeling any moral pressure to do it ... If reality is like it is experienced by the ecological self, our behaviour naturally and beautifully follows norms of strict environmental ethics.[7]

During the year 1984, George Sessions and Arne Naess drew up eight basic principles that describe deep ecology. These have been listed on the Deep Ecology foundation page (www.heureka.clara.net/gaia/deep-eco.htm):

- The well-being and flourishing of human and nonhuman life on Earth have value in themselves. These values are independent of the usefulness of the non-human world for human purposes.
- Richness and diversity of life forms contribute to the realisation of these values and are also values in themselves.
- Humans have no right to reduce this richness and diversity except to satisfy *vital* needs.
- The flourishing of human life and cultures is compatible with a substantial decrease of the human population. The flourishing of non-human life demands such a decrease.
- Present human interference with the non-human world is excessive and the situation is rapidly worsening.
- Policies must, therefore, be changed. These policies affect basic economic, technological and ideological structures. The resulting state of affairs will be deeply different from the present.

- The ideological change is mainly in appreciating *life quality* rather than adhering to an increasingly higher standard of living. There will be a profound awareness of the difference between big and great.
- Those who subscribe to the foregoing points have an obligation, directly or indirectly, to try and implement the necessary change.

This discussion may be summed up by saying that if we acquire deep ecological awareness we become intuitively aware of ineffable knowledge and tribal wisdom: 'The connection between an ecological perception of the world and corresponding behaviour is not a logical but a psychological connection.'[8] Like the 'deep ecology' tradition, the Vedas (knowledge) or the oldest written scriptures of ancient Indian literature (as early as 1500 BCE); the Upanishads or the philosophical texts of ancient India; the Puranas or stories on various ancient Indian gods and goddesses, and other Indian classical literature clearly promoted a nature-friendly world view that encouraged ancient Indian people not merely to respect the environment with reverence, but also create a feeling amongst themselves that the great natural forces—the earth, the sky, the air, the water and the fire—as well as various flora and fauna are all bound to each other. The Dalai Lama's interconnectivity was already voiced as existing and real long back in the era of the Vedas.

The Vedic scriptures and classical literature uniquely assert interconnectivity when compared to Ashoka or even the current ecologists who are reminiscent of similar qualities; qualities that make Gandhi stand out in his ahimsa stance amidst others. Gandhi remarked that ahimsa was integral to human species; that is why we have existed over time, notwithstanding our ability and propensity for wars and violence.

In the same way, the Vedic scriptures stand out in their documentation of nature as an *already* recognised, acknowledged and legitimatised part of human existence. On the contrary, for Ashoka, the legacy of nature becomes prominent post severe loss of natural resources. Similar Ashokan concerns also haunt the contemporary ecologist. Thus, nature has never been a fiction for the ancients, though copiously divinised in their poetry, arts and scriptures, or a resource to be saved; it was always saving us! In the following passages, we will look at the mythological, the legal and the fictional narratives of nature in ancient Indian scriptures in our attempt to historicise the interconnectivity and hence the *inclusion* of nature in human practices, the echoes of which are so compelling in contemporary discourse.

The ancients offered many prayers for a peaceful environment. The Atharva Veda, one of the famous Vedas, calls out for peace in the hymn translated below:

Now let the earth be peace and
the air, the sky,
the waters, the herbs, the trees be peace.
Let the gods give us peace and peace
comes from these calls for peace.
With these peace calls that assuage everything,

I give peace to the terrible here,
to the cruel here, to the evil,
let them now be quiet, mean well,
let everything be good to us.[9]

Ishavasya Upanishad says that the entire universe belongs to God. One should not covet anything. One should treat everything around one equally and reverently. One should enjoy but neither hoard nor kill.[10] The ancient Indian seers firmly believed that people's duty is to follow the eternal law of nature without any violation, and if they do so, nature will honour them with bounty. The hymn is given below in translation:

For one that lives according to eternal law,
The winds are full of sweetness.
The rivers pour sweets.
So many plants be full of sweetness for us.
Sweet be the night and sweet the dawns.
Sweet be our Father Heaven to us.
May the forest trees be full of sweets for us.
And full of sweetness the Sun,
May the kine be full of sweetness.[11]

Yajur Veda states that service to animals is a heavenly act. No person should kill animals that are helpful to all; by serving them one should obtain happiness.[12]

The Atharva Veda has a whole prayer named 'Prithvi-Sukta', or Hymn on Earth, in praise of the earth.[13] The earth is considered here as the abode of all beings—human as well as others. Mother Earth nourishes all, but 'when angered by misdeeds of her children, punishes them with disaster'. Verse 11 in the Sukta is translated below:

> Oh, Earth! Sacred are thy hills, snowy mountains and deep forests. Be kind to us and bestow upon us happiness. May you be fertile, arable and nourisher of all. May you continue supporting people of all races and nations. May you protect us from your anger (natural disasters). And may no one exploit and subjugate your children.

We must note that the prayer is for support from nature for 'people of all races and nations', a prayer dating back to the early era!

The concerns for nature as an intrinsic part of the divinity is found in ancient rituals, daily practices and prayers. The five sacred obligations called *rinas* are exemplary. Among these obligations, *deva-rina* and *bhuta-rina* are directly related to the environment. The first obligation is called the *deva-rina* which human beings owe to the gods (*devas*), who control nature and its various phenomena. Offerings to the gods (*deva-yajna*) are made through sacrifices (*yajnas*) and prayers (*prarthanas*) to express one's gratitude for the great gifts of nature such as water, light and air.

Human beings *also* have a duty towards all those who contribute directly or even indirectly to their sustenance. In other words, *they owe a debt* to all sub-human species (*bhuta-rina*). They can discharge this debt by observing *bhuta-yajna*, a sacrifice mainly to the animals and birds.[14]

The animals and birds too contribute to human welfare and, therefore, humans too should feed them. The directions to give food to dogs and birds, both in the morning and evening, in a ceremony known as *vaishvadeva* is the outcome of universal kindness and charity. It is said that the food to be offered should be sprinkled with ghee, curd or milk but not with oil or salt. Thus, it is prohibited to offer food that is mixed up with what has been considered inferior food to birds and insects. It is prescribed that even when people are not going to eat on a particular day, they must offer *vaishvadeva*. If they could afford no food, they must offer fruits, roots or in the least, water. Sacred scriptures condemn to hell those who take their own meal without offering *vaishvadeva* when they are not in distress or difficulty.[15]

It is significant to note here that rice flour is used for making designs or *rangoli* in front of houses in the morning. This practice is still prevalent in southern parts of India. This is to feed small insects such as ants every day.

Cattle is also treated reverentially. The ancient literature encouraged the construction of tanks, leaving at least one side as an earthen ramp for animals, near pasture lands so that cattle coming to graze may drink water. In other words, the scriptures broadly classify dharma as *ista* and *purta*. *Ista* comprises those duties that spiritually elevate the individual. The *purta* is related to social duties such as digging wells, building tanks, planting trees, not cutting trees, laying pathways and roads, looking after orphanages, providing resting places for the tired wayfarer and so on.[16]

Reverence for animals is also found in the ancient Indian mythologies. The bull, the eagle, the lion, the elephant, the swan, the cow, the mouse and many more are the vehicles of various gods and goddesses. The message conveyed here is that the animals are not to be exploited but to be treated as partners with human beings. Even if one does not have any love for the frog, at least one's self-love should dictate that one's survival is tied up with the survival of the frog[17]; a theory that is very reminiscent of the inevitable interconnectivity discussed by the Dalai Lama.

The quintessential messages of the Upanishads, like *sarvam khalvidam brahma* or 'all that exists is verily the Brahman' or *ishavasyam idam sarvam* or 'everything is enveloped by the ultimate reality', speak of the highest condition of interconnectedness and inclusiveness. The equation between the living and the non-living has been the base for scientific discourse. Let us look at a few definitions from the Western sciences as well that reinforce the scriptural harmony and balance:

- Einstein's famous equation: $E=MC^2$

On the most basic level, the equation says that energy and mass (matter) are interchangeable; they are different forms of the same thing.

Under the right conditions, energy can become mass and vice versa. We humans do not see them that way—how can a beam of light and a walnut, say, be different forms of the same thing?—but Nature does.[18]

- Johannes Kepler in his book *Harmonices Mundi* or *The Harmony of the World* (1619) discusses harmony in geometrical forms and the planetary motions, equating them with musical harmony as well.

In this regard, Swami Vivekananda observes:

> In science, every day they are coming to a similar broad view of matter. You speak of matter, the whole universe as one mass, one ocean of matter, in which you and I, the sun and the moon, and everything else are but the names of different little whirlpools and nothing more... It is one unchangeable, unbroken, homogeneous Atman.[19]

The ancient Indian seers also believed in the Supreme Being as existing in all forms in the world. According to the Bhagavad Gita, the cosmic life is manifesting itself as the human beings, as animals, as birds, as the vegetable kingdom and other species, as listed below:[20]

- The Himalaya mountain is divine.
- The Ashvattha (Peepal tree) that yields no edible fruit has always been associated with the worship of the divine.
- The cows, the horses and the elephants are manifestations of the divine glory.
- The serpent is a venomous creature but it is considered as divine.
- The Nagas are non-poisonous snakes and the Lord rests on Ananta and hence it is divine.
- The lion is the lord of beasts and he is the vehicle of the cosmic mother.

- Vainateya is another name for Garuda and Lord's presence is found in this bird also.

Finally, Bhagavad Gita says that there is no being, whether moving or unmoving, in which the Supreme is not present.

The Vishnupurana says that humans, animals, birds, trees and crawling creatures are forms of Lord Vishnu. It says that equal consideration of all is the real worship of Lord Vishnu.[21]

Thus, nature is part of our existence; it is us, it is ours and as dear to us as our children or all that we love or own. Ironically, the ancient Vedic seers were able to revere nature; we as descendants of that civilisation are not able to and hence are embroiled in discourses to save nature. The contemporary inevitability of consideration of nature through evils of deforestation is way different from the natural *inclusion* of nature in human habitat in ancient times. We need to echo Auden's lines from the previous chapter again:

> About suffering they were never wrong,
> The Old Masters: how well, they understood.[22]

The ancient seers, like Auden's Old Masters, had a larger picture of the universe and human existence was just one part of it. They knew that inconsiderate consumption and the accelerated exploitation of natural resources and destruction of the precious environment could not go on forever. The resources of the earth had to be protected and sustained not only for humankind, but also for other species, and not only for this generation, but for generations to follow, even if in the name of divinity. They had the common sense to understand that to sustain the resources of the earth, the approach *cannot* be centred on any one species like the human being, but should encompass the entire life-support system. In fact, the ancient seers considered the earth itself as a gigantic super-organism, which is living, dynamic, evolving and continuing.

The human being, the universe and the God were generally regarded as the three main themes of humankind's religio-philosophical speculations. Three of the ancient civilisations had their respective watchwords. The watchword of the ancient Western thought was 'I' (*aham*); that of the ancient Chinese thought was 'we' (*vayam*); and that of the ancient Indian thought was 'all' (*vishvam*).[23] Yet, the 'I', the 'we' and the 'all' have in their own way contributed to nature discourses with similar concerns.

For instance, the individual or the 'I' has always had an important position in Western philosophies, with the famous French philosopher René Descartes making it a philosophical mandate with his legendary statement, '*Cogito Ergo Sum*' (I think, therefore, I am). Notwithstanding the power of fate and destiny in civilisations as old as the Greek myths, there was a Daedalus who did attempt wax wings like the League of Nations attempted to broker peace during the world wars, both unsuccessful in their attempts but attempts they were. Not just this, but the famous

20th-century German philosopher Martin Heidegger in *The Question Concerning Technology* (*Die Frage nach der Technik*, 1954) discussed the utilitarian nature of the modern technological individual, where the whole universe is made to be a standing reserve for him/her to put to use as and when required.

In other words, technology has changed the relationship between nature and humankind. However, like the ancient sages, we need to realise that we can make use of the standing reserve only as long as it exists. If we do not care for the reserve, it would slowly not function as a reserve any more. This is where Heidegger is unusually contemporary when he asks us to think, ponder and reflect upon the windmill and the hydroelectric power plant on the river Rhine. The windmill arrives from an ancient civilisation, where some typical forces of nature were harmoniously channelised for a certain productive aim. In contrast to the simplicity of the windmills,

> [t]he hydroelectric plant is set into the current of the Rhine. It sets the Rhine to supplying its hydraulic pressure, which then sets the turbines turning. This turning sets those machines in motion whose thrust sets going the electric current for which the long-distance power station and its network of cables are set up to dispatch electricity. In the context of the interlocking processes pertaining to the orderly disposition of electrical energy, even the Rhine itself appears to be something at our command.[24]

Thus, whether the essence of technology is about 'supreme danger' or 'saving power' is a debate that lies in the reflective capacity of the makers and users of technology—humankind. Can technology be seen to be more than an instrument of use is the question the philosopher asks the Western modern individual. The Heideggerian individual is one who is listening and reflecting on technology as unfolding the essences of discovery to harbour newer and harmonious relationships with nature rather than be an instrument that needs to be mastered for use to command and control nature. We contend that the Heideggerian individual is perhaps the hope for the 'doom' created by the utilitarian technologist; the foreboder of the Dalai Lama's responsible humanitarian and compassionate individual, the Western answer to the criticism of the 'I'-centric modernity.

The ancient Chinese philosophies had their fair share of contemplation on the relationship between nature and humankind. The *Huai-Nan Tzu* says it all:

> The Tao of Heaven operates mysteriously and secretly; it has no fixed shape; it follows no definite rules; it is so great that you can never come to the end of it, it is so deep that you can never fathom it.[25]

Unlike the Western 'I', the central position in Chinese Eastern philosophy of Taoism, in particular, has been the 'relationship' itself. So, nature cannot be mastered but lived as a 'partner in relationship'. Unlike the Western obsession with rationalism (metaphorically represented by 'I'), Taoism ventured to understand nature as infinitely irrational and irrationality was seen as an enviable state of enlightenment.

It was not nature that was required to be perfected, it was us. We needed to be part of the original order, the order of nature, which was interestingly orderless, undifferentiated and irrational; we needed to be irrational to get enlightened, as opposed to the Western Descartian rational 'I'.

The need to return to nature is also evident in the Taoist valorisation of animals and children as beings closer to the sacred order of nature: 'The wise person becomes like an animal or a child, participating joyfully in the profoundly irrational order. He or she learns to trust the chaos.'[26] Moreover, in the order of nature, human beings are not central to the scheme of things:

> The Taoists have always avoided anthropocentrism. Unlike other religions, they have never lost their animal gods. Ancient Chinese shamans put on animal masks in order to communicate with these animal gods. Their spirit-animals were links between the worlds of people, ancestors and gods. There was a tradition of animal frolics during which one became a particular animal, such as a crane or a bear. These rituals are still meaningful.[27]

Our reverential relationship with nature has been integral to most ancient traditions. As per the famous 19th-century French anthropologist Claude Lévi-Strauss, the Greeks were believers of the myth that human beings have sprung from nature. Hence, their myths always dealt with the contradictions between the scientific explanation of the anthropomorphic nature of human beings (we are born from man and woman) and the mythical contemplation of the autochthonous origin of humankind (born straight from the earth). Even the famous Zuni myths or the North American lores believed in the vegetal origins of the earth and its entire species.[28] For instance, not unlike the Indian scriptures, in some North American myths, the buffalo was seen to be the sacred knowledge carriers and were spiritually powerful, having gods and spirits named after them, such as Mosairu Kachina or Hopi. In some others, they were special because they readily gave themselves up for human consumption.[29] Hence, humankind has consistently been seen as a part of nature and not the most substantial representation of nature.

If the North American saw humankind as vegetal, the Indian scriptures looked at the entire creation with a unified vision—a non-differentiating, distinction-less vision; the Taoists looked at nature as heavenly chaos and the Western mind looked at nature as potential enfolder of wonders or as an instrument for saving or destroying. In all these capacities, the humankind (Eastern or Western) is entrusted with the responsibility to maintain harmony with nature.

Thus, the technologised world today calls for human collaboration to save planet Earth, while we have had actual measured ethical and legal practices documented in our scriptures, centuries ago. Our scriptures, hence, should make paramount sense today, far more than they did then.

Let us look at the ancient legal and ethical codes that would make sense even today. The legal codes instruct people not to kill animals like bullocks useful for agriculture or like cows that give us milk and all other helpful animals. The ancient Indian medical system, Ayurveda, regards the presence of animals, birds and other creatures as necessary for a healing and balanced environment. According to *Charaka Samhita*, the destruction of forests is most dangerous for the nation and for human beings.[30] According to it, the vegetable kingdom has a direct relationship with the wellbeing of society. According to *Sushruta Samhita*, a physician must not render any medical aid to hunters, bird-catchers and others. According to these writers, vegetable life and animals must be protected because they are useful to humankind.[31] These instances are not mere instances of instrumentality, it is showing reverence and care to those that we use.

The belief that a god dwelt in a tree or that the tree was the spirit naturally made the cutting down of trees a very undesirable act. The healing power of plants and their utility in curing human diseases were known to people during the ancient age. Some thinkers, such as Manu, were of the opinion that according to the usefulness of the several kinds of trees, graded fines should be imposed for injuring them. Vasistha, another thinker, felt that even the king should not be allowed to injure trees that bore fruits and flowers.[32]

It may be pointed out here that Kautilya, the author of *Arthashastra*, who was known for his valorisation of economics, interestingly took great pains to state that every creature has its own role to play in maintaining the environment. According to him, notified carnivorous and herbivorous animals, birds and aquatic animals, as well as animals in the notified areas, are neither to be caught and killed nor molested. 'The female that has just given birth to a young one of any species, or in any area, shall not be killed or injured.' This reveals Kautilya's concern to ensure the preservation of all species; a compelling task today.

Kautilya lays down rules to ensure punishment for injuring trees that were situated in city parks and bore flowers, fruits and yielded shade—punishments were to vary according to the part of the trees damaged. He firmly believed that human beings have no right to use the animals for their luxury because he states that skin, hair, bones and other things are to be collected from dead animals. According to him, causing pain or killing animals is a cognisable offence;[33] a legal rule still accountable, even if for notified animals and plants.

Trees played a considerable part in the administration of ancient Indian kingdoms. The practice of planting saplings of shady fruit trees along public roads and laying out gardens for public use dates back to remote antiquity. The practice had a religious sanction and public gardens were solemnly consecrated. The planting of trees has been proclaimed as conducive to great merit.[34]

Trees came to be regarded as so important that their felling or deforestation without reason and permission was looked upon as a penal offence. Today, green corporate gifts such as saplings are gradually being imagined in an Archies- and Hallmark-driven society.

Sage Patanjali's *Yoga Sutra* contains many ethical guidelines related to the environment. Yoga means discipline and control over body and mind, through physical practices and ethical code of conduct. Yoga has eight formal disciplines of which the first two (*yamas* and *niyamas*) have direct relevance to the environment and the ethics of using natural resources. *Yamas* are essentially moral commandments or ethical guidelines that deal with underlying principles governing our relation with other human beings, other species in the biosphere and our surroundings. *Yama* deals with what human beings should refrain from doing to the environment.

The first *yama* is ahimsa, that is non-violence against all living creatures and all non-living materials in the universe.[35] It also includes shunning violence in thought, word and deed. Pollution of air, water and land is also violence because it affects not only the life of other human beings but of all other creations, both living and non-living. As an example of this in the present context, one can think of passive smoking and the injuries it causes to innocent people around the smoker.

The second *yama* is satya, that is truth. One truth is that all living creatures are a part of one living universal family (*vasudhaiva kutumbakam*) and all have equal rights. Another truth is that human beings have no right to harm any animate or inanimate creation for their own greed.

The third *yama* is *asteya*, that is not stealing or using materials acquired through illegitimate means. For its own good and welfare, humankind must avoid overuse and wanton destruction of the ecological assets. The last *yama* is *aparigraha*, that is not coveting wealth or pleasures that are unnecessary or those that belong to others, or amassing wealth and worldly possessions out of greed.

Five *niyamas* are self-based codes of conduct. The first *niyama* is *shaucha*, that is cleanliness both in one's person and in one's surroundings. The mind must become clean of lust (*kama*) and greed (*lobha*). The second *niyama* is *santosha*, that is contentment that pertains to the use of materials and other facilities afforded by the universe to satisfy essential needs and comforts. The third *niyama* is *tapas*, that is austerity and penance and it involves simple living. The fourth *niyama* is *swadhyaya*, that is the study of the self. This leads to the study of oneself and enlightens one about the interconnectedness and interdependence of the entire world besides pointing out one's place in the universe, and the duties and responsibilities of an enlightened human being.

The fifth *niyama* is *ishvara pranidhana*, that is surrender to almighty—prayer, meditation and dedication of all action unto the universal spirit. Surrender to almighty and considering that everything belongs to God prevents indulging in any anti-environmental activity.[36]

Along with other ancient religions, India could never discard Buddhism from its soil—Buddhism had its interconnected presence with the Indian scriptures. The interdependence and inclusivity towards nature was essential to the fabric of the religion. It is well known that the middle path propagated by Gautam Buddha is the harmonious development of the multiple dimensions of the human personality that lies between the two extremes—vile pleasure-seeking and extreme asceticism. The middle path includes a bit of everything and maintains a harmonious balance. We must remember Einstein and Kepler when we think of the greatest takeaway of the middle path—harmony and balance. In effect, the Dalai Lama propagates the four pillars of world peace as the middle path and calls them the 'bedrock' of Mahayana Buddhism. The middle path is more than evident in Buddha's often quoted four states of mind. In Pali, the language of the Buddhist scriptures, these four states are known as *Brahma-viharas*.[37] They are considered to be the ideal social attitudes that are the foundations of ethical modes of conduct towards living beings.

The four 'sublime states' are:

- *Metta* (*maitri*): loving-kindness towards all; 'the wish that all sentient beings, without any exception, be happy.'
- *Karuna*: compassion; 'the wish for all sentient beings to be free from suffering.'
- *Mudita*: sympathetic joy; 'the wholesome attitude of rejoicing in the happiness and virtues of all sentient beings.'
- *Upekkha* (*upeksha*): equanimity; 'not to distinguish between friend, enemy or stranger, but regard every sentient being as equal.'[38]

Thus, the Dalai Lama's four pillars are definitely reminiscent of the *Brahama-viharas*.

It is here that Ashoka becomes even more characteristic because his inclusivity of nature is an important historical and mythological discourse of India. Like Kautilya, Ashoka had a prescription of nature legalities in his edicts. It is stated in Rock Edit I:

> No living being should be slaughtered for sacrifice. Many hundreds of thousands of living beings were formerly killed every day in the royal kitchen. But now only three living creatures i.e. two peacocks and one animal are killed for the sake of curry. Even this animal is not regularly killed. These three living beings shall not be slaughtered in the future.[39]

It is recorded in his Rock Edict II that:

> [King Piyadasi, Beloved-of-the-Gods], (Ashoka) has arranged for medical treatment of both humans and animals all over his empire and in the territories beyond the borders as those of the Chola, Pandya, the Satiyaputra and the Keralaputra up to Tampraparni and those of the Greek king Aniyoka and also his neighbours. He has arranged also for planting medical herbs, roots and fruit-yielding trees. Wells have also been dug and trees have been planted on the roads for the enjoyment of animals and men.

Shar-i-Kuna Edict of Ashoka states that ten years (since the coronation) having been completed, King Piyadasi proclaimed piety (truth) to people: 'No animal or bird is killed for feeding the king and people have also given up the same. Hunters and fishermen have stopped killing.'

The Pillar Edict V of Ashoka becomes significant in this regard. In a nutshell, it says that twenty-six years after Ashoka's coronation, the following species of animals were declared to be protected from slaughter: parrots, *mainas*, ruddy geese, wild geese, waterborne birds, bats, queen ants, terrapins, boneless fish, skate fish, tortoise and porcupines, leaf-hares, twelve-antler stags, free-roaming bulls, cats and rats, rhinoceroses, pigeons, village pigeons and all the quadrupeds. Those she-goats, ewes and cows that are pregnant should not be killed. Also, their young ones, less than six months old, should not be killed. This reveals Ashoka's concern to ensure the preservation of all species. Further, the inscription states that cocks are not to be caponed. Husks containing living beings should not be burnt. Forests should not be burnt without purpose or just to destroy living beings. Living beings must not be fed to living beings.

Fish should neither be killed nor sold on the three days of every three-month period: the full-moon day in the month of *Tishya* (Jan-Feb), the 14th, the 15th of every bright fortnight, and the first of the dark fortnight in each case and in every fast day. These and other species of animals should not be killed in the forests and the fisherman's localities.

It is to be noted here that *Tishya*, also called *Pushya*, was the birth star of Ashoka. Bulls and other animals are not to be castrated on those days, also on the 8th, 14th and 15th days of the fortnight and on the days of *Tishya* and *Punarvasu*, on the three days of every three-monthly period and on every auspicious day. Horses and bullocks should not be branded on those days.[40]

The wonderful results achieved through the persuasive efforts of Ashoka are recorded in Rock Edict IV:

> For hundreds of years in the past the killing of living beings, cruelty to them, etc. increased… but now as a result of both precept and practice on the part of the king, the practice of *Dhamma* has increased… Abstention from the killing of living beings, non-violence… and similar other acts of *Dhamma* have developed.
>
> [Beloved-of-the-Gods] will encourage their further development. His sons, grandsons and great-grandsons will exert similarly and instruct the people for all time.

Thus, we leave the readers to compare Ashoka's edicts and Kautilya's ethical environmental laws with the contemporary wildlife protection acts and then compare the list of endangered animals and birds *then* and *now*.

It is not merely ancient scriptures, meditations, politics, legal codes, ethical laws and philosophies that discussed environmental inclusivity and sustainability, even art and literature purported to that. We have Sanskrit poetry from ancient India, motifs from ancient China and the Romantic poets from the West, amidst many. They all discuss nature and interconnectivity.

Sanskrit poetry was a product of those who lived amidst hills, lakes, animals, trees and flowers and had all the time to feel the full impact of nature in its beauty, severity and sublimity. Technology had yet not destroyed the relationship between nature and human beings. The great Sanskrit poet Kalidasa was a powerful advocate of discipline in individual and public life. In one of his dramas, *Abhijnana Shakuntala,* King Dushyanta asks: 'Is it that my sins have checked the flowering of the plants?'[41]

Kalidasa does not tolerate the teasing of the animals. In *Abhijnana Shakuntala* again, the son of Dushyanta, Sarvadamana, violates the practice of forbearance by teasing the cub of a lion in a hermitage, which was a place of refuge for animals. So, Sarvadamana was rebuked by a female anchorite for his offence. Violence to creatures was strictly forbidden in the hermitages. When King Dushyanta was about to shoot the deer in the hermitage of Kanva, the sages requested him earnestly to withdraw his arrow as the deer belonged to the hermitage and he readily obliged them.[42] According to Kalidasa, it is the duty of a king to prevent the killing of animals.

The description of Shakuntala, who is the heroine in *Abhijnana Shakuntala*, leaving her surroundings in Kanva's hermitage is one of the most moving scenes in the world's entire dramatic literature. Goethe, the famous German poet, expressed his admiration of Kalidasa's portrayal of Shakuntala in 1792 in four well-known lines, which are worth quoting here (as translated by E.B. Eastwick):

> Wouldst thou the young year's blossom and the fruits of its decline.
> And all by which the soul is charmed, enraptured, feasted fed,

> Wouldst thou the earth, and heaven itself in one sole name combine?
> I name thee, O Shakuntala! and all at once is said.[43]

In one of the scenes, Kalidasa movingly presents the farewell occasion, depicting the departure of Shakuntala to her husband's home. Brought up from infancy in the lap of nature, Shakuntala had a sisterly affection for the flora and fauna of the place. The strings that connected Shakuntala's heart to the flora and fauna seemed to be coming apart as she said a tearful goodbye to them.[44] Let us look at a few of the poetic descriptions that represent the reciprocity of emotions between Shakuntala and nature. Her foster father addresses nature when she is about to depart to her husband's palace. The simplified translation of the verse is given below:

> This Shakuntala who never wishes to drink water while before watering you; who, fond though she is of decorating, never plucks a sprout from you through affection, who enjoys festival celebration on the occasion of your first blossoming—she, this Shakuntala, is today leaving for her husband's home, Pray, let her receive the permission of you all![45]

A cuckoo's note is heard and then an invisible voice wishes her a safe and pleasant journey:

> May lily-dotted lakes delight your eye;
> May shade-trees bid the heat of noonday cease;
> May soft winds blow the lotus-pollen nigh;
> May all your path be pleasantness and peace.[46]

The agony of separation is felt not only by Shakuntala but also by the entire hermitage. Feeling sad at Shakuntala's immanent farewell, the whole grove cries at parting from her:

> The grass drops from the feeding doe;
> The peahen stops her dance;
> Pale, trembling leaves are falling slow,
> The tears of clinging plants.[47]

Next, Shakuntala tells her foster father about the pregnant doe wandering near the cottage. Shakuntala requests that when the doe becomes a happy mother, he must send someone to bring her the good news without fail. Her father promises to do that. Then Shakuntala stumbled when somebody pulled her dress as if to hinder her. She turned around to see and her father said:

> It is the fawn whose lip, when torn
> By *kusha*-grass, you soothed with oil;
> The fawn who gladly nibbled corn
> Held in your hand; with loving toil
> You have adopted him, and he
> Would never leave you willingly.[48]

Then she said:

> My dear, why should you follow me when I am going away from home? Your mother died when you were born and I brought you up. Now I am leaving you, and my Father will take care of you. Go back, dear! Go back! (She walks away, weeping).[49]

Thus, emotionally she takes leave of her pet fawn, plants and creepers of the hermitage. The poet imaginatively describes nature in full sympathy with human sentiments.

The sylvan deities offer garments and ornaments for Shakuntala's adornment, birds bid farewell in sweet sounds and the animals and creepers vent their grief on the occasion of her departure.

When King Dushyanta asks Shakuntala to convince him about her marriage with him, she talked about the fawn Dirghapanga, whom she used to give water with her hands.[50]

Another example from Kalidasa's works is from *Vikramorvashiya* where Ayush (son of Indra and Urvashi) kills a vulture. The sage Chyavana considers that a serious transgression of the traditional law of the hermitage. Sage Chyavana asks the female ascetic to take Ayush back to his relatives for this fault.[51]

In Banabhatta's (another famous poet) *Kadambari*, sage Harita takes pity on the baby parrot, which in its attempt to escape a hunter, fell from the nest on account of its immature wings. The sage brings the parrot to the hermitage. The poet narrates the story of compassion from an injured parrot's point of view. The poet then tries to imagine what the bird would be thinking of us:

> While I was thus reflecting, by that very path (where I lay) came a young ascetic called Harita followed by sons of other ascetics to bathe in that very lotus-lake…

Generally, the hearts of good persons are ever ever-friendly (towards others) without any (apparent) cause, and exceedingly compassionate. For, when he saw me in that condition, he felt pity, and thus spoke to one of the many young ascetic-boys, who was near him:

'This young parrot here has somehow fallen from this tree-top, even when his wings have not yet (fully) grown. Or (probably) he might have fallen down from the beak of a hawk... For, owing to his having fallen from a very great height, very little of life is left... he is not able to hold up his neck. Come, take him up before he dies and carry him down to the water-side.'

With these words, he carried me to the shore of the lake. He then... opened my beak and made me drink a few drops of water with his finger... He took me up and slowly walked in the direction of the penance-grove.

Harita placed me in a certain spot in the shadow, underneath a tree, he sat on a seat of grass which lay not very close to his father. Seeing me, all those sages asked him, after he had taken his seat: 'Whence did you get this young parrot?' He replied to them: 'I found this young parrot when I went off from this place to my bath. He had fallen down from his nest on the tree... Suffering from the heat of the sun, he was lying upon a heap of hot dust; his body had lost all its strength on account of his fall from a great height, and very little life seemed left in him. I took pity on him and brought him here... As long, therefore, as he may be unable to fly up into the sky on account of his wings not being fully grown, so long let him stay here, in a hollow of some hermitage-tree nourished with juices of fruits and collections of grain brought to him by the sons of the ascetics and by myself. It is the duty of persons like us to protect those who have no protector. With the wings grown, and able to fly into the sky, he may go where he likes or may continue to stay here if he becomes (so much) attached to us.'[52]

The Sanskrit poets and writers have cast their admiring eyes on trees also. With a passion for learning, they have sought to derive lessons from them. Out of many such beautiful verses carrying great messages, we quote below a few samples in simplified translation.

Among the didactic verses, we find what trees have to teach us. In the *Abhijnana Shakuntala* (V.12), Kalidasa observes that trees, laden with fruits, bend low. This teaches us that a good human being should not be puffed up with prosperity. Even fables in the form of the *Panchatantra*, the Jataka tales and didactic fables in the *Hitopadesha* establish the value of nature for us.

As said in a popular Sanskrit verse, a sandal tree, even while it is cut down perfumes the blade of the axe. From this, we should learn that we should not refrain from being good to even an enemy who seeks shelter with us. The tree bears the scorching heat on its head, but assuages the fatigue of one who resorts to its shade. The big trees provide shadow for others, but they stand in the sun. They produce fruits for others and not for themselves.[53] There is an elegant tribute paid to a tree in the following verse occurring in the *Panchatantra*:

Deer recline in its shade;
birds in multitudes gather to roost,
darkening its dark-green canopy of leaves;
troops of monkeys cling to the trunk;
while hollows hum with insect-throngs;
flowers are boldly kissed by honey-bees;
Oh! What happiness its every limb showers
on assemblages of various creatures.
Such a tree deserves all praise
Others only burden the Earth.[54]

And here are the responsibilities of trees, very elegantly explicated: 'The whole life of these trees is to serve. With their leaves, flowers, fruits, branches, roots, shade, fragrance, sap, bark, wood, and finally even their ashes and coal, they exist for the purpose of others.'[55] The list of kindnesses of the trees are pragmatically aligned: 'Trees have five sorts of kindnesses which are also their daily sacrifices. To families, they give fuel; to passers-by, they give shade and a resting place; to birds, they give shelter; with their leaves, roots and bark, they give medicines.'[56] Thus, ancient Indians did not rest content by merely utilising the object of nature such as trees and rivers for their comfort and convenience but they also tried to derive lessons from them. Some more lessons are listed below:

- The sun causes the group of sun-lotuses to expand without a solicitation; the moon, though unasked, causes the moon-lotuses to bloom; and the cloud yields water without being solicited; good people direct their efforts towards the good of others of their own accord.[57]

- The rivers do not drink their own water; nor do the trees consume their own fruits; nor do clouds swallow the crops they water. Thus, the wealth of good persons is only for helping others.[58]
- The clouds take in saltwater, but give us back the same having made it (pure and) sweet. Even so, good persons listen to the foul words of the wicked and (in reply) utter only good words.[59]

Thus, we cannot but remember Gandhi's self-suffering and ahimsa here or the Dalai Lama's compassion. The Chinese are no different in their symbolic takeaways from nature. Look at the following list selected from *Chinese Symbols and Art Motifs*[60]:

- Bamboo:

  Always green in colour, bamboo is a symbol of old age and modesty. Bamboo and plums together represent man and wife. Bamboo, pine trees and plums, commonly seen together in a painting, are the 'Friends in Winter'.
- Banana:

  The symbol for self-discipline.
- Bear:

  Symbolises man and stands for strength and courage.
- Bee:

  Symbolises industriousness and thrift.
- Cricket:

Symbolises summer. It also represents courage and a fighting spirit.

- Eagle:
  A symbol of strength, an eagle shown perched in a pine tree is a suitable gift for an older man, wishing him the strength of an eagle and longevity of a pine tree. An eagle on a rock in the sea symbolises 'hero' who fights a lone battle.
- Elephant:
  The elephant can symbolise strength and astuteness. It is regarded as an animal with very high moral standards and is often shown along with the tiger, lion and leopard.
- Mountains:
  In most religions, mountains have an important symbolic role. They are the geographic point at which followers believe they are the closest to their gods or to the highest points of the universe.
- Pine:
  The favourite tree of Chinese painters, the pine symbolises longevity and steadfastness. Pine trees rank above all other trees and epitomise self-discipline. Pine, bamboos and plum trees are the 'Three Friends in Winter' as mentioned before.
- Yin and Yang:
  The negative and positive forces of universal life; they are represented by the symbol which is a diagram of an egg showing the yolk and the white, in dark and light colours to distinguish the two principles.
  The Yin embodies the female principle and is associated with the earth, with the North and the cold. The original meaning of the word means 'shady side'; the side of the

> mountain not facing the sun. The Yang signifies heaven, sun, light, vigour. Together the Yin and Yang make up the Tao, the eternal principle of heaven and earth and the origin of all things human and divine. This, in turn, produces Chi, the perfect balance of all things.

The Western modern world has had the technological utilitarian transforming the relationship between humankind and nature, as reflected by Heidegger. The English Romantic poets in the 19th century hierarchised the value of nature in their poetry—Wordsworth, Keats, Shelley and the rest become famous as nature poets. The Romantics, as they were popularly called, reacted and revolted to the utilitarian nature of industrialisation that had taken over the Western world in the later part of the 18th century. And subsequently, their art presented nature as a symbolic mutation of values and not a utilitarian resource to be used, particularly at a time when the instrumentality of nature through industrialisation was gradually escalating.

One of the finest and often-quoted nature poems is William Henry Davies's 'Leisure' (1911):

> What is this life if, full of care,
> We have no time to stand and stare.
> No time to stand beneath the boughs
> And stare as long as sheep or cows.
> No time to see, when woods we pass,
> Where squirrels hide their nuts in grass.
> No time to see, in broad daylight,
> Streams full of stars, like skies at night.

No time to turn at Beauty's glance,
And watch her feet, how they can dance.
No time to wait till her mouth can
Enrich that smile her eyes began.
A poor life this if, full of care,
We have no time to stand and stare.[61]

We can also look at perhaps the most-celebrated Western nature poet, Wordsworth, when he puns on the word 'wealth' in his poem 'Daffodils'. 'Wealth' between the 1750s and 1850s was all about money, industry and economic position, due to the popularisation of the famous treatise by the Scottish economist Adam Smith, *The Wealth of Nations* (1776). We must remind our readers that this, 'Daffodils', was the very poem that formed the subtext in a classroom where Swami Vivekananda,[62] as a young student, asked the English teacher the meaning of the word 'trance'—Wordsworth fell into a 'trance' when he looked at the 'wealth of daffodils'. Wordsworth *mutates* the value of 'wealth' from money to nature:

I wandered lonely as a cloud
That floats on high o'er vales and hills,
When all at once I saw a crowd,
A host, of golden daffodils;
Beside the lake, beneath the trees,
Fluttering and dancing in the breeze.
...
The waves beside them danced; but they
Out-did the sparkling waves in glee:

A poet could not but be gay,
In such a jocund company:
I gazed—and gazed—but little thought
What *wealth* [emphasis added] the show to me had brought:

For oft, when on my couch I lie
In vacant or in pensive mood,
They flash upon that inward eye
Which is the bliss of solitude;
And then my heart with pleasure fills,
And dances with the daffodils.[63]

If Wordsworth established the images of a group of daffodils as wealth, Keats in 1819 established the month of autumn as resplendent with human characters, personalities and emotions and activities:

Season of mists and mellow fruitfulness,
Close bosom-friend of the maturing sun;
Conspiring with him how to load and bless
With fruit the vines that round the thatch-eves run;
To bend with apples the moss'd cottage-trees,
And fill all fruit with ripeness to the core;
To swell the gourd, and plump the hazel shells
With a sweet kernel; to set budding more,
And still more, later flowers for the bees,
Until they think warm days will never cease,
For summer has o'er-brimm'd their clammy cells.[64]

Keats even laments that human beings can never be free like the nightingale since we are doomed with our knowledge of time and death, but which, as per Keats, the nightingale is blissfully unaware of and need not know, and hence can sing like it would sing forever, with no limitations, fear, envy or restrain. In other words, there is an underlying envy of the innocence and purity of nature, which is lacking in human beings. In fact, the passage below establishes the emotional dependence on the songs of the nightingale through history, through time:

> Thou wast not born for death, immortal Bird!
> No hungry generations tread thee down;
> The voice I hear this passing night was heard
> In ancient days by emperor and clown:
> Perhaps the self-same song that found a path
> Through the sad heart of Ruth, when, sick for home,
> She stood in tears amid the alien corn;
> The same that oft-times hath
> Charm'd magic casements, opening on the foam
> Of perilous seas, in faery lands forlorn.[65]

Shelley tells us all to learn the art of revolution that is natural to the west wind:

> Make me thy lyre, ev'n as the forest is:
> What if my leaves are falling like its own!
> The tumult of thy mighty harmonies
> Will take from both a deep, autumnal tone,
> Sweet though in sadness. Be thou, spirit fierce,
> My spirit! be thou me, impetuous one!
> Drive my dead thoughts over the universe,
> Like wither'd leaves to quicken a new birth!

> And, by the incantation of this verse,
> Scatter, as from an unextinguish'd hearth
> Ashes and sparks, my words among mankind!
> Be through my lips to unawaken'd Earth
> The trumpet of a prophecy! O Wind!
> If Winter comes, can Spring be far behind?[66]

And perhaps the best ode to nature comes from the dramatist Oscar Wilde in the late 19th century when he writes about the 'selfish humankind' and the 'selfless nightingale'. 'The Nightingale and The Rose' is a story of a young student who wants to dance with a girl, but she wants a red rose. He could not find any red rose, they are all white. A nightingale promises to help him. She negotiates with a tree:

> 'If you want a red rose,' said the Tree, 'you must build it out of music by moonlight, and stain it with your own heart's-blood. You must sing to me with your breast against a thorn. All night long you must sing to me, and the thorn must pierce your heart, and your life-blood must flow into my veins, and become mine.'[67]

The bird knows she will die, but she wants to help the lover. She tells the boy about her sacrifice but with the promise that he would be a true lover. She did what she had promised and finally died, and there was the red rose in the morning. When the boy gave the girl the rose, she had changed her mind. She felt the rose did not go with her dress and diamonds would suit her more. The boy gets frustrated and throws the rose into the street, where it was crushed by the wheels of a cart. He gave up his suit altogether and consoled himself with a dusty book of metaphysics.[68]

Not unlike the Indian and the North American lores, birds have been symbols of God even in the Holy Bible. The first such reference comes from the second verse in Genesis, the book of The Old Testament, where the reference to bird is by the connotation of the action expressed through the verb hovering: '...The Spirit of God was hovering over the waters'. Here, the Spirit of God is presented as a bird because, evidently, hovering is what birds usually do. To confirm the Spirit of God symbolised as a bird, the New Testament reads as follows in the verses from the Gospel of Matthew (3:16 and 17):

> As soon as Jesus was baptized, he went out of the water. At the moment heaven was opened, and he saw the Spirit of God descending like a dove and lighting on him. And a voice from heaven said, 'This is my Son, whom I love; with him, I am well pleased.'[69]

The albatross in another British poet Coleridge's poem 'The Rime of the ancient Mariner' is a pure innocent spirit, like that of Christ, and it is called Christian.[70] Thomas Hardy's thrush, 'The Darkling Thrush', stands for hope against a bleak landscape.[71] And there are many.

Concluding Remarks

This reverence for nature and all forms of life, vegetable or animal, represents powerful traditions that need to be re-nurtured and reapplied in our contemporary context. What is needed today is to remind ourselves that nature cannot be destroyed without humankind ultimately being destroyed itself. There is a need to incorporate these traditional and literary environmental values in the formal and non-formal educational systems. Most contemporary schools in the primary sections have a special class and examination on environmental studies. There is also a need for a coordinated programme of awareness through every available medium to build up public opinion to renew these ancient concepts of environment-friendly lifestyles. An example would be the Discovery Channel that works to engage the audience. The heritage of the past of thousands of years codified in sacred scriptures and literary works is becoming more and more relevant today.

As the environmental crisis looms ominously, the limitations of our dominant self-centred lifestyle and a throwaway culture must give way to a more sustainable civilisation that recognises the fundamental interconnectedness of all peoples and nature—a state of existence that ancient traditions have been trying to awaken humankind to for the past several thousand years.

6

Religious Pluralism Is the Need of the Hour

All religions should reside everywhere,
for all of them desire self-control and purity of heart.
—Ashoka the Great

The Politics of Inclusive Harmony

The Dalai Lama's third pillar described in 'A Human Approach to World Peace' is the intrinsic responsibility of world religions to maintain world peace. And he furthers his claim on religious inclusivity when he states that universal humanitarianism and compassion 'are in accordance with the ethical teachings of all world religions':

> I maintain that every major religion of the world—Buddhism, Christianity, Confucianism, Hinduism, Islam, Jainism, Judaism, Sikhism, Taoism, Zoroastrianism—has similar ideals of love, the same goal of benefiting humanity through spiritual practice, and the same effect of making their followers into better human beings. … The common goal of all moral precepts laid down by the great teachers of humanity is unselfishness.[1]

What is then interesting about the Dalai Lama's religious humanitarianism? He significantly *does not* proclaim religious conversion or a 'new world religion', but 'better interfaith understanding so as to create a workable degree of unity among all religions'. We must remember Arun Gandhi here for his concern for a more 'interfaith' international foreign policy. Hence, as stated by the Dalai Lama: a) we need to respect each other's beliefs and b) do so by emphasising 'the common denominator of all world religions—humanitarian ideals'. Evidence of common humanitarian ideals is amazingly found in the following precepts from multireligious texts:[2]

> This is the sum of duty; do naught unto others
> which would cause you pain if done to you.
>
> —Hinduism

> Hurt not others in ways that you
> Yourself would find hurtful.
>
> —Buddhism

> In happiness and suffering, in joy and grief,
> we should regard all creatures
> as we regard our own self.
>
> —Jainism

> That nature only is good
> when it shall not do unto another
> whatever is not good for its own self.
>
> —Zoroastrianism

Do not unto others
what you would not
have them do unto you.

—Confucianism

No one of you is a believer
until he desires for his brother
that which he desires for himself.

—Islam

All things whatsoever ye would
that men do to you,
do ye even so to them.

—Christianity

What is hateful to you,
do not to your fellow men,
that is the law
all the rest is commentary.

—Judaism

Every religion has the following components:

- Metaphysics and concept of God
- Ways to salvation or liberation
- Mythology
- Rules or customs governing social institutions and rituals
- Basic ethics

Religions may differ from each other significantly in the first four components. But they more or less agree on the basic ethical principles such as commitment to truth, compassion for the weak and self-control. While the other components of religion divide people, ethics has the powerful potential to unite them on a common footing as illustrated in the golden rule appearing in almost all religions, as quoted above.[3]

We return to the ancient Indian scriptures for the religious inclusivity insights. This is no news that India has always been a laboratory for religious diversity and pluralism, which has been singularly responsible for India's pride in the world map. India has had an unrivalled tradition of religious freedom and tolerance. The oldest written document amongst the Vedas, namely the Rig Veda (1500 BCE), states, '*ekam sat vipra bahudha vadanti*' (reality is the One, whom the wise call by many names—which forms the basis of pluralism). The concluding verse of this Veda strikes a highly significant note in this regard. It exhorts, 's*amgacchadhvam, samvadadhvam, sam vo manamsi janatam*', meaning:

> meet together, talk together in an accommodative spirit,
> so as to give and take, to live and let live and
> may your mind apprehend the truth alike.[4]

Another interesting verse found in this Veda says: '*a no bhadrah kratavo yantu vishvatah*' (let noble thoughts come to us from all quarters of the world). At another place, it also says '*ma vidvishavahai*' (let us not be intolerant of each other).

A famous Sanskrit verse occurring in the Mahabharata talks about the contradictions in the revealed texts and other authorities on religion and hence urges us to follow the path of great persons. We give the verse in translation below:

> Argument leads to no certain conclusion, the Vedas (*srutis*) are different from one another; there is not even one sage (*rishi*) whose opinion can be accepted by all; the truth about religion and duty is hid in caves: therefore, that alone is the path along which the great have trod.[5]

Noteworthily, the Sanskrit word *neti* means 'not this alone'. According to this, one should not claim one's definition is absolute or final; the door for discussion must remain open but there can be sufficient grounds for taking positions.[6]

The *Narada Bhakti Sutra* says clearly (in simple translation):

> It is not proper to enter into a controversy about God, or spiritual truths, or about comparative merits of different devotees.
> For there is room for diversity in views; no one view based upon mere reasons is conclusive in itself.[7]

The *Shivamahimna Stotra* of Pushpadanta makes this point clear in the following prayer (simple translation):

> There are many religions—that of the Vedas, Sankhya, Yoga, Pasupatas, Vaishnavas, and one person chooses one path, another person another path; because of the variety of preferences, favourably a straight path or a winding, you are the goal for men, as the ocean is the goal for all rivers.[8]

Hinduism's view that there is one divine, which may be reached by many paths, has proven throughout the centuries to be a powerful influence upon Hinduism's interaction with other religions. This point of view is expressed clearly in the famous speech delivered by Swami Vivekananda in Chicago on 11 September 1893, an extract of which follows:

> I am proud to belong to a religion which has taught the world both tolerance and universal acceptance. We believe not only in universal toleration, but we accept all religions as true. I am proud to belong to a nation which has sheltered the persecuted and the refugees of all religions and all nations of the earth ... I will quote to you, brethren, a few lines from a hymn which I remember to have repeated from my earliest boyhood, which is every day repeated by millions of human beings: 'As the different streams having their sources in different places all mingle their water in the sea, so, O Lord, the different paths which men take through different tendencies, various though they appear, crooked or straight, all lead to Thee.' ...
>
> I fervently hope that the bell that tolled this morning in honour of this convention may be the death-knell of all fanaticism, of all persecutions with the sword or with the pen, and of all uncharitable feelings between persons wending their way to same goal.[9]

To substantiate Swami Vivekananda's hope that was translated into action, we produce one outstanding case below. The case of an Indian king Maharaja Digvijay Sinhji Ranjit Sinhji (reign 1933–1948 CE), Jadeja of Nawanagar in Gujarat, is worth recapitulating here.

During the Second World War, Poland was almost destroyed by enemy forces and its people were held captive in concentration camps and hundreds of its children became orphans. Many Polish children and women managed to escape their country. But they were turned back from many countries they approached for support and help. When their ship arrived in Mumbai, the British governor too refused them entry. When Maharaja Digvijay Sinhji came to know the pitiable conditions of the refugees, tried to help them and requested the British government to allow the refugees to disembark. Even though the government did not act in his favour, the Maharaja allowed the ship to dock at Rosi port in his province. When the people disembarked, the Maharaja himself gracefully received the Polish women and children and said: 'Do not consider yourself orphans. You are now Nawnagaris and I am Bapu, father of all the people of Nawanagar, so also yours.'

The children were provided with tented accommodations till the Maharaja constructed a permanent structure famously known as the Balachadi camp, 25 km away from the capital city of Jamnagar. Even though he faced severe objection from the British government for taking in foreign refugees, the Maharaja proudly claimed they were part of his family and even provided the government with adoption certificates for them! The Maharaja took many personal risks to ensure that more than 640 women and children found a safe dwelling in Balachadi. Some of the survivors have made eye-opening remarks.

Wieslaw Stypula, a Polish survivor, remembers the Maharaja's concern for their eating habits: 'When we arrived at the camp, the Maharaja gave a party but he did not know what we children liked to eat… Despite being hungry, we didn't like to eat at all. Bapu saw this and said, "Don't worry, I will fix this." He brought seven young cooks for us from Goa!'

Another survivor Jadwiga Tomaszek remarked: 'We never liked the spinach that was cooked in the camp and so we decided to have a spinach strike. When Bapu heard this, he immediately ordered the cooks not to make spinach anymore.'

The refugees spent four years under his care and remembered him forever.

It is worth noting here that being inspired by the Maharaja's noble gesture many others opened their hearts and homes to the innocent victims of the war, not just in India but throughout the world. His act of benevolence is still remembered in Poland, where he was posthumously awarded the Commander's Cross of the Order of Merit by the president. Poland has also named the Maharaja the Honorary Patron of the popular Warsaw Bednarska High School. In 2013, the Government of Poland inaugurated the 'Good Maharaja Square' in Warsaw.

It is heartening to hear Starczewska, principal of Bednarska High School who says that the legacy of kindness experienced in India continues. The school provides free education to the children of refugees in

Poland from Chechnya, Vietnam, Sri Lanka, Tibet and African countries. Many roads in the capital of Warsaw are named after Maharaja Jam Sahib (Digvijay Sinhji). Poland government has named many schemes in Poland after him. Every year Poland newspapers publish articles about Maharaja Digvijay Sinhji.

In her doctoral thesis, submitted to the University of Pune in 2006, Anuradha Bhattacharjee documents the comprehensive history of Polish refugees in India. Bhattacharjee's book quotes Polish survivor Marian Raba from Balachadi paying a tribute to Digvijay Sinhji:

> He welcomed us to Nawanagar saying he was Bapu, father, to all, which meant a lot to us. He lived up to it by involving himself in our lives and taking pride in our achievements and later we heard that he had even adopted us to prevent our forcible removal to communist Poland. In his farewell speech, he said that he would always be Bapu to us and we could return to Nawanagar in our lives.

Children of Jamnagar, a film directed by Anuradha Bhattacharjee and Sumit Osmand Shaw and co-produced by India and Poland, acknowledges the contribution made by the Maharaja. It has been shown on Polish TV channels multiple times.[10]

The Indian soil was fertile for the birth of many religions. The ancient Hindu religion went through many transformations, absorbing the tenets of Jainism, Buddhism and Sikhism, to name a few. They may be considered as reform movements attempted from within the fold of Hinduism in order to meet the requirements of the various stages of its faith. Zoroastrianism, Islam and Christianity that have been prevalent in the country for so long have become native to the soil and are deeply influenced by the general atmosphere of Hinduism. The popular Sufi saint Kabir also expresses a similar view: 'The same God is sought after all in all religions which differ only in naming Him.'[11]

This makes all religious quarrels–those between Hindus and Muslims and those among all other religions–futile. Kabir's religious view is that every person must give up ego and vanity and consider the other as one's own self. A remarkable feature of another religious track in the Adi Granth, the holy book for the Sikhs, is that it contains the writings of the religious teachers of Hinduism, Islam and other religions.[12]

Secularism as a Western concept has been influencing the world fabric today, and not just the Indian. Yet, the Dalai Lama emphasises on the significance of religion and the acceptance and legitimisation of religion. What is important here for us is the Dalai Lama' stance: 'Rather, I try to think of how I as a Buddhist humanitarian can contribute to human happiness.' That religion matters and religious identity matters is a fascinating thing to say in today's secular discourse. In the Dalai Lama's poignant words:

> While pointing out the fundamental similarities between world religions, I do not advocate one particular

> religion at the expense of all others, nor do I seek a new 'world religion'. All the different religions of the world are needed to enrich human experience and world civilization. Our human minds, being of different calibre and disposition, need different approaches to peace and happiness.

Thus, the interest should be not secularism at the expense of religion, but to respect the social and cultural identity of an individual first. As the Dalai Lama has rightly commented, it is important to identify and eulogise efforts made in any part of the world to 'better understanding among religions', rather than eradicate religious identity. That makes the Dalai Lama different in his approach to religious pluralism. If interconnected and inclusive humanitarianism is the common denominator of every religion, then why should any religious identity not be eulogised and appreciated? Hence, we contend, that just like Gandhi's philosophy of ahimsa being integral to the human constitution, religious inclusivity is also integral to religious identity. The need to appreciate individual religions is necessary to maintain harmony and balance of humankind; not deriding of religions in the name of political secularism. Hence, the Dalai Lama's caution is mandatory—there can be no universal religion; but interfaith understanding: 'The need for this is particularly urgent now. If all religions make the betterment of humanity their main concern, then they can easily work together in harmony for world peace.'

Interfaith understanding will bring about the unity necessary for all religions to work together. However, although this is indeed an important step, we must remember that there are no quick or easy solutions. We cannot hide the doctrinal differences that exist among various faiths, nor can we hope to replace the existing religions by a new universal belief. Each religion has its own distinctive contributions to make, and each in its own way is suitable to a particular group of people as they understand life. The world needs them all.[13] Every individual's opinion counts! Why? The Dalai Lama answers:

> Despite the progressive secularization brought about by worldwide modernization and despite systematic attempts in some parts of the world to destroy spiritual values, the vast majority of humanity continues to believe in one religion or another.
>
> The undying faith in religion, evident even under irreligious political systems, clearly demonstrates the potency of religion as such. This spiritual energy and power can be purposefully used to bring about the spiritual conditions necessary for world peace. Religious leaders and humanitarians all over the world have a special role to play in this respect.

Thus, religious leaders have as much role to play in maintaining world peace as is the political leader of any nation. In this context, we can further justify King Ashoka's global religiosity even *then* as is evident in his Rock Edict XII:

> Beloved-of-the-Gods, King Piyadasi, desires that there should be growth in the essentials of all religions.

> Growth in essentials can be done in different ways, but all of them have as their root, restraint in speech, that is, not praising one's own religion, or condemning the religion of others without good cause. And if there is cause for criticism, it should be done in a mild way. But it is better to honour other religions for this reason.
>
> By so doing, one's own religion benefits, and so do other religions, while doing otherwise harms one's own religion and the religions of others.
>
> Whoever praises his own religion, due to excessive devotion, and condemns others with the thought 'Let me glorify my own religion', only harms his own religion. Therefore contact (between religions) is good. One should listen to and respect the doctrines professed by others. Beloved-of-the-Gods, King Piyadasi, desires that all should be well-learned in the good doctrines of other religions.

Ashoka is saying this *then*, the Dalai Lama is justifying the importance *now*! If Swami Vivekananda popularised the tolerance of Hinduism in Chicago in the 19th century, we must not forget the 'critical tolerance' attitude mentioned in the Buddhist mandate for their missionary goals. Buddhism has spread widely from India to Sri Lanka, Southeast Asia, Tibet, China and Japan, and recently to Europe and North America. Although Buddhism encountered established religions in all of these regions, there is little evidence of war or persecution. Buddhism has demonstrated a remarkable degree of tolerance and flexibility throughout the course of its expansion.

Now, we present an artistic enterprise that establishes the significance of religious pluralism as not merely essential but the inevitable character of secular politics today.

If Hinduism and India have been noted for religious pluralism, notwithstanding fanaticism as well, America is perhaps one of the most multiracial nations, and in that capacity, not unlike Indian multireligions. The 2004 Oscar-winning movie *Crash* is fictional, but the depiction of the American pluralism is poignant and significant in the contemporary era. Why? Because of the inevitability of interconnectivity and inclusivity of differences as depicted in the movie. It is amazing that so many different cultures exist in the same continent, even country, and despite the other cultures, which they feel have invaded their spaces. The film strategically highlights the despise, the anger, the racism, the fanaticism and the fascism that are all existing together, ironically inclusive of each other, yet hating each other. It is here that the quote from the Japanese Prince Shōtoku is of great value:

> Let us cease from wrath, and refrain from angry looks. Nor let us be resentful just because others oppose us. Every person has a mind of his own; each heart has its own leaning. We may regard as wrong that others hold as right. We are not unquestioningly sages, nor are they assuredly fools. Both of us are simply ordinary men. Who is wise enough to judge which of us is good or bad? For we are all wise and foolish alternately, like a ring which has no end. Therefore, although others may give way to anger, let us on the contrary dread our faults, and

though we may be sure that we are in the right, let us act in harmony with many others.[14]

And *Crash* is all about that. The plural cultures that inhabit America reach their peak of global existence in the strategically chosen racial backgrounds of the various characters that inhabit the screen. Let us look at Table 6.1 that contextualises the race and connected turmoil of the characters depicted in the movie.

TABLE 6.1 Crash *Characters and Their Local Context/Prejudice*

Character	*Colour / Race*	*Prejudice/Context*
Peter, detective's younger brother and gang associate	African-American	Petty criminal
Anthony, Peter's associate	African-American	Petty criminal
Rick Cabot, District Attorney	White	Has a suspicious and difficult wife
Jean, attorney's wife	White	Irritated and pampered; suspicious of the coloured sections
Ryan, police officer	White	Racist; had been through bad times due to some African-Americans, particularly relating to health insurance coverage for his father's health problems
Officer's younger partner, Hansen	White	Idealistic; for the African-Americans; hates Ryan for his prejudice against them

Character	*Colour / Race*	*Prejudice/Context*
Hollywood actor, Cameron and his wife Christine	African-American	Suffer racist attacks from the White police officer, Ryan
Father Farhad and daughter Dorri	Persian immigrant	Wary of others who look down upon him for his race
Daniel Ruiz, locksmith, and his daughter Lara	Hispanic	Looked down upon for his race

Source: Author's compilation

We can tabulate the characters into races and individual problems but the uniqueness of the movie lies in the fact that we cannot categorise them into 'sages' or 'villains', or victims and offenders. Each one has suffered at someone else's hands and bears prejudice against that someone and that someone's entire race. Yet, compellingly, the despised enemy turns out to be the messiah in difficult situations for the contextual victim; the inevitable interconnectivity is like an inescapable Shōtoku ring, which has no end.

Table 6.2 establishes the inclusive and interconnected ring of human differences that nevertheless help, include and harmonise, even when they have been excluding, hating and reacting.

TABLE 6.2 *The Interconnectivity of the* Crash *Characters*

Character	*Offender?*	*Victim/Offender?*
Anthony	Along with Peter, when in a moment of heated argumentation, they run over an Asian. They argue what to do with him, then dump him in front of a hospital and run away.	Much later, Anthony finds a white van that belonged to the Asian, who they (Peter and he) had run over. He drives the van away since the keys were still there. Later, when he decides to sell the van illegally and the van is opened, a number of Asian immigrants are found chained in the back of the van. *Thus the Asian victim of hit-and-run is a human trafficker!* Anthony is offered $500 for each person in the van. In the last scene, Anthony parks the van elsewhere, opens the back door and sets the Asians free. He tells them 'this is America' and hands them money so that they could all buy some 'chop suey' to eat! *Thus, the African-American hit-and-run offender actually is not a human trafficker; he sets them free.*
Jean	She and her attorney husband are carjacked by Anthony and Peter. Later, in their house, she is found suspecting aloud that the heavily tattooed Hispanic blacksmith, who is changing their locks, will surely go and give copies of the new keys to other possible gang members. She is wary of her housekeeper, also coloured. Her husband as a political leader wants votes from the coloured community.	She realises through a phone conversation with her friend Carol that she is always angry and she does not know why. Post the phone call, she falls down the stairs. Later, she calls her husband, who is busy with his politics of winning votes from the coloured communities. Her friend Carol is equally busy. She breaks down and hugs her housemaid, who is taking care of her, and she says, 'you are the only friend that I have'.

Character	*Offender?*	*Victim/Offender?*
		Thus, the well-off white suspicious wife of a politician finds solace and friendship only from her coloured housekeeper, who she often hated.
Ryan	He stops the actor and his wife Christine in their car, and sexually assaults the wife under the pretext of searching for illegal possessions. Christine is mad at her husband for letting Ryan touch her and for not doing anything about it. She felt deep humiliation. The husband sheepishly claimed that he had no other option since Ryan was a white cop.	In a car accident, Christine gets trapped. Ryan reaches the accident spot, and without prior knowledge rushes towards the car to get the victim safely out. He is shocked to realise that the victim is Christine and Christine is shocked to realise that her saviour is the molester. *In an amazingly sensitive manner, Ryan calms a hysterical Christine and gets her out! Christine has a baffled 'thank you' expression, and Ryan an equally baffled 'you'll be fine' expression on his face.*
Hansen	He detests Ryan's racist prejudice and requests headquarters to allow him a new patrol partner. He is sympathetic to the injustice meted out to the coloured people.	In one of his kind and broadminded moods, he gives a lift to Peter. Yet, he is suspicious about Peter since he picks up an African-American guy in the night. He is worried about weapons that Peter might be hiding. Notwithstanding his external projection of broadmindedness for African-Americans, he is hounded by internal suspicion. Peter finds a small statuette of a Saint in Hansen's car, and he is amused because he has a similar statuette of his culture with him. He realises *how similar people and their beliefs are*. But Hansen

Character	*Offender?*	*Victim/Offender?*
		suspects Peter's laughter, and in fear and suspicion, he asks Peter to get down as quickly as possible. In an attempt to defend himself, Peter says that he would show Hansen what he had in his mind and he puts his hand in his pocket to bring out the statuette. Hansen thinks this is a gun, and immediately shoots Peter. Peter dies and Hansen belatedly realises about the statuette!
Daniel and Farhad	Daniel rectifies Farhad's lock but finds his shop doors faulty. He warns Farhad that his doors need rectification. Farhad screams at him, accusing him of cheating. Daniel refuses to take the money and goes off. Farhad's shop is later looted and the insurance does not pay for the disaster since it is declared that this was a case of negligence—he was advised to replace the door and he did not. Farhad finds Daniel's name on the invoice and decides to take revenge.	Farhad locates Daniel's house and attempts to shoot Daniel. Daniel's daughter jumps to rescue her father and gets shot. She is miraculously unharmed because the ammunition with Farhad, bought by his understanding daughter, was a box of blanks. *A dazed Farhad later admits that Daniel's daughter was his 'farishtey', or angel, who saved him from such a ghastly crime.*

Source: Author's compilation

Thus, the difference in culture, race, religion, caste, ideology and even nationality does not remove the chance of humanity, love, care, help, understanding and respect. In the end, many religions have statuettes and many do not, many are similar or dissimilar in the same way! Yet, each one has the capacity, the context and, fascinatingly, even the desire to be useful to society, consciously or otherwise, and each is. We all contribute to society significantly. All we need to do is consciously do so.

Now let us look at a few instances of geographical collaboration of religious sentiments. It may be appropriate to mention here that there is a place called Dharmasthala in Karnataka where three faiths—Jainism, Vaishnavism and Shaivism—are followed in harmony. Here, the Jain tirthankara (prophet) is worshipped on the same consecrated grounds with Lord Shiva (Manjunatha).

The priests come from the Vaishnava community and the guardian of the temple, a Heggade, is a Jain by faith. This centre for religious and communal harmony exists for the last 800 years, the quintessence of which is religious tolerance, compassion and spirit of oneness. Dharmasthala Sri Manjayya Heggade, who was the head of this temple from 1918 to 1955 started the *Sarvadharma Sammelana* (the conference of all religions) to emphasise the oneness of all religions and propagate religious tolerance. This unique conference is hosted annually since 1933, wherein heads of various religions, scholars, poets and other distinguished personalities get together on a common platform, forging a religious bond that helps in encouraging solidarity, unity and above all universal brotherhood.[15]

Another example is that of Sringeri, a small town situated in the very western extremity of the same state. It is a sacred place for the followers of Hinduism. It is of special interest to note that in this centre, so sacred to

Hindus, there are evidences of a time when Buddhism was allowed to lift up its head without fear of persecution. It is a fact that inside the main temple, there are several pillars of distinctly Buddhist origin, while in a neighbouring village, a Buddhist image is still worshipped by the devotees of the sage of Sringeri.[16] It may be recalled that one of the sages of Sringeri, Jagadguru Bharathi Teertha Mahaswami (born 1951), visited the famous Buddhist shrine at Saranath on 5 December 1994. He was felicitated by the Maha Bodhi Society of India. It is perhaps the first time in the annals of Hinduism and Buddhism that a Shankaracharya has accepted the hospitality of a Buddhist organisation. Shankaracharya was received near Dhamek Stupa, the place where Lord Buddha delivered his first sermon to his five disciples. In his address, the Shankaracharya said: 'The principles of non-violence, compassion, truth, self-restraint and purity were meant for every individual, one might go to a temple, *vihara* or church, but the faith and belief were the same.'[17]

The credit also goes to the Maha Bodhi Society for having extended a welcome to the successor of Adi Shankaracharya, widely considered as the one who contributed significantly to the decline of Buddhism in India. Thus, religious concord is not new for a country equally besotted with communalism as depicted in the 1947 partition and the 1992 Babri Masjid incident.

When we were about to complete this section, we came across a very relevant news item that strengthens our point and hence the same is recorded here. This is about Indonesia, the country with the largest Muslim population in the world, gifting an imposing 16-feet tall statue of Saraswati, the Hindu goddess of learning and wisdom, to the American capital city of Washington DC. The statue has been positioned in front of the Indian Embassy in Washington DC. It is significant to note here that Hinduism is the primarily practised religion among Balinese people in Indonesia. A spokesperson of the Indonesian Embassy said that this gift of the statue was not decided only on any religious grounds, but more because its symbolic values that match several key principles of Indonesian–US relations under a comprehensive partnership, in particular education and people-to-people contact. In the statue, Goddess Saraswati is depicted to be holding in her hands an *aksamala* (prayer beads) symbolising the eternal process of learning; *vina* (a string instrument) symbolising arts and culture; a *lontar* (manuscript) symbolising the source of knowledge.

> Additionally, the lotus that she stands on illustrates holiness and purity of knowledge, while the white goose depicts wisdom that knowledge is hoped to bring.
>
> 'With these culturally dense symbolizations, it is expected that the erection of this statue could help promote the importance of mutual understanding within the diverse society we are increasingly having today,' the Indonesian spokesperson said.[18]

It makes sense here to bring in Narayana Murthy, the founder of Infosys and the contemporary corporate leader, who also talks about the importance of religious inclusivity.

We refer to both his convocation address and his Darbari Seth Memorial lecture, delivered on 28 December 2001 and 21 August 2002, respectively:

> As we enter the twenty-first century, I am reminded of the famous words of Albert Einstein that science without religion is lame; and religion without science is blind. In fact, as the influence of technology on our lives increases, the social and human aspects of our lives become all the more important.
>
> The founding fathers of independent India wanted a nation where every religion would flourish and every voice would be heard. Thus, India, very rightly, adopted secularism as its credo... However, our education system has consistently downplayed religion. Consequently, we do not know much about other religions because people do not speak openly about them. Such ignorance leads to suspicion and mistrust. In fact, such suspicion and mistrust have resulted in attacks by people professing one religious pursuit on people practising other religions. We cannot let this continue. The heritage of this country is too precious to be left to goons and illiterates to destroy it in their bigotry and hatred...
>
> Importantly, religious beliefs manifest themselves in ethical questions and disputes, not only within nations and communities but sometimes even within organizations. As you go on to become the leaders of this country and the world, an understanding of the religious beliefs of your colleagues will be of vital importance.

> We operate today in a globalized world. We interact with people of different cultures and different religions. Today... high-energy units operate as unified teams and transcend barriers imposed by nationality, race and religious belief. Thus, it is important that we understand and appreciate the religious beliefs, convictions and practices of our colleagues...
>
> For me, secularism is about respecting every religion and appreciating the positive aspects of each faith. 'Religion consists not of mere talk. He who looks on all alike and he who considers all to be equal is truly religious,' says the Adi Granth (Holy Book of Sikhism).
>
> In fact, every religion teaches man to be good and has its positive aspects, be it the quest for knowledge of Hinduism, the tolerance of Sikhism, the sacrifice embodied by Christianity, the brotherhood of Islam or the compassion of Buddhism.[19]

Again:

> Leaders should act as change agents of progress by raising the aspirations and confidence of all the people—Hindus, Muslims, Christians, Sikhs and every other religion flourishing in our country. They have to bring about a big-ticket change in the secular orientation of the masses. They should be 'uniters and not dividers'. This is the responsibility of the leaders of all communities, not just the majority community. The best way to do

> this is by walking the talk to demonstrate their total commitment to secularism.
>
> 'We must become the change we want to see in the world,' said Mahatma Gandhi. Our leaders have to demonstrate their belief in secularism in every action of theirs…
>
> We should honour and publicize role models of secularism from every religion.
>
> Successful leadership today is about dealing with the contemporary and future issues of development. It is not about fighting for relics, icons and ideas of the past. A nation is judged by its contemporary status and not by its past. A confident leader looks at what he can do in the future to better the lives of people rather than digging up the past.[20]

Equal importance was given by Einstein to religion and science, as quoted by Murthy at the beginning of his lecture, and can be illustrated beautifully through an incident narrated by the Dalai Lama, while interacting with the students of IIM Calcutta on 1 December 2011. The narration provides more insights on the complementary aspect of religion and science. A day before the Dalai Lama's gall bladder operation, his secretary informed him that many people were praying for the success of the operation. Immediately, the Dalai Lama remarked that it is good to know that so many people were praying; prayer has its own benefits and effectiveness. But, the Dalai Lama also wanted to know from the secretary about the competence of the surgeon. In other words, science has its significance notwithstanding one's faith in religion.

Murthy's reference to religious beliefs manifesting themselves in ethical questions is clearly evident in the case of Savita Halappanavar, a young dentist of Indian origin who died at the University Hospital Galway in Ireland in October 2012. She was refused abortion at a government hospital even though her life was in danger. The refusal has been popularly cited to have been influenced by Ireland's strict anti-abortion law based on religious views. The conduct of doctors at University Hospital Galway, who refused to perform an abortion on grounds that 'this is a Catholic country' was criticised all over the world.[21]

The Inclusive Individual: Swami Vivekananda as the Internationalist and Obama as the Nationalist

The final pillar for world peace as discussed by His Holiness is individual responsibility for initiating inclusive organisations, movements, culture. One man stands out for his incredible feat: he took the trouble in the 19th century to travel from India to Chicago, address the international diaspora of religious bodies and talk about Hinduism and its inherent value of 'acceptance'. If the Dalai Lama in his speech in the 1990s says: 'Rather, I try to think of how I as a Buddhist humanitarian can contribute to human happiness'; then, Vivekananda does the same with Hinduism, but in the 19th century.

That Hinduism is a uniquely plural religion is not the point of discussion here, but Swami Vivekananda's *need* to address a world forum to establish the plurality of Hinduism is what makes Swami, the individual and not necessarily the religion, even more remarkable for us. Vivekananda was instrumental in being that 'individual power' that 'shaped' the Ramakrishna Math as an 'institution' of 'religious acceptance' in India and abroad. Our interest is in his *inclusive* method of institutionalising the Ramakrishna Math, which is a lesson in organisational inclusivity.

Vivekananda was the follower of Ramakrishna Paramahamsa. In Swamiji's words from his own writings: 'Sri Ramakrishna never spoke a harsh word against anyone. So beautifully tolerant was he that every sect thought that he belonged to them. He loved everyone. To him, all religions were true. He found a place for each one.'[22]

So, the 'leader' was himself pluralistic and loving. And he preached or rather lived a religion in a time (19th century) that was entangled in mutually exclusive divisions, sects and systems. Amidst these meshes of interpretations of a very old religion—Hinduism—Vivekananda was mesmerised by the simplicity and inclusivity of Sri Ramakrishna's interpretations of the same. In Swamiji's words again:

> When the degraded Aryans had almost turned India, the land of religion, into hell, Bhagavan Sri Ramakrishna incarnated himself to demonstrate the true religion of the Aryan race. He made visible the unity among the innumerable sects and denominations of the Hindu

> religion that had cropped up throughout the country over a vast period of time. At that time, the Hindu religion had been devastated by continuous sectarian fights and was seemingly divided into many sects. Its various sects were overrun by hideous customs, and Hinduism had become confusing to Indians and an object of contempt to foreigners.
>
> Over time, this eternal religion had been debased, but Sri Ramakrishna incorporated its universal and eternal aspects in his own life to become a living example of the eternal religion, which he lived before all for the good of humanity...[23]

The significant point, then, is the *choice of the leader* made by Vivekananda. What made him even want to follow Ramakrishna? In his own words, Ramakrishna was the living embodiment of the new and modern interpretation of Hinduism—a religion that *includes* every sect, the poor, the weak, the outcast, the downtrodden and not the mutually exclusive religion it was becoming due to some sects:

> for everyone in this world, inside India or outside India; and at the same time whose grand brilliant intellect would conceive of such noble thoughts as would harmonise all conflicting sects, not only in India but outside of India, and bring a marvellous harmony, the universal religion of head and heart, into existence. Such a man was born, and I had the good fortune to sit at his feet for years ...[24]

We must remember that Vivekananda was interpreting in a time when popular customs were more prevailing embodiments of the religion and Ramakrishna cut a queer figure because he was not into customs (he even cleaned the house of a pariah, the street cleaner, when he was a Brahmin).[25] He was poor, he renounced studies and hence got labelled as illiterate, but he talked about god through every tenet of every religion and that was a *new* value, which Vivekananda called the 'new religion of the age'.[26] For any old movement to be 'revivified', for any new movement to start, it needs 'a character, a life, a centre, a god-man that must lead the way, that must be the centre around which all other elements will gather themselves and then fall like a tidal wave upon the society, carrying all before it, washing away all impurities'.[27]

The 'centre' is not so much the point of introspection here as is the interpreter of the 'centre'—Vivekananda himself, as mentioned earlier. There are two points of introspection:

- The choice of the centre as an access point to 'manage' a humanitarian world.
- The individual who made it possible to propagate the values emanating from *that* centre to a whole geopolitical expanse beyond the localised concentration of the centre.

These are precisely the reasons why Vivekananda is important for the understanding of the role of a leader in the contemporary world of globalisation and cosmopolitanism.

A centre would always mean a totalitarian point of power; a point that holds a structure together and hence itself is a point of non-dialogue. But what is new about the centre that Vivekananda vociferously advocated for a *newer* institutionalisation of an age-old religion? The characterisation, the life of the god-man is itself uncentred, inclusive and plural. In Vivekananda's words, though Ramakrishna knew only one religion, he had a strong urge to know the others:

> He wanted to understand what other religions were like... He found a Mohammedan saint and placed himself under him; he underwent the disciplines prescribed by him, and to his astonishment found that when faithfully carried out, these devotional methods led him to the same goal he had already attained. He gathered similar experience from following the true religion of Jesus the Christ. He went to all sects he could find, and whatever he took up he went into with his whole heart. He did exactly as he was told, and in every instance, he arrived at the same result. Thus, from actual experience he came to know that the goal of every religion is the same, that each is trying to teach the same thing, the difference being largely in method, and still more in language...
>
> That is what my Master found, and he then set about to learn humanity, because he had found that the one idea in all religions is, 'Not me, but Thou...'[28]

The religion became a means to serve humanity and not *vice versa*. Hence, 'he then set about to learn humanity' and in the process, he found plural paths leading towards similar humanitarian goals. Vivekananda says about Ramakrishna:

> That is a glorious thing, that there should be so many paths, because if there were only one path, perhaps it would suit only an individual man. The more the number of paths, the more the chance for every one of us to know the truth.
>
> If I cannot be taught in one language, I will try another ... Thus, his benediction was for every religion.[29]

This is where Ramakrishna is important. He overcame the external barriers of religious discourse. For him, '[T]he more the number of paths, the more the chance for every one of us to know the truth.' It is this loving acceptance of other paths that propelled Vivekananda to spread the same as the doctrine of modern religion: 'That new life-force which he [Ramakrishna] brought with him has to be instilled into learning and education.'[30]

The rise of the Ramakrishna Mission as an organisation is no less a study in the managerial organisation, marketing and in brand-building, what with the commander himself admitting that he was chosen to 'organise', he was 'advertised'[31] in Chicago; he has a 'project'[32] that he needs to accomplish, or the way truth has to be 'broadcast'[33]. So, what are the important facets of marketing and brand-building? They include:

- The values of the brand, or the 'ideals'

- The qualifications of the salesperson, or 'service for order'
- The publicity of the same, or 'broadcast'

First, the master and a group of very young boys decided upon the values of their brand; the ideals that were hugely inclusive from the mutually exclusive Hindu practices of the time: '[W]e must show the spirituality of the Hindus, the mercifulness of the Buddhists, the activity of the Christians, the brotherhood of the Mohammedans, by our practical lives. "We shall start a universal religion now and here," he said, "we will not wait."'[34] The tenants of the math as a brand have been laid down.

Next, let's look at why is Vivekananda the organiser at the helm of affairs? Can we manufacture a possible portfolio for a salesperson or, 'what kind of service was required for the order'?

- His absolute appreciation in the Ideal, come what may: 'If it is in failure great sage laid down his life after having attained superhuman heights of Jnana, Bhakti, love and powers, and after having practiced for forty years stern renunciation, non-attachment, holiness and great austerities, then where is there anything for us to count on? So, I am obliged to trust his words as the words of one identified with truth.'[35]
- His belief in himself that *he was* 'born to organise'.
- His belief in the process notwithstanding results: 'His command was that his all-renouncing devotees should group themselves together, and I am entrusted with

seeing to this. Of course, it matters not if any one of us goes out on visits to this place or that, but these shall be but visits…'[36]

- Unflinching category for inclusion (recruitment) of other members (employees): 'order of all-renouncing devotees'.[37]

Next, what are the publicity methods? Vivekananda learnt two important points in this regard, from his master:

- 'Religion can be given and taken more tangibly, more really than anything else in the world', (in our words, religion can be shared; it is not mutually exclusive)
- All religions of the world are not contradictory or antagonistic; rather, '[t]hat one central religion is applied to different planes of existence, is applied to the opinions of various minds and various races'[38]

With these points in mind, he first started the 'broadcast' of the new ideals at home. But it was difficult with only a few followers: 'After Sri Ramakrishna's passing away, all forsook us as so many worthless, ragged boys. Only people like Balaram, Suresh, Master… and Chuni Babu… were our friends at that hour of need.'[39]

The difficulty was even more in the reception of the attempts of the handful of boys in the homeland itself or as we put it, the paths of exclusion they had to face: 'The only thing we got from those around us was a kick and a curse—that was all.'[40]

And yet, the perseverance amidst the 'kicked' group had another LCD: '"No compromise!" was the watchword. "This is the ideal, and this has got to be carried out. If we meet the king, though we die, we must give him a bit of our minds; if the peasant, the same."' [41]

Thus, the tag line for the spirit of advocacy was 'No compromise!' and the target group for advocation of new ideals was 'borderless', in any capacity, from the kings to the pariahs, from nationals to the internationals. And the method of advocation was personal, tangible, word of mouth and peripatetic communication. Do we remember Ashoka's method of communication of his Dhamma doctrine through edicts here? The differences between Ashoka and Vivekananda are:

- Ashoka was a king who had to incorporate a new institution in his territory and Vivekananda was a common man who had to establish a new institution in a territory that was not under his governance.
- Ashoka planted edicts all over his territories with the Dhamma principles inscribed on them and Vivekananda along with his group of men travelled like the Sophists, the *sanyasi*, the monks, to deliver knowledge, from door to door, seeking alms.
- Ashoka had inscribed in some of the edicts the *inclusive* treatment for people beyond his territories and Vivekananda travelled across waters to advocate his religion in foreign shores.

Vivekananda's speech had manifold opportunities for the publicity of the math.

- The press coverage as quoted by Vivekananda in his Chicago speech:

> These I quote from the journals: 'But eloquent as were many of the brief speeches, no one expressed as well the spirit of the Parliament (of religions) and its limitations as the Hindu monk. [. . .]' *New York Critique*
>
> He has preached in clubs and churches until his faith has become familiar to us. … His culture, his eloquence, and his fascinating personality have given us *a new idea of Hindu civilization…* (*Ibid.*)
>
> Vivekananda is undoubtedly the greatest figure in the Parliament of Religions. After hearing him we feel how foolish it is to send missionaries to this learned nation. [42]

Thus, the foreign media coverage is able to get to the nook and corner of the world, which could not have been possible in simple peripatetic travels in India. The same salesmanship spirit was advertised by Gandhi when he stood in the court of law in Britain in his simple dhoti (the common cloth that the Indian farmers wore) and yet showed great intellectualism in his answers, with the foreign media reporting his exotic look yet powerful determination in galore. The whole world was a witness to the anti-colonial fight of India through the power of ahimsa due to the Western media coverage, including the enemy media. Vivekananda was in his turban, which the American was trivialising or looking down upon. But his communication skills—'deep musical voice', 'speaks without notes' and 'rising often to rich inspiring eloquence'[43]—got the same Americans mesmerised.

Intellectualism lay in communication, in the thoughts and the *sanyasi*'s habit was that of a peripatetic speaker, oral, from the heart, and hence never requiring notes and making possible tangible transference of religious ideas.

✦ Help from the West

Vivekananda admits that Indians did not initially help him, his own brethren *excluded* him:

> I am the same here as in India, only here in this highly cultural land there is an appreciation, a sympathy which our ignorant fools never dream of. There, our people grudge us monks a crumb of bread, here they are ready to pay one thousand rupees a lecture and remain grateful for the instructions for ever.[44]

He also mentions how each of his lectures earned him hefty amounts in dollars, which he sent back to India to help the math. His popularity grew manifold in India due to his popular lectures in America and the rest of the world. The use of the West to institutionalise the East is what makes Vivekananda an interesting personality for a discourse on leadership in the contemporary world. If the Dalai Lama stated, years later, 'As all nations are economically dependent upon one another more than ever before, human understanding must go beyond national boundaries and embrace the international community at large', Vivekananda stated centuries earlier, in a time when the world was not termed *global*: 'I belong as much to India as to the world... What country has any special claim on me? Am I any nation's slave?'[45]

Not just that, he set about finding the Dalai Lama's common denominator in Hinduism, and the Western religions: 'I am one of those monks who have been described as beggarly. That is the pride of my life. I am proud in that sense to be Christlike.'[46]; 'I have a superstition—it is nothing, you know, but a personal superstition—that the same soul who came once as Buddha came afterwards as Christ.'[47]

And even more striking is his understanding of the interconnectedness of nations, religions and individuals: 'I am thoroughly convinced that no individual or nation can live by holding itself apart from the community of others, and whenever such an attempt has been made under the false ideas of greatness, policy, or holiness—the result has always been disastrous to the secluding one.'[48]

Thus, Vivekananda becomes a lesson for the present politics of an interconnected world, a politics established even more strongly in the next point regarding the impact of the foreign platform.

✦ Use of the West

Vivekananda knew that the Chicago Parliament of Religions (11–27 September 1893) was organised by the Roman Catholics, with the intention to make it a Catholic show. Such an inference comes from the news that a similar venture in Paris was being opposed by the same organisers. But the Parliament eventually became the best platform for the 'broadcast' of the Indian thought and India:

> The Parliament of Religions, as it seems to me, was intended for a 'heathen show' before the world: but it turned out that heathens had the upper hand and made it a Christian show all around. ... It helped on the tide of Vedanta, which is flooding the world. The American people—of course, *minus* the fanatical priests and Church-women—are very glad of the results of the Parliament.[49]

When the President of the United States addressed the Indian Parliament[50] on 8 November 2010, it was a déjà vu of sorts. Swami Vivekananda as the 'commander' of an order initiated by Ramakrishna, travelled across shores to address the Parliament of Religions organised in Chicago in the 19th century to advocate a religion as the 'national consciousness' of his country, an advocation that was on shaky grounds in the home nation itself. Obama as the President of America, aware of the rising champion of economic and geopolitics, China and Asia, makes a political visit to India and addresses the Indian Parliament in a manner and with an agenda, not different from Vivekananda's. It is an astute inclusion of the 19th century Chicago event in Obama's speech in the 21st century: 'It's the richness of faiths celebrated by a visitor to my hometown of Chicago more than a century ago—the renowned Swami Vivekananda.' He said that, 'holiness, purity and charity are not the exclusive possessions of any church in the world, and that every system has produced men and women of the most exalted character.'

Again, the 'common denominator' set by Vivekananda and Obama are strikingly similar. Vivekananda mentions his beggarly appraisal as similar to Christ; he equates the soul of Buddha with the soul of Christ; he equates Buddha's renunciation to the basic renunciation doctrine of Hinduism. Obama equates the democratic ideals of India with America—America as the oldest democracy and India as the largest democracy. Look at the interconnectedness highlighted in Obama's description of the American population: 'I bring the greetings and friendship of the world's oldest democracy—the United States of America, including nearly three million proud and patriotic Indian-Americans.'

Again, he establishes a 'common denominator' between America and India through the heroes produced; Vivekananda set the tone by equating the beggarly appearance of a *sanyasi* with that of Christ, Obama sets the tone through Vivekananda, to establish the interconnectedness in exalted ideals from 'exalted character'. Gandhi and his championing of equality was an influence for Martin Luther King, a similar champion of equality in the US. Quoting Obama again: 'After making his pilgrimage to India a half-century ago, Dr King called Gandhi's philosophy of non-violent resistance "the only logical and moral approach" in the struggle for justice and progress.'

What is interesting about Obama's speech is his positioning of India as a significant contributor to world politics, economics and culture. He is almost selling India to India, as is evident in the following excerpts from his speech:

- One billion Indians establishing the largest democracy (think market and consumer reach).
- Around 3 billion Indian-Americans as part of American population itself (remember Arun Gandhi and his problematisation of the 'us' and 'our' when talking about US and 9/11).
- Indian contribution to information age through 'zero', and hence 'ancient civilization of science and innovation'.
- The diversity in race, caste and creed existing in harmony in one country, representative of how the world with diverse race and creed should live.
- Democratic politics and voting system, through 'free and fair elections, which enable citizens to choose their own leaders without recourse to arms... an independent judiciary and the rule of law, which allows people to address their grievances; and a thriving free press and vibrant civil society which allows every voice to be heard'. The inference is that the law of the land is above all customs, and everyone must be treated equally in the eyes of the law.
- '[M]oral imagination' from religious and artistic texts about dignity, discipline and fearlessness (Vivekananda had already started the process of advertising the Indian consciousness centuries ago).
- Non-violence from Gandhi that the world followed (including Martin Luther King).

- Creating the world's largest middle classes (consumer base) by supporting the global economy rather than resisting it through feats like the reformation of the licensing raj and many others.

Perhaps, the following is the clinching statement that says it all: 'This year, as India marks 60 years with a strong and democratic constitution, the lesson is clear—India has succeeded, not in spite of democracy; India has succeeded because of democracy.'

But what is the need to sell India to India? Vivekananda was advertising the Indian consciousness to the Western world. But America comes to India to advertise India to India and the Eastern world? Obama's statement regarding the Indian population in America and the largest middle class in India perhaps establishes the inevitable interconnectedness between the Western and the Eastern bloc. Arun Gandhi had mentioned the political division that materialised significantly during the world wars.

The Dalai Lama further established the division as the main exponent of world disharmony. Obama astutely meets the division as a division that must be left in history:

> Now, just as India has changed, so, too, has the relationship between our two nations. In the decades after independence, India advanced its interests as a proud leader of the nonaligned movement. Yet, too often, the United States and India found ourselves on opposite sides of a North-South divide, estranged by a long Cold War. Those days are over.

So, as Obama mentions very frankly, what is left now is the 'natural' necessity to collaborate: 'Here in India, two successive governments led by different parties have recognised that deeper partnership with America is both natural and necessary. And in the United States, both of my predecessors—one a Democrat, one a Republican—worked to bring us closer, leading to increased trade and a landmark civil nuclear agreement.' He sets the ground for the 'natural' necessity of collaboration between India and America by establishing 'common denominator' of ideals or 'shared values':

- Both are democratic nations, hence belief in equality is similar
- Gandhi and Martin Luther King: similar fights in similar fashions—non-violence
- Both support the global economy, rather than resist
- 26/11 and 9/11—both condemn terrorism
- Similar contributions in Green Revolution
- Both nations entertain diverse races, castes and creeds

So, what is the difference between Vivekananda's visit and Obama's visit? Vivekananda was setting up a unified religious or spiritual integration of Hinduism in the face of sectism, divisions and prejudices. He was establishing the national character of the Indian religion—Hinduism. Obama establishes a national character of India but it is a character of progress—material, spiritual, political, technical and idealistic. We must bring in the Dalai Lama again at this interesting point of Indian characterisation by an American President. The Dalai Lama is contemporary in his spiritualism and his managerial understanding of material development as an inevitable human condition:

> Finally, a few words about material progress. I have heard a great deal of complaint against material progress from Westerners, and yet, paradoxically, it has been the very pride of the Western world. I see nothing wrong with material progress per se, provided people are always given precedence.
>
> It is my firm belief that in order to solve human problems in all their dimensions, we must combine and harmonise economic development with spiritual growth.

The greatest spiritual and material resource for India as an emerging economy is its people, mentioned in no uncertain words by President Obama: 'Instead of becoming dependent on commodities and exports, you invested in science and technology and in your greatest resource—the Indian people.'

The repeated inclusion of the Indian population—Indian people, largest middle class, Indian-Americans—in the presidential speech favours the need for 'wise self-interest'. Why would a Hollywood movie, say *James Bond*, open in India now along with its Western release? On 10 July 2012, *The Times of India* featured an article titled 'Spiderman director thanks India':

> 'The Amazing Spiderman' director Marc Webb, wrote a letter to the Indian audiences, thanking them for all the support and love they have showered upon his Superhero. The Spider-Man reboot released in India, a week before the US. ... The movie The Amazing Spider-man made a comeback with its reboot in the franchise a week ago but set a record within 3 days of its release. The figures were enough to prove the love of the Indian fans for their favorite super hero.

The spirit of inclusion that started after the end of the Cold War and the current power of Asian consumer base favours the need for 'compromised self-interest' between two large populations through political partnerships. Such a partnership between India and the US can be illustrated by the following points covered by President Obama in his speech:

- Inclusion of India in the United Nations Security Council: 'I look forward to a reformed United Nations Security Council that includes India as a permanent member'
- India's major role in G20
- India's major role in international financial institutions
- Inclusion of India in climate change projects in Copenhagen
- Indian contributions in United Nations Peace-keeping Missions
- The civil nuclear agreement will 'help meet India's growing energy needs and create thousands of jobs in both of our countries...'

- Amiable export: '[W]e've removed Indian organizations from our so-called "entity list". And we'll work to remove—and reform our controls on exports. Both of these steps will ensure that Indian companies seeking high-tech trade and technologies from America are treated the same as our very closest allies and partners...'
- Agricultural facilities: 'We aim to help millions of Indian farmers—farming households save water and increase productivity, improve food processing so crops don't spoil on the way to market, and enhance climate and crop forecasting to avoid losses that cripple communities and drive up food prices...'
- Global health: '[W]e'll continue to support India's effort against diseases like tuberculosis and HIV/AIDS, and as global partners, we'll work to improve global health by preventing the spread of pandemic flu...'
- Education exchange: '[W]e will increase exchanges between our students, our colleges and our universities...'

Perhaps the most contemporary global and inclusive statement of interconnected inevitability is exemplified in the President's request for Indian aid, not for themselves but for Africa: 'And as part of our food security initiative, we're going to share India's expertise with farmers in Africa. And this is an indication of India's rise—that we can now export hard-earned expertise to countries that see India as a model for agricultural development.' It is another powerful example of how American and Indian partnership can address an urgent global challenge. It is the Dalai Lama's 'mutual interest' that is praiseworthily evident in a partnership that is desired for not merely each other's benefit, but for the benefit of the whole world, which President Obama, like the Dalai Lama, also describes as 'interconnected world':

> That's what I want to address today—the future that the United States seeks in an interconnected world, and why I believe that India is indispensable to this vision; how we can forge a truly global partnership—not just in one or two areas, but across many; not just for our mutual benefit, but for the benefit of the world.

So, the shared vision for a global future is being laid down by President Obama as a possible venture in collaborative partnership, with world peace and world progress in their agenda rather than mere 'self' or only Indian–American futures. The shared vision spelt out is not out of sync with the Dalai Lama's interconnected humanitarian role, Arun Gandhi's statement to America in their role of humanitarian responsibility towards Afghanistan, Ashoka's concern for people beyond his territories, Gandhi's notions of ahimsa, and Vivekananda's broadcasting 'visits' in foreign shores to establish national character and consciousness of inclusivity. A few more examples from the speech are given below:

- The admittance that America needs to forge 'deeper cooperation with 21st-century centres of influence' like India to 'seek a just and sustainable international order that promotes peace and security by meeting global challenges through stronger global cooperation'.

- Fight against terrorism: 'America's fight against Al-Qaeda and its terrorist affiliates is why we persevere in Afghanistan, where major development assistance from India has improved the lives of the Afghan people. We're making progress in our mission to break the Taliban's momentum and to train Afghan forces so they can take the lead for their security. And while I have made it clear that American forces will begin the transition to Afghan responsibility next summer, I've also made it clear that America's commitment to the Afghan people will endure. The United States will not abandon the people of Afghanistan—or the region—to violent extremists who threaten us all.'
- Engaging Asia: 'More broadly, India and the United States can partner in Asia. Today, the United States is once again playing a leadership role in Asia—strengthening old alliances; deepening relationships, as we are doing with China; and we're re-engaging with regional organizations like ASEAN and joining the East Asia summit—organizations in which India is also a partner. Like your neighbors in Southeast Asia, we want India not only to "look East", we want India to "engage East"—because it will increase the security and prosperity of all our nations.'

- Reducing nuclear weapons: 'This includes our responsibility to prevent the spread of nuclear weapons. Since I took office, the United States has reduced the role of nuclear weapons in our national security strategy, and we've agreed with Russia to reduce our own arsenals. We have put preventing nuclear proliferation and nuclear terrorism at the top of our nuclear agenda, and we have strengthened the cornerstone of the global non-proliferation regime, which is the Nuclear Non-Proliferation Treaty.' Hence, there is a need to 'pursue our goal of securing the world's vulnerable nuclear materials. We can make it clear that even as every nation has the right to peaceful nuclear energy, every nation must also meet its international obligations—and that includes the Islamic Republic of Iran'.
- 'Visits' and 'broadcast': 'And in another example of how American and Indian partnership can address global challenges, we're going to share these innovations with civil society groups and countries around the world.' India as a democracy has already made transparent its Right to Information Act, the e-panchayat system and so on. 'Likewise, when Indians vote, the whole world watches. Thousands of political parties; hundreds of thousands of polling centres; millions of candidates and poll workers—and 700 million voters.'
- Objection to loss of freedom in any nation: 'As the world's two largest democracies, we must never

> forget that the price of our own freedom is standing up for the freedom of others. ... Before he ever began his struggle for Indian independence, Gandhi stood up for the rights of Indians in South Africa. Just as others, including the United States, supported Indian independence, India championed the self-determination of peoples from Africa to Asia as they, too, broke free from colonialism. ... But when peaceful democratic movements are suppressed—as they have been in Burma, for example—then the democracies of the world cannot remain silent. For it is unacceptable to gun down peaceful protestors and incarcerate political prisoners, decade after decade. It is unacceptable to hold the aspirations of an entire people hostage to the greed and paranoia of bankrupt regimes. It is unacceptable to steal elections, as the regime in Burma has done again for all the world to see.' And India has been slow in interrupting, but it must.

Thus, Obama's speech stands testimony to a turn of events where politics has to explain itself to a global audience; where partnerships are no more about the partners alone; where 'self-interest' has to project an interconnectedness, which it cannot avoid—even if I am the most powerful, I cannot ignore the weaker sections; because ironically I am dependent on the weaker sections for my economic progress. I cannot but empower them as I empower myself. Otherwise, there is no empowerment.

Concluding Remarks

Great Sanskrit works such as Vedas, Upanishads and classical poetry promote an attitude and spirit that can make it possible for the human race to grow together into a single family (*vasudhaiva kutumbakam*). The basic tenets of Jainism, one of the major religious sects of India, can be summed up in two words: non-violence (ahimsa) and many-sidedness (*anekanta*). These tenets promote peaceful coexistence, philosophically and socially. Mahatma Gandhi was a champion of *anekanta*, which promotes the comprehension of a thing from different points of view through the development of compassion and tolerance necessary for peaceful coexistence. *Anekanta* also makes one investigate as to how and why others hold a different view and how the apparent contradictions can be reconciled in a peaceful manner. Positive insights provided by the great religions of the world need to be rearticulated to suit present-day requirements. Concepts like peace, human brotherhood and compassion leading to benevolent actions need to be properly interpreted and reactivated for developing peaceful societies and good human and international relations.

7

Universal Welfare Is Business Welfare

One cannot be happy unless everyone around is happy.
—Sir M. Visvesvaraya

Introductory Remarks

The ancient Indian cultural wisdom talks of universal welfare as an eternal guiding principle for effective leadership.[1] Most of the concepts covered under *rajadharma* are related to peace and welfare of all. It is also implied therein that the leaders who promote universal welfare also contribute to world peace. Kalidasa beautifully expresses the concept of universal welfare through a prayer quoted below with translation:

sarvastaratu durgani
sarvo bhadrani pashyatu
sarva kamanavapnotu
sarvah sarvatra nandatu[2]

May all get across the difficulties
May all come by happy events

May all realise their wishes
May all be joyous everywhere

As noted in Chapters 1 and 2, kings and rulers of ancient India both preached and practised universal welfare-oriented leadership style.

We also discussed how Ashoka provided help and support to his neighbours in order to maintain harmonious relations with them. From the earlier Indological examples, we take our learnings into the contemporary era. In this chapter, we provide examples of corporate leaders and industrial houses that are known for executing projects in the area of social sectors benefitting everyone. We hope this would inspire others to follow their examples and contribute to society in a manner that suits their area of work or expertise.

Corporate culture is popularised as a profit-oriented universe. Yet, how can we have profit, if the economy is not sound and harmonious, and that would also include the world economy. And the world economy can remain sound, only if world peace is maintained and interfaith amidst nations flourish. Thus, universal welfare (*lokasamgraha*) is not an unknown concept in corporate culture, and today, it no longer can be an unknown practice.

Corporate Social Responsibility (CSR) is now a familiar phrase in the managerial and industrial world; a phrase that had lived a different existence in the times of kings and emperors, but nevertheless existed as their duties for their states. When elected democracies and nation-states developed, it existed as duties of the elected governments towards their citizens. Similarly, the corporate also has duty towards its 'corporate citizens', its consumer market; in short, towards the society that it exists in, exists for and exists by. Does the corporate like the kings, presidents, prime ministers, philanthropists, social activists, environmentalists and spiritual seers have social obligations? Perhaps the following writings and speeches from several famous corporate personalities and corporations would help answer the question.

Matsushita Electric Industrial Company (renamed Panasonic Corporation)

The concept of universal welfare had inspired some of the greatest contemporary corporate leaders. Kōnosuke Matsushita, founder chairman of Matsushita Electric Industrial Company, had a unique philosophy for his business—to achieve material abundance for all people, for the whole world. Once, he made it the pillar of his management philosophy, his leadership of Matsushita Electric became incomparably more dynamic and confident. This shows it is important to have long-term goals. They assure improvement and advancement, and Matsushita believed that employees would only strive to improve themselves if their company has some overarching goals. He expanded on his ideas at every opportunity he had to speak to his employees: 'I ran Matsushita Electric on the premise that it had a duty to perform in the industry, that it had to contribute to a better world.' He later explained, '... that approach won it the understanding and patronage of many people all over the country'.[3]

Tata

Ratan Naval Tata, chairman of Tata trusts (Sir Dorabji Tata Trust and Sir Ratan Tata Trust), observes:

> I believe the Tata model of business is a more sustainable one—simply because we really do care. If the industry is numb to the concerns of civil society, if it considers itself beyond the pale of the public good, or even if it needs government diktat and monitoring to do the right thing, then I don't see how such an industry can survive for long.
>
> Tata companies are different in this respect because they have always done what is required by the letter and the spirit of the laws of the land, and often times much more. It's our duty to play whatever role we can, in whichever way we can, to diminish disparities. This is the guiding principle for all of us at Tata. We are not in it for propaganda or visibility. Rather, we are in it for the satisfaction gained from knowing that we have achieved something meaningful, that we have put our shoulder to the wheel of nation-building, that we are serving the country that provides us sustenance. The Tata ethos demands no less.[4]

In his foreword to *The Art of Effective Giving* (2011) by R.M. Lala, he says:

> All these business persons [J.R.D. Tata, Bill Gates, Warren Buffet] practiced constructive philosophy with

> the same vigour and purpose they showed in their business. What is more, their sense of self-fulfilment came not from the act of creating their vast wealth but from putting it to social use through their foundations and trusts.
>
> This message needs to be adopted by more business persons across the world, especially at this time when the image of capitalism and capitalists is at a historical low because of rising inequality [remember Arun Gandhi's foreign policies] across the world[5]
>
> ...
>
> Not satisfied with their own contributions, which are substantial, Bill Gates and Warren Buffet decided to widen their scope by getting other American billionaires to subscribe to their philosophy through The Giving Pledge campaign, and till 2011 about sixty-nine have pledged to give at least half their wealth for philanthropic causes, some in their lifetime, others on their demise.[6]

Moreover, the objectives of the Sir Dorabji Tata Trust are similarly exemplary

- Maintenance and support of educational institutions and hospitals.
- Providing help and assistance to people suffering from natural disasters such as earthquake, flood, famine, fire or any such calamity.
- Supporting learning, particularly medical and industrial research.

- Extending financial support to the Indian Institute of Science, Bangalore, to aid in setting up of endowments for professorships or lectureships or giving scholarships.
- Assisting students to study abroad by providing lump sum money or with regular instalments and awarding fellowships in any branch of science.
- Helping any other charitable institutions or objects.[7]

Jamsetjee Jeejeebhoy, the youngest son of a cloth weaver, was born in Bombay on 15 July 1783. He believed in the principle that service to humankind is service to God. Most of the charities and institutions set up by him, based on the philosophy of inclusion, were open to all irrespective of caste, community or creed at a time when the communal divide in India was very rigid. Jamsetjee made large-hearted donations to unfortunate victims of fire, flood and famine. He demonstrated the global mindset when he donated a large sum to relieve the sufferings of the Irish during the famine in Ireland in 1822. He sent a considerable amount to help the victims of floods in France in 1856 and helped the victims of the great fire in Surat (India) in 1837. The District Benevolent Society later known as the Sir J.J. Dharamshala started by him in 1831 was the first free cosmopolitan home for the aged in Asia. The Dharmshala survives to this day providing food, clothing, shelter and medical help for innumerable old people irrespective of caste, colour, language, creed or religion.

Sir Jamshetjee Jeejeebhoy Group of Hospitals in Mumbai, for which Jamsetjee gave ₹10 million, is open to all communities and even today renders medical services to poor suffering from many types of illness. It is very pertinent to note here that Jamsetjee's charity was not confined only to human beings—he contributed to a home for animals, constructed water places for cattle and horses and gave much for regular feeding of stray dogs. This reminds us of innovative social services rendered by King Ashoka.

In continuation with the Tata philosophy, we reproduce some portions of the transcripts of a video talk delivered by B. Muthuraman, former vice-chairman of Tata Steel Limited, formerly Tata Iron and Steel Company Limited (TISCO), that establish some practical hints on discharging corporate social responsibility:

> [C]orporates not only have the responsibility of transforming their own organization through their own people but they have a responsibility of transforming society through their own people. It is a very important dimension of a corporate function, and let me give you two examples.
>
> In Jamshedpur—just like any other city in India, any other town of India—there are schools, some good and some bad and some indifferent. About a year and a half back, we decided that we would impact on the process of education in various schools in Jamshedpur… the Malcolm Baldrige Model is an educational excellence model and we adopted that and, some two years ago, we

introduced it at various schools in Jamshedpur—some 20 or 30 schools. In the last one year, I can see some major changes happening in the educational quality.

A second example from outside the company: Jamshedpur is in Jharkand [India], a tribal state dominated by tribals. We are all sitting on tribal lands, originally owned by the tribals ... we have a responsibility towards their well-being. And some time ago, between Tata Steel, the XLRI in Jamshedpur and the government of Jharkhand, we started an institute called the Tribal Institute Centre, where every year we pick up about 40–50 boys and girls and prepare them for competitive examinations. Tata Steel has provided certain infrastructure and educational facilities, and XLRI faculty come and teach the students free of cost.

I was quite doubtful when we selected them on day 1, but now I see a remarkable difference. These tribals didn't have confidence and they didn't have the gumption to face the world; and in just one year's time, they are as good as any one of us.

You cannot distinguish a tribal girl or a boy who has been through college (Tribal Education Centre) for a year, from any one of us, or any one of you sitting in this hall. And it gave us a tremendous amount of satisfaction that we have been able to impact society.

...

I often tell my people, I often tell the students, I often tell the people I talk to, that when they go to shop next time, whether to buy toothpaste, soap or steel or a steel product, they should look at the price tag and the quality. I think you should also ask yourself the question, 'What is the kind of organization that has produced this product that I want to buy?'[8]

Infosys

In 1996, Infosys established the Infosys Foundation to support the underprivileged sections of society. Infosys contributes 1 per cent of their profit after tax to the foundation for its campaign to improve the welfare of people in rural areas of India. It operates on the principle—*bahujana hithaya, bahujana sukhaya* (for the benefit of many, for the happiness of many).

The Infosys Foundation improves healthcare infrastructure, supports primary education, rehabilitates abandoned women and children, and preserves Indian art and culture. It partners with non-government organisations (NGOs) to make a difference among local communities.

The Infosys Foundation has supported the Akshaya Patra Foundation, an organisation that runs lunch programmes in schools. This initiative is the largest NGO-led lunch programme in the world and feeds 1.8 million school children every day in India. This NGO serves locally palatable wholesome meals from its 51 kitchens operating in 12 states and 2 union territories.

The Infosys Foundation has also helped create libraries for underprivileged children in 15,000 villages across India, has provided scholarships to thousands of children, built hospitals, rehabilitated children, sex workers and destitute, and supported cultural activities.[9]

Narayana Murthy, the co-founder of Infosys, says:

> Corporations must remember that businesses cannot succeed in societies that fail. The need, therefore, is to create companies which want to make a difference to the context through society-oriented and charitable activities…
>
> It is in this context that business leaders like us have to take the lead in encouraging and promoting philanthropy and compassionate capitalism in our society. I believe that we have all at some time eaten the fruit from trees that we did not plant. In the fullness of time, when it is our turn to give, we must, in turn, plant gardens that we may never eat the fruit of, which will benefit the generations to come.[10]

Murthy's talk on compassionate capitalism is an eye-opener. To illustrate this we provide here a few excerpts from a lecture delivered by Murthy on compassionate capitalism at the Global Brand Forum, Singapore, on 1 December 2003:

> Compassionate capitalism is about bringing the power of capitalism to the benefit of large masses… It is about creating a community that believes in the concept of *vasudhaiva kutumbakam* (the world is one family).
>
> We will do well to remember the words of John F. Kennedy who said, 'If a society cannot help the many

who are poor, it cannot save the few who are rich.' It is our duty to create a mandate for an ideology that we believe in—one which allows unfettered opportunities to create an upward spiral of wealth and prosperity for everyone.[11]

...

Now I come to the most important question—how do we practise compassionate capitalism? The people at the vanguard of the capitalist movement have to make themselves more acceptable to those left behind by shunning a vulgarly rich life.

Compassionate capitalism is about putting community interest ahead of private interest in the short term and being a good corporate citizen. It is about civilized behavior and about long-term orientation. It is about making life better for the next generation. This is what civilized societies are about and history has shown that it is such civilized societies that have always progressed.

...

We have arrived at a time in our history when we are equipped with the strength of knowledge, the power of globalization and the convenience of technology to accomplish seemingly impossible goals—elimination of poverty, hunger and disease from this world. Let us derive the best out of free markets and open competition and, at the same time, show compassion to the less fortunate in this world. Let us proudly stand up and proclaim, as Anita Roddick has done. 'That's what I want to do to the business world – nurture a revolution in kindness.' Let us make this a time, in David Korten's words, 'filled with hope

> for a new millennium in which societies will be freed from the concerns of basic survival to pursue new frontiers of social and intellectual advancement'. This is the only way we can continue to grasp the incomparable advantages that capitalism can offer. Let compassionate capitalism flourish.[12]

Wipro

The mission statement from Azim Premji, founding chairman of Wipro Limited, is:

> With utmost respect to Human Values,
> we promise to serve our customer with Integrity,
> through a variety of Innovative,
> Value for Money Products and Services,
> By Applying Thought, day after day.[13]

In one interview, he says:

> I suppose the driving force changes from time to time. At this point of time, apart from being successful in my job, one wants to give back to society what one has received from it.[14]

Premji had started a substantial trust for primary education with a ₹700 million donation. He ran it for 10 years, taking an intense personal interest in it and not leaving it to a CEO to run. The trust's main objective is to raise the level of school education in India. He says:

> I am completely committed to supporting a larger ambition of creating the required social change...
>
> All our efforts including the university (which is also in Bengaluru) are focused on the underprivileged and disadvantaged members of the society. Our experience of the past ten years has motivated us to significantly scale up our initiatives...[15]

Narayana Health

Narayana Hrudayalaya rebranded as Narayana Health, based in Bengaluru has 24 hospitals, 7 heart centres and a network of primary care facilities across India and an international hospital in the Cayman Islands. It was the only Indian firm featured on Fortune's 2018 'Change the World' list (at number 33) and were number 462 on 'Fortune India 500' list in 2018. Dr Devi Prasad Shetty, founder and chairman of this group, is a recipient of the highest civilian awards of the Government of India—Padma Shri in 2004 and Padma Bhushan in 2012.

In a letter written in 1997 by Dr Shetty to children for whom he had performed heart surgery free of cost, he said:[16]

> As a heart surgeon, I have performed more than 4,000 operations on children like you suffering from heart disease. Most of them came from poor families. Despite their backgrounds, I treat all for free.
>
> I think this is the best way *I can repay God* who has given me everything I wanted... For me this world is

> such a happy place to live in and *in my own small way, I strive hard to make it happy for others around me* who are not so fortunate [emphasis added].

This reminds us of Ashoka's inscription from Rock Edict VI: 'There is no better work than promoting the welfare of all the people and whatever efforts I am making *is to repay the debt I owe to all beings* [emphasis added] to assure their happiness in this life.'

Dr Shetty's letter continues:

> One day you will become an adult and probably a very important member of our society. You will have a lot of responsibilities and commitments.
>
> All I ask of you for is, *can you spare a few moments of your precious time every day for someone who needs it* [emphasis added] and that too without expecting anything back in return. Did you know, to save your life, a few hundred people worked sincerely without expecting any remuneration other than the joy of making your family, friends and relatives happy?

The following narrative beautifully illustrates how Dr Shetty's wish came true—three members of a family visited Dr Raghuvanshi, vice-chairman of Narayana Hrudayalaya in his chamber. One of them was an 18-year-old girl on whom Dr Raghuvanshi had operated on in 2001 when she was just a year old. She needed three surgeries over 15 years as she had a complicated heart problem. The family could partly pay the expenses of the first surgery, but they did not have the means to afford the second and third surgeries in 2007 and 2015. The father, who was a primary school teacher, had lost his job. Narayana Hrudayalaya's foundation chipped in and the surgeries were done at almost no cost. A few years later, when the family had come for a final check-up and the girl asked if she could work at the hospital to extend her gratitude. 'This is what we live for, it's so fulfilling,' said Dr Raghuvanshi. This is in keeping with the philosophy the hospital follows—to provide high quality, affordable healthcare to the masses so that no patient is turned down from a medical procedure for lack of money.[17]

Narayana Health tries to live up to its purpose in spite of tough situations. The hospital chain caters to over 2.6 million patients annually and nearly 40 per cent of them are provided with financial assistance, which comes via the foundation, financial sponsors such as merchant groups and corporates, or crowdfunding platforms such as Milaap.org.

Narayana Health spends nearly 5 per cent of its revenues on subsidies.

That's the purpose of the business and if ever this business of caring for the poor and the working class becomes so bad that it becomes unsustainable then Dr Shetty does not want to be in the business.[18]

Dr Shetty believes that everyone should have a purpose. Narayana Health's mission is to deliver high-quality, affordable healthcare services to the broader population in India.

Its core values are represented by the acronym 'iCare', which encompasses innovation and efficiency, compassionate care, accountability, respect for all and excellence as a culture. At the same time, it seeks to generate a strong financial performance and deliver long-term value to its shareholders through the execution of its business strategy.[19]

Once Dr Shetty got a call that had a significant impact on him and his business strategy. He narrates:

When I was working in the hospital in Calcutta, in the middle of an operation my anaesthetic took a call and he told me that some patient wants me to make a house call. And I politely told him that I am a heart surgeon, what do I do at home? And then the caller insisted that I visit the patient saying that it might perhaps transform my life. And that patient happened to be Mother Teresa. She introduced me to the power of simplicity, power of compassion, power of love. One of her very famous statements which I have in my office says that 'Hands which help are holier than the lips that pray.' She's a nun. Her job is supposed to pray but she herself believes that helping other human beings is the best form to reach out to God. ... When a patient comes to me... he has to trust me. I have to look into his eyes. Talk to him. Connect with him. And that's very important. That has larger healing power than all the surgical tools and medicines I have in this world. But unfortunately, the whole philosophy of touch, compassion and caring is gradually losing ground. It is a sad situation. I hope it gets restored.[20]

A very interesting physical structure that attracts our attention is the prayer hall which Dr Shetty has created in his hospital campus in Bengaluru. Anyone can offer prayers in this unique hall that welcomes people following different religions—Hinduism, Christianity, Islam, Buddhism, Jainism and others. Different religious symbols are boldly depicted so that people following different religions can come and offer prayers to the gods of their choice without fear.

Again, we are reminded of Ashoka's Rock Edict VII: 'Beloved-of-the-Gods, King Piyadasi, desires that all religions should reside everywhere, for all of them desire self-control and purity of heart.'

Aravind Eye Hospital

We will now present an extraordinary case that we are proud to share as an Indian example of universal-welfare business model.

In 1976, Dr Govindappa Venkataswamy (popularly known as Dr V) founded Aravind, an 11-bed eye hospital in Tamil Nadu, India.

Over the next three decades, his humble establishment grew to become a reckoned eye care service provider in the world. At Aravind, patients choose whether to pay or not; yet the organisation remains considerably profitable. The business model is now being imitated everywhere, from

Tanzania to the United States of America. The Aravind growth model has become a staple diet for all MBA students at Harvard Business School. Dr V realised that his clinic alone will not be able to eradicate blindness all over the world, but it can be achieved through replication of Aravind model across states, countries and even continents. His ambition was to make a global effort to conquer cataract blindness. In a systematic manner that spanned over decades, he lifted Aravind's relevance from the 'provincial' to the 'planetary'. In early 1980, he wrote in a journal:

> Last night I dreamt of expanding the work of Aravind Hospitals to other places. Get involved, [and include] people from other states and countries [emphasis added].[21]

His futuristic vision aligned Aravind's work with a much broader effort, making it one of the strongest links in a global chain of contribution. Lions Aravind Institute of Community Ophthalmology (LAICO) was opened in 1992. It is Aravind's training and consultancy institute. It aims to replicate the Aravind model to build international capacity for eye care and by 2011, had trained more than 6,000 people from 69 countries. LAICO endeavours to reposition competition as a form of sharing as evident in the following statement by Dr Thulsi (executive director of Aravind Eye Care System):

> People ask us why we spend so much effort on training our competition. By definition, competition would

> mean a situation where the service supply is greater than the demand. Right now, that may be the case, but only because the demand is a small fraction of the need. Aravind's focus is making the need manifest itself as demand through market penetration, awareness building and outreach. The work to be done there is enormous, and when you take that into account, there is no competition.[22]
>
> We could try to create dominance with Aravind's level of expertise, but we don't. Instead, we try and create training programmes around those competitive skills. We see training as a form of sharing.
>
> This ethos of formally transferring knowledge and capability outside its walls is why, today, one in ten eye doctors across India has undergone some form of training at Aravind... That is how Aravind's brand recognition happens. Not just through volume growth or the bottom line but through its spirit of sharing.[23]

Surprisingly, the business model is almost built on the very virtue that, in the conventional sense, was opposed to competition. Paradoxically, an ancient popular verse composed in Sanskrit (produced in translation below) points to the unique significance of sharing:

> Oh, Goddess of Learning! You have a unique treasure.
> When spent (shared) increases and when hoarded (not shared) diminishes.[24]

Aditya Birla Group

An observation made by Kumar Mangalam Birla, chairman of the Aditya Birla Group:

> The days are long past when the business of business was just business. The idea that a corporation is merely a legal abstraction, devoid of heart and soul, no longer has legitimacy. The corporation may be an economic wunderkind, but it falls short and often falls apart if it does not meet the needs of society, or if it does not act with a conscience. Today, no stakeholder—be it a shareholder, an employee, the community or the government—would accept a business whose rationale is limited to profit at any cost, or only to the compulsion of its immediate business.[25]

Microsoft

Bill & Melinda Gates Foundation was established in 2000 based on the principle—'All lives have equal value'. The life of an impoverished child in a developing country is as precious as that of a middle-class child in the developed world. The focus of the Bill & Melinda Gates Foundation is on global health, global development and improving access to education and information technology in the US. The reasons for starting the foundation becomes clear if we look at Bill Gates' Harvard Commencement Speech. He said:

> I left Harvard with no real awareness of the awful inequities in the world—the appalling disparities of

health, and wealth, and opportunity that condemn millions of people to lives of despair ... It took me decades to find out.

You graduates came to Harvard at a different time. You know more about the world's inequities than the classes that came before...

If you believe that every life has equal value, it's revolting to learn that some lives are seen as worth saving and others are not. We said to ourselves: 'This can't be true. But if it is true, it deserves to be the priority of our giving.'

So we began our work in the same way anyone here would begin it. We asked: 'How could the world let these children die?'

The answer is simple and harsh. The market did not reward saving the lives of these children, and governments did not subsidize it. So the children died because their mothers and their fathers had no power in the market and no voice in the system.

But you and I have both ... [A]t the close of the letter [that Gates' mother wrote to Melinda during their bridal event] she said: 'From those to whom much is given, much is expected.'

When you consider what those of us here in this yard have been given—in talent, privilege and opportunity—there is almost no limit to what the world has a right to expect from us ... And I hope you will come back here to Harvard 30 years from now and reflect on what you have done with your talent and your energy.

I hope you will judge yourselves not on your professional accomplishments alone, but also on how

> well you have addressed the world's deepest inequities … on how well you treated people a world away who have nothing in common with you but their humanity.[26]

Delhi Metro Rail Corporation

E. Sreedharan, former managing director of Delhi Metro Rail Corporation (India), shares an example related to the tree planting initiative of his organisation:

> Tree cutting in Delhi is considered as a crime and we had to get permission from ten authorities to cut a tree going up to Lt Colonel of Delhi.
>
> But we had planned and started implementing across every construction site that we will plant and grow minimum ten trees for every tree cut and this made people realize that we will not do any wrong and the total cooperative attitude of people came to our support.[27]

Ashoka: Innovators for the Public

It is impossible to capture the persons, policies and events on which King Ashoka's influence is clearly seen as the number is countless and spread all over the world. We record here one of the 20th-century personalities who had a great influence on world population. Bill Drayton contemplated on what distinguished Ashoka from other historical figures and found out that it is Ashoka's 'how-to'.

As is well known, Ashoka established the world's first large-scale class of civil servants devoted to public welfare. These workers were mainly responsible for building India's Grand Trunk Road—the popular travellers' route extending from Afghanistan to West Bengal—and arranging watering sheds, rest houses and trees along much of its length. They also established hospitals for people and animals, food-for-work programmes comparable to the Kibbutzim in Israel. Ashoka realised the economic power of the continental scale empire and he used that power for a social purpose.

Drayton thought of naming his organisation after King Ashoka, who unified much of South Asia in the 3rd century BCE and pioneered innovations in both economic development and social welfare. He considered Ashoka to be one of history's most tolerant, global-minded and creative leaders. Hence, Drayton opted for the name—Ashoka: Innovators for the Public. In Sanskrit, Ashoka means the 'active absence of sorrow'.

The Ashoka is the largest network of social entrepreneurs worldwide, with more than 3,200 Ashoka Fellows in 83 countries putting their system-changing ideas into practice on a global scale. Founded by Bill Drayton in 1980, after he resigned his fabulous job at McKinsey, Ashoka has provided financial support, professional pro-bono partnerships and connections to a global network of peers and a platform for people dedicated to changing the world. The Ashoka launched the field of social entrepreneurship and has influenced key global players across sectors to recognise and nurture the potential of entrepreneurial talent to solve social problems. With Ashoka Fellows at the centre, Ashoka is enabling an 'everyone a changemaker' world in which everyone uses their own potential to see a problem, develop a solution and put the idea into action.[28]

Mokshagati

An example for including the excluded comes from Alokananda Roy who created the dance-drama called *Mokshagati*. She is an internationally acclaimed exponent of Indian classical dance, a reformer of souls and a mother. For years now, Roy has been using the arts, especially traditional dance and music, to change the lives of inmates of correctional homes in Kolkata. She also started a school for children of female inmates. Through her 'movement', she is helping them 'return to a world they once knew'. Her work to try and reform jail inmates, particularly for convicts under trials, through her art and love-therapy has provided new life to hardened criminals and earned her fame that has crossed the borders of India into faraway lands where her work is used as a template for reforms.

Roy's concern is about criminals coming out of prisons after completing their terms at a young age. No one will offer any job to them and they will be left without any social support. As we know, society's tag line is 'once a criminal is always a criminal'. No one is ready to help them to live a normal life.

If they remain excluded, chances are that they may get back to a life of crime again. So, Roy's twin concerns are to find a place for them in society by helping them get a decent job and preventing them from committing a crime again. This inspired her to start dance-drama classes inside the prisons. Apart from the highly professional production of dance-dramas, what is path-breaking is the fact that everyone from wardens and their families to prison authorities and inmates come together in not just performing the drama but also in designing the costumes and constructing the props for these performances. This has manifested in a bond of a different nature—not of 'the jailor and the jailed', but of talent coming together on equal terms.

According to Roy, everyone wants to be *free*. In fact, one of the basic pillars of modern-day democracy is freedom. It is the birthright of every individual and hence is correctly considered priceless. But everyone is not fortunate and being *free* for some is a struggle.

They seek freedom not only from the oppressions of the outside world but also from one's own internal demons. Manacles like drug addiction, alcohol abuse and criminal offences incapacitate a person from taking holistic decisions and their acts destroy the very fabric of their life completely.[29] Hence, to break free from such shackles, a therapeutic balm becomes an essential antidote to the sufferers. Roy has initiated a very unique salutary cultural therapy for many such distressed souls to guide them on the path of redemption. Roy reveals the secret of her inspiration in an email sent to one of the authors reproduced below:

As a school student, when I studied Ashoka the Great... little did I know that I will come across real-life

Ashokas, later in life, who have been transformed from Chandashoka to Dharmashoka.

In the correctional homes in West Bengal, where dance, music, rhythm and, above all, love and compassion touched numerous souls, I found my Ashoka the Great in each one of them, who have learned the true meaning of human values.

Our production, *Mokshagati*, a unique presentation through film and stage, is based on Emperor Ashoka's transformation, performed by the prisoners. The story is narrated through the eyes of a Universal Mother, who is pained when any one of her children is hurt and seeks forgiveness and redemption for the one who has wronged and realises his mistakes.

Prison transformed me as well. As a maa (mother) to all of them I learned to love unconditionally, learned to be non-judgmental and [realised] the most precious human emotion of forgiveness. While teaching them, I learnt that victory can only be achieved through love, compassion and forgiveness—not war or revenge.

In Mahatma Gandhi's words, 'an eye for an eye will make the whole humanity blind.'[30]

Concluding Remarks

In short, we have to agree with the Mahabharata:

> The power of production in the merchants should be always encouraged. They make the realm strong,

> enhance agriculture and develop its trade. A wise king should be studiously favourable to them... There is no wealth in a kingdom greater than its merchants.[31]

On the other hand, we must also remember the following:

- Bill Gates (Harvard Commencement Speech): 'So, the children died because their mothers and their fathers had no power in the market and no voice in the system.'
- Narayana Murthy: 'While tremendous progress has been made in enhancing the economic well-being of people, the chasm between the haves and the have-nots of the world has widened, especially in the developing world. No corporation can sustain its progress unless it makes a difference to its context.'

Thus, the contradiction of profit and social obligation for the corporate is here to stay, but the movement towards social welfare is encouraging. In a gripping survey of European companies conducted by Harris Research, it is revealed that 70 per cent of companies view corporate responsibility as a very important issue; that 88 per cent regard corporate reputation as exerting a big influence on corporate value and that a quarter see greater expectations of social responsibility as the main reason that reputation management is rising in importance.[32] Thus, even if we consider 'self-interest', corporate social responsibility as 'reputation management', image and credibility building is also a viable metre of corporate sustainability. The following then might anchor our concerns perhaps less idealistically, but more practically:

- Corporations are more powerful than the market. This was not so 50 years ago. Thus, if Tata and Reliance Fresh retail outlets decide to sell sustainable products, things might change.
- Consumers are more powerful than citizens. Citizens vote in five years; consumers vote daily.
- Social issues are business issues as well. And that is the basic nature of CSR that we need to encounter, accept, challenge and perhaps appropriate for a better social future.[33]

Thus, the discussion becomes important because it does not say corporations must be socially responsible. No, it says corporations are also social responsibilities and social responsibilities are also businesses. And that is what makes CSR relevant to us—the gradual inevitability that such a function carries in contemporary world activities. This takes us to a survival economy.

Survival economy has mostly been popularised by C.K. Prahalad in his famous conceptualisation of the 'Bottom of the Pyramid' (BOP). Rapid industrialisation in economies such as China and India has squeezed the survival economy to the brink. It is estimated that about 150 million people in China are refugees from the survival economy who have been forced to leave their roots due to deforestation, soil erosion, floods or droughts (Prahalad). Rural population is finding it very difficult to continue their traditional lifestyle.

Never before has the world seen so much poverty, hunger and deficit in education and health. Paradoxically, never before, business corporations were so much empowered to provide solutions to this rising poverty. The vectors of social responsibility, technological enablers and market incentives have aligned to give tomorrow's managers new empowerment.

Prahalad argued that 4 billion people in the bottom of the economic pyramid provided a great challenge for business, government and civil society to work together. He also argued that by pursuing strategies for the BOP, business leaders of tomorrow can move beyond the boundaries of free trade and capitalism on the one hand and the proponents of social sustainability on the other.[34] The response from Hindustan Lever Limited (now Hindustan Unilever Limited, HUL) to the challenge of reaching out to the BOP customers through a product called 'wheel' is instructive. After serving India's elite for five decades, HUL was forced to change its business model by substantially reducing the ratio of oil to water in the product by recognising that consumers in survival economy washed their clothes in rivers and public water systems.

The role of business in creating and maintaining a sustainable social balance includes the creation of buying power, shaping of aspirations, improving infrastructure and innovating local solutions. Some of the examples of sustainable business practices may be:

- Siemans AG in 2010 earned more than €25 billion (nearly 30 per cent of its revenue) from the environmental and climate-related products. These include waste water reuse systems and carbon abatement products.

- Hybrid cars: Combining the two critical energy components, for example, petrol and electricity, to produce hyper low emission.
- Biofuels and solar power: Alternative and renewable energy source is critical to sustainability.
- GE's 'ecomagination strategy' generated around 20 billion in 2009 in eco-innovations such as wind turbines and water desalination.
- Strange it may appear, but overall US consumers were expected to spend $220 million in 2010 on goods and services related to sustainable ideas in health, environment, social justice and others.
- Socially screened mutual funds: More than 250 fund products are available for ventures to be funded if they can justify their social purpose.
- Dow Jones Sustainability World Index (DJSWI): This index reports on global companies driving sustainability worldwide. The size of the index grew by 36 per cent in 2009.
- Goldman Sachs index: Goldman Sachs indices called 'GS Sustain' outperformed the market in 2010 by incorporating the ESG data.
- J.P. Morgan: In late 2009, J.P. Morgan initiated a new network called Global Impacting Investing Network (GIIN). This is a private-public partnership initiative supported by J.P. Morgan, Citigroup, US Aid and the Rockefeller Foundation. GIIN's character is

to develop a better industry infrastructure with enhanced metrics and reporting standards for socially responsible investing.

Social change is no longer an agenda outside the scope of business leadership. Social change has become an economic commodity, and this is what we are harping on. The key question is that the corporate sector around the world appears to be unclear as to how to become involved in a meaningful way.

Over the next few decades, the major challenge of business leadership is to gain mastery over the role of business in society as well as transform the role of society in business.

Corporate success today increasingly depends on social change and developing of *social* products and services is the key pathway. This market of 'social capital' needs to be the guiding light for companies. This role is essential in leading the process of social innovation. This is very different from the commonly known concepts of philanthropy or social innovation. The distinguishing feature is that social innovations rely not on social responsibility concepts but on the strategic core of a business. This is not pretending to do good—it is a measurable and transparent engagement.

As the Cambridge University research team suggested, the role is to do 'more for "more for less"' through what they term 'disruptive innovation'. The idea of disruptive innovation is the paradigm shift that businesses engage in, to leverage the rising social capital market.

Integrating sustainability is not for improving the image of modern business, it is essential for it to survive and grow. Corporations are increasingly in demand from institutional investors to become involved in social business as for them responsible business is becoming a matter of risk management. External pressure from media, NGOs and other stakeholders is also increasing. Overall, the cost of 'writing off' the big business on ideological grounds is a very high-cost option for society. The challenge for a society is how to make business part of the solution. In 2010, the Indian government spent ₹90 billion on rural development, but not more than 15 per cent reached the rural poor.

Over the past decade, megacorporations around the world have become more powerful than markets. For example, McDonald's is responsible for 90 per cent of new jobs in the US. They have been recruiting about 1 million employees annually. If Tata Company in India or Heier Group in China decides to sell only sustainable products, the impact will trigger a multiplier effect of immense proportions.

Another significant development has been the rise of consumer power as globalisation spreads its wings and market ideology prevails. McKinsey Global Survey 2010 asked leading global managers to prioritise their critical business issues with a surprising response. They considered the following issues as critical for their future success:

- 50 per cent of CEOs selected 'educational systems and talent shortage'

- 44 per cent of CEOs considered improving public governance as a critical issue
- 38 per cent of CEOs considered climate change as a challenging issue
- 36 per cent of CEOs considered engagement in 'disruptive innovation' through the development of BOP products as a challenge
- 35 per cent of CEOs considered 'energy security' as the most critical issue
- 12 per cent considered access to clean water as the key issue

The McKinsey survey provides evidence that social capital market is challenging ways to create value. As a corollary, the social capital market, in turn, offers the possibility of staggering growth for these companies as well. The market in insuring the uninsured, delivering alternative energy, alleviating poverty or engaging in disease eradication creates some of the areas where a business that wants to grow has infinite possibilities.

The challenge before future business leaders is to extend their mindsets beyond eco-efficiency, environmental performance or social and ethical responsibilities. The new framework for a sustainable world needs to include the following:

- Moving beyond corporate social responsibility, philanthropy and ethical practices to embrace the concepts of sustainable social business.
- Key to this engagement in sustainable social business is to focus on 'survival economy' through

BOP collaboration. Developing social agenda and collaboration with community, NGOs, government, universities and other stakeholders will need a very different type of business leadership for tomorrow.

- Making social problems as the strategic focus and working on internal operational stability rather than the other way round.
- Emphasising 'disruptive innovation': This lies in addressing the social problems at the holistic system level rather than in parts. The idea is to innovate new solutions relevant to the context rather than extrapolating the future based on the present strategic platforms.

It can be argued that companies that are most sustainable will be the most successful. Businesses that are willing to lead through strategies, culture, operations, products and services will benefit as the society enriches. So, how do we understand sustainability? In India, the Housing Development Finance Corporation (HDFC) build a cooperation-based relationship even with competitors—an instance of corporate cooperation.

Instead of trying to derail the potential competitors to protect its near-monopoly position, the HDFC management took a very different view. HDFC's mission was to contribute to solving the housing problem in India by helping middle-class Indians own their homes, particularly in the 1980s. Given the enormously large market, HDFC could not possibly serve all the potential customers and more housing financing companies were necessary for HDFC to achieve its core mission. So, the company encouraged many new entrants in the field and fully supported them on strategy and training, helping them to become stand-alone entities. Each of these companies operated independently in the market and competed for business against HDFC. Meeting an important social need rather than personal profit was the key motivator. Thus, as represented in Figure 7.1, the mutating gene of cooperation was in the act of building competitors, rather than monopolising the market.

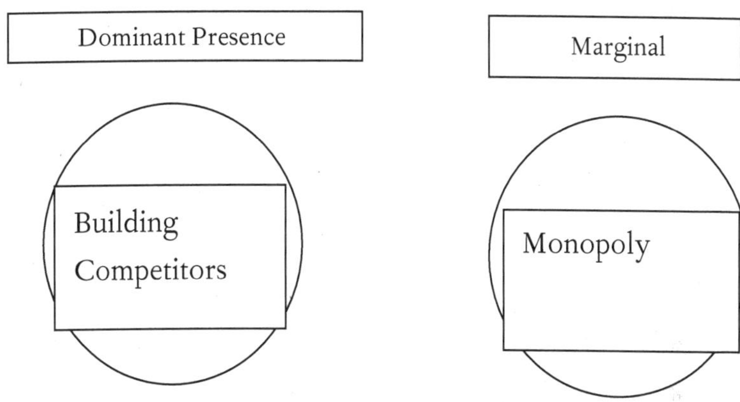

FIGURE 7.1 *The Model of Cooperation*

It is important to refer to the Derridian pluralities again. For instance, an ordinary wooden table has a natural *use-value*, which the German thinker Karl Marx also called the ontological value. But when the table becomes a *commodity*, something to be sold—it develops an exchange value, a market value, a commodity form.[35] On a similar note, just being kind on one's own is like a use-value—I am being of some use to the other person, who is needy. When HDFC is being useful for those who need HDFC's help, it produces a social change; the action becomes an exchange value for society, making social change an economic commodity.

What Derrida contends is that every use-value is 'haunted' by its probable market value.[36] We, therefore, contend two propositions. HDFC has been able to establish the potential market value for otherwise ethical practices of *lokasamgraha*. On the other, every corporate *lokasamgraha* practice is haunted by traces of contexts, histories, traditions with possibilities of social change, as is HDFC, which is and has been unconsciously haunted by the *lokasamgraha* philosophy, and each philosophy and action is and would further haunt the rest of the activities of humankind. This is depicted in Figure 7.2.

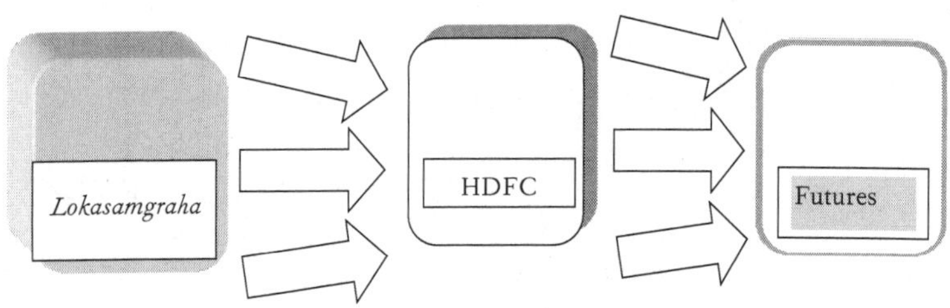

FIGURE 7.2 *Lokasamgraha*–HDFC Legacy

This relationship between ancient Indian ethos and contemporary corporate cooperation business models may inspire many other corporations to continue the legacy of cooperation, and thus, cooperation as a mutating value is *sustained* over time; and if the value is sustained, so is the corporation and the cooperation.

Therefore, we argue for responsible awareness of present actions because they have the potential for shaping the future, perhaps without our conscious awareness of even the context, or the person, or the organisation. In short, we *haunt* the futures; we must be responsible in the manner in which we *haunt*.

As Hart pointed out in his prize-winning 1997 *Harvard Business Review* article titled 'Beyond Greening: Strategies for a Sustainable World', '[F]aced with impoverished customers, degraded environment and unravelling societies, it will be increasingly difficult for corporations to do business.'[37] Unfortunately, few business leaders realise the potential revenue growth through their immersion in socially responsive business.

Thus, we can reiterate Milton Friedman here. His precept of 'business of business is business' has come a long way as social contribution emerges as the major source of revenue for business organisations. The businesses in environment, education, healthcare and other infrastructure are no longer in the soft domain. They have a significant economic impact.

The debates on corporate social compliance and corporate social responsibility have come a long way towards value creation through the leveraging of 'social arbitrage'. This entails a fundamental re-conceptualisation of the concepts and practices of strategy. New business leaders become involved in sustainable business ecosystems, innovate new products and services for the survival economy, and enrich and transform new frontiers through collaboration and entrepreneurship.

Thus, we have come a full circle from where we started—from the leader (who was the technology of code and surveillance of the code of conduct) to the firms and their leaders (that exemplifies social corporate responsibility). Thus, we have the responsibility loop—a historical loop on leadership, care, economy and sustenance, as depicted in Figure 7.3.

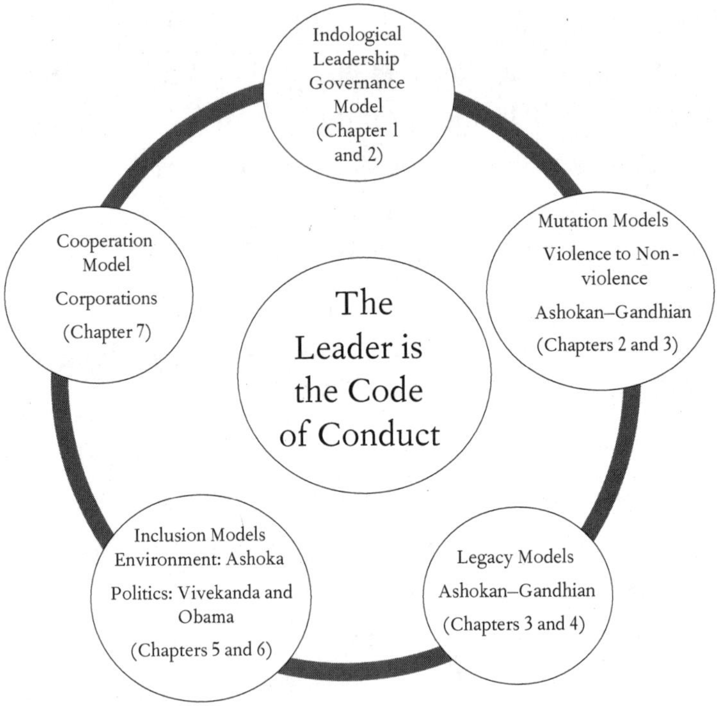

FIGURE 7.3 *The Responsible Leadership Loop*

NOTES AND REFERENCES

CHAPTER 1

1 Laureen Zanotti. 'Text Summary of Michel Foucault's *What is an Author?*' Available at: http://laureen.zanotti.me/wordpress/wp-content/uploads/summary_foucault.pdf (accessed on 15 May 2014).
2 Ibid.
3 *Aitareya Brahmana*. I.14.1.
4 The Mahabharata. 'Shanti Parva', 59.14. See also M. Rama Jois. 1996. *Dharma*, 108–111. Mumbai: Bharatiya Vidya Bhavan.
5 The Mahabharata. 'Shanti Parva', 59.14, 68.19–35 (simplified translation). See also Badrinath Chaturvedi. 2006. *The Mahabharata: An Inquiry in the Human Condition*, 422ff. Hyderabad: Orient Longman.
6 Ibid.
7 Shekhar Sen. 2001. 'Management of Power in ancient Indian Literature'. In *Leadership and Power, Ethical Explorations*, edited by S.K. Chakraborty and Pradip Bhattacharya, 398ff. New Delhi: Oxford University Press.
8 A.S. Altekar. 1992 (reprint). *State and Government in ancient India*, 89–90. New Delhi: Motilal Banarsidass.
9 Ibid.
10 The Mahabharata. XII. 67. 41ff.
A.S. Altekar. 1992. *State and Government in ancient India*, 92.
11 The Mahabharata. XII.39.128. (simplified translation)
12 Kalidasa. *Raghuvamsha*. IV, Verses 12, 86.
13 Kalidasa. *Abhijnana Shakuntalam*. Act V, Verse 4.
14 A.S. Altekar. 1992. *State and Government in ancient India*, 92.
15 Ibid.
16 *Agnipurana*. 226, 17–20.
17 A.S. Altekar. 1992. *State and Government in ancient India*, 92–93.

18 *Manusmriti*. VII. 45. See also Altekar. 1992. *State and Government in ancient India*, 93.
19 A.S. Altekar. 1992. *State and Government in ancient India*, 95.
20 Ibid., 93.
21 Ibid., 95.
22 Elizabeth I. 1601. 'The Golden Speech'. The Elizabeth Files. Available at: http://www.elizabethfiles.com/resources/speeches/the-golden-speech/ (accessed on 13 September 2016).
23 A.S. Altekar. 1992. *State and Government in ancient India*, 95.
24 Ibid., 93.
25 *Digha-nikaya*. XXVIII, 17. See also Hajime Nakamura. 1992. *A Comparative History of Ideas*, 317ff. New Delhi: Motilal Banarasidass.
26 Hajime Nakamura. *A Comparative History of Ideas*.
27 M.R. Kale. 1968 (fourth revised edition). *Bana's Kadambari*, 150ff. New Delhi: Motilal Banarsidass.
28 Ibid., 150–152.
29 Article 4 of 'Hymns in Praise of Prince Shōtoku'. In *The Shinshu Seiten: The Holy Scriptures of Shinshu*. Compiled and published by the Hompa Hongwanji Mission of Hawaii, Honolulu, Hawaii, 247. As cited in Hajime Nakamura. *A Comparative History of Ideas*, 336, 339.
30 Charles Drekmeier. 1962. *Kingship and Community in Early India*, *255*. Stanford, CA: Stanford University Press. See also A.S. Altekar. 1992. *State and Government in ancient India*, 78.
31 Max Anderson and Peter Escher. 2010. *The MBA Oath*. New York: Portfolio.
32 C. Panduranga Bhatta. 2003. 'Timeless Fundamentals for Effective Leadership: Classical and Empirical Insights'. *OORJA*, 1(1, Sept–Dec): 9.
33 The Mahabharata. 'Shanti Parva', 57, 4–5, 11–19, 30–39, 67, 37–38, 69, 31, 71, 1–11, 108, 15–23. See also G.P. Singh and Premananda Singh. 2008. *Kingship in ancient India: Genesis and Growth*, 60ff. New Delhi: Akansha Publishing House.
34 Ibid.
35 Available at: https://www.wisdomlib.org/definition/bhumipala (accessed on 28 April 2019).
36 The Mahabharata. 'Shanti Parva', 69, 79. See also Suryanarayana Hegde. 2005. 'Raja Kalasya Karanam: In Modern Perspective'. In *The Concept of Rajadharma*, edited by Dr Michael, 41–49. New Delhi: Sundeep Prakashan.

37 Ibid., chapters 66, 44–46, 68–73, 80–98, 103–105 (abridged and simplified translation).

38 *Varaha Purana*. Chapter 32. *Manusmriti*. I.81–86.

39 The Ramayana. I.8.16 (simplified translation).

40 Ibid., II.1.7–32 (simplified translation).

41 The Mahabharata. 'Shanti Parva', 66.44–46 (simplified translation). Based on *The Mahabharata*. 1975. Translated by Kisari Mohan Ganguli. New Delhi: Munshiram Manoharlal.

42 The Mahabharata. 'Shanti Parva', chapters, 58, 63, 71, 81. See also Badrinath Chaturvedi. 2006. *The Mahabharata: An Inquiry in the Human Condition*, 418–464. Hyderabad: Orient Longman. Jack Hawley. 1993. *Reawakening The Spirit in Work: The Power of Dharmic Management*, 181–185. San Francisco: Berrett-Koehler Publishers. The Mahabharata, translated by Kisari Mohan Ganguli, Munshiram Manoharlar, 1975.

43 *Abhijnana Shakuntala*. VIII Act, last verse.

44 *Manimekalai*. VII, 5, 8–12 (translated from Tamil). A.S. Altekar. 1992. *State and Government in ancient India*, 96.

45 *Arthashastra*. VI.2.

46 *Bhagavad Gita*. XVI, 1–3, 7–16.

47 M.R. Kale. 1968 (fourth revised edition). *Kadambari* (*Purvabhaga*), 141–149. Bombay: Motilal Banarsidass (simplified translation of select lines from *Shukanasa Upadesha* (A Minister's Advice to Young Prince).

48 Plato. 1976. *Republic*. Translated by A.D. Lindsay with an introduction by J.M. Dent Renford. London: Bambrough.

49 Aurobindo. 1927. *The Mother*. Available at: https://www.auro-ebooks.com/mother/ (accessed on 10 March 2020).

50 'Social function' is a reference to Foucault's *What is an Author?* mentioned in the opening paragraph of this chapter.

51 Jacques Derrida. 'Structure, Sign And Play In The Discourse Of Human Sciences'. Available at: http://www2.csudh.edu/ccauthen/576f13/DrrdaSSP.pdf (accessed on 15 March 2020).

52 The idea of 'technology of surveillance' is borrowed from Foucault's concept of surveillance in *Discipline and Punish*. To know more, read Michel Foucault. 1991. *Discipline and Punish: The Birth of the Prison*. Penguin.

CHAPTER 2

1 S.K. Chakraborty. 1997. *Ethics in Management: Vedantic Perspectives*, 152. Delhi: Oxford University Press.

2 The Ramayana. IV, 25.4–7.
3 Ibid., II.2.28.
4 Ibid., VII. 59.1–14.
5 Ibid., I.14.1; II.3.42, II.14.18, II. 100.27; II.109.9–10, 20; III. 41.6, 12; IV. 29.5; VII. 45.3, 14; VII.62.6. See also C. Panduranga Bhatta. 2001. 'Management of Power: Lessons from the Ramayana'. In *Leadership and Power: Ethical Explorations*, edited by S.K. Chakraborty and Pradip Bhattacharya, 423–424. New Delhi: Oxford University Press.
6 Bhatta. 'Management of Power: Lessons from the Ramayana'.
7 The Ramayana. II.3.9.ff.
8 Ibid., II.2.15–16.
9 Ibid., II.3.27.
10 Ibid., II.3.9–21.
11 Ibid., IV.16.58.
12 Ibid., II.73.30; II. 114. 66–8, III. 40.6. K.P. Jayaswal, 1943. *Hindu Polity*. New Delhi: Chaukhamba Sanskrit Pratishthan.
13 P. Sorokin and Walter Lunden. 1994. *Power and Morality*, 31. Bombay: Bharatiya Vidya Bhavan.
14 Bhatta. 'Management of Power: Lessons from the Ramayana', 426–427.
15 The Ramayana. Vl. 36.11. See also V. Raghavan. 1976. *Two Brothers, Rama and Lakshmana*, 1–44. Madras.
16 Ibid., Vl. 49, 17–18.
17 Ibid., II, 100, 64–67.
18 Ibid., III. 37.2; VI.16.20.
19 *Raghuvamsha*. I.7, 18.
20 G.K. Bhat. 1982. *Appointment with Kalidasa*, 69–74. L.D. Series 83. Ahmedabad: L.D. Institute of Indology.
21 *Raghuvamsha*. IV.76.
22 Jitendra Bajaj and M.D. Srinivas. 1996. *Annam Bahukurvita*, 125. Madras: Centre for Policy Studies.
23 Hiuen-Tsiang. *The Biography of Hiuen-Tsiang*. Compiled by his disciples, Sramanas Hwu Li and Yen-Tsung, 183–187. See also Bajaj and Srinivas. *Annam Bahukurvita*, 120.
24 M. Rama Jois. 1997. *Dharma: A Global Ethic*, 129. Mumbai: Bharatiya Vidya Bhavan.
25 Sorokin and Lunden. 1994. *Power and Morality*, 38–39.
26 *Arthashastra*. 1.19, 34, 47, 'The Duties of a King, Concerning Discipline'.

27 U. Ghosal. 1923. *A History of Hindu Political Theories*, 144–145. London: Oxford University Press.

28 *Arthashastra*. 2.23.11, 2.1.26, 57; 13.5.11. See also L.N. Rangarajan. 1992. *Kauṭilya's Arthaśāstra*, 41. India: Penguin. C. Panduranga Bhatta. 2019. 'Revolutionary Political Ideas of Kauṭilya'. *Viśvabhāratī* (Felicitation Volume of Professor C.S. Radhakrishnan), V, 57–58.

29 Bhatta. 2019. 'Revolutionary Political Ideas of Kauṭilya'.

30 *Arthashastra*. 1.19.34, 47; 3.20.22.23, 253.

31 Ghosal. 1923. *A History of Hindu Political Theories*.

32 *Arthashastra*. 2.23.11, 147.

33 Ibid. See also Bhatta. 2019. 'Revolutionary Political Ideas of Kauṭilya'.

34 *Arthashastra*. I.19.

35 C. Panduranga Bhatta. 2003. 'Exploring Eternal Leadership Values and Practices for Organisational Excellence'. *Review of Business Research*, 4–6.

36 Ibid.

37 Radhakumud Mookerji. 1995. *Asoka*. New Delhi: Motilal Banarsidass.

38 D.C. Sircar. 1967. *Inscriptions of Ashoka*. New Delhi: Publications Division, Government of India.

39 *Rock Edict* of Ashoka, VI.

40 *Kalinga Rock Edict* of Ashoka, II.

41 Ibid.

42 Ibid.

43 See https://www.mkgandhi.org/voiceoftruth/worldfederation.htm (accessed on 5 March 2020). https://www.mkgandhi.org/momgandhi/chap91.htm (accessed on 8 March 2020). https://www.mkgandhi.org/ebks/gandhis-india.pdf (accessed on 9 March 2020). https://www.mkgandhi.org/voiceoftruth/nationalism.htm (accessed on 8 March 2020).

44 The Dalai Lama. 1993. Speech delivered on 2 October 1993 at the inaugural ceremony of the Budhha, Jayanti Park, New Delhi.

45 Bhatta. 2003. 'Timeless Fundamentals for Effective Leadership: Classical and Empirical Insights'.

46 Giles Lionel. 1907. *The Saying of Confucius, A New translation of the greater part of the Confucian Analects with introduction and notes*, 39. London: John Murry.

47 Chundar (tr). 1995. *Kautilya's Arthashastra*, 303–304. Calcutta: The M.P. Birla Foundation.

48 Ibid. See also Shekar Sen. 2001. 'Management of Power in ancient Indian Literature'. In *Leadership and Power Ethical Explorations*, 397.

49 Vinayaka Bhatta. 1999. 'Vrddhasamyoga in the Education of the King'. In *Kautilya's Arthashastra and Social Welfare*, edited by V.N. Jha, 26–30. New Delhi: Sahitya Akademi.
S. Manik Thakar. 1999. 'Moral Values Reflected in the Kautilya Arthashastra'. In *Kautilya's Arthashastra and Social Welfare*, 31–37.

50 Bhatta. 2003. 'Timeless Fundamentals for Effective Leadership: Classical and Empirical Insights'.

51 Badrinath Chaturvedi. 2006. *The Mahabharata: An Inquiry in the Human Condition*, 418–463. New Delhi: Orient Longman.

52 Ibid, 430–431.

53 Ibid.

54 Ibid.

55 Vidyaranya. 2008. *Panchadashi*, 176. Translated by Nanda Lal Dhole. New Delhi: Sri Satguru Publications.

56 Aung San Suu Kyi. 1995. *Freedom From Fear*, 170–173. London: Penguin Books.

57 Ibid.

58 Bhatta. 2003. 'Exploring Eternal Leadership Values and Practices for Organisational Excellence'.

59 *Rock Edict* of Ashoka, XII.

60 C. Panduranga Bhatta. 1997. *Contribution of Karnataka to Sanskrit*, 519–522. Chennai: Institute of Asian Studies.

61 *Epigraphia Carnatica*. VI. Inscriptions in the Bangalore District. Compiled by B. Lewis Rice. 1905. Bangalore: Mysore Government Central Press.

62 Ahmed Bashir. 2009. *Akbar: The Great Mughul: His New Policy and His New Religion*, 133–169. New Delhi: Akbar Books.

63 Ibid.

64 Shireen Moosvi. 1994. *Episodes in the Life of Akbar: Contemporary Records and Reminiscences*. New Delhi: National Book Trust.
M.L. Roychoudhury. 1941. *The Din-i-llahi*. Calcutta: University of Calcutta.

65 Dirk Collier. 2011. *The Emperor's Writings: Memories of Akbar the Great*, Annexure I. New Delhi: Amaryllis.

66 Ibid., 592.

67 Ravindra Varma. 2006. *The Spiritual Perceptions of Mahatma Gandhi*, 141. New Delhi: Rupa & Co.

68 *Collected Works of Mahatma Gandhi* (1958–1994), XXIX, 411. New Delhi: Publications Division, Government of India.

69 Ibid, VII, 338.

70 K.R. Kripalani (ed.). 1960. *All Men are Brothers*,56. Ahmedabad: Jitendra Desai, Navajivan Mudranalaya.

71 K.G. Saiyidain. 1994. *Significance of Gandhi As a Man and Thinker*, 36. Publications Division, Ministry of Information and Broadcasting, Government of India.

72 Narasimha H.V. Murthy. 2005. 'Concept of Ramarajya and its Relevance'. In *The Concept of Rajadharama*, edited by Michael, 25. New Delhi: Sundeep Prakashan.

73 Ravindra Varma. 2006. *The Spiritual Perceptions of Mahatma Gandhi*, 64.

74 Available at: http://abdulkalam.nic.in/sp011004-2.html (accessed on 8 March 2020). See also A.P.J. Kalam. 2012. *Indomitable Spirit*, 201–202. New Delhi: Rajpal & Sons.

75 The full interview is available at https://bangaloremirror.indiatimes.com/bangalore/others/when-i-can-go-to-masjids-why-cant-they-come-to-our-mutt/articleshow/59345211.cms (accessed on 10 August 2019).

CHAPTER 3

1 Ven S. Dhammika in *The Edicts of King Ashoka* (1993, Sri Lanka: Wheel Publication) writes:

> Asoka's edicts are to be found scattered in more than thirty places throughout India, Nepal, Pakistan and Afghanistan. Most of them are written in Brahmi script from which all Indian scripts and many of those used in Southeast Asia later developed. The language used in the edicts found in the eastern part of the sub-continent is a type of Magadhi, probably the official language of Asoka's court. The language used in the edicts found in the western part of India is closer to Sanskrit although one bilingual edict in Afghanistan is written in Aramaic and Greek. Asoka's edicts, which comprise the earliest decipherable corpus of written documents from India, have survived throughout the centuries because they are written on rocks and stone pillars. These pillars in particular are testimony to the technological and artistic genius of ancient Indian civilization.

See also Rich Bruce. 'The Great Conquest'. In *To Uphold the World*, 112–116.

2 Rich Bruce. 2010. *To Uphold the World: A Call for a New Global Ethic from ancient India*, 114. Boston: Beacon.

3 The edict quotes have been taken from Dhammika. This practice remains throughout the chapter, unless specified otherwise.

4 Percy Bysshe Shelley. 'Ozymandias'. *The Literature Network* (Site Copyright © Jalic Inc). Available at: http://www.online-literature.com/shelley_percy/672/ (accessed on 15 September 2012).

5 Dhammika writes: 'Dhamma sadhu, kiyam cu dhamme ti? Apasinave, bahu kayane, daya, dane, sace, socaye. (Dhamma is good, but what constitutes Dhamma? It includes little evil, much good, kindness, generosity, truthfulness and purity).' Dhamma, as defined in Rich (115):

The Dhamma of which Ashoka speaks is related to Buddhist and Older Brahmin teachings of dharma, but Ashoka defines it in his various edicts and inscriptions as a secular ethic of nonviolence, charity, compassion, tolerance, social welfare, good governance, purity of heart, respect for parents and kin, protection of animal and plant life, and frugality.

6 M.R. Yardi. 1996. *The Yoga of Patanjali*, 40–41. Poona: Bhandarkar Oriental Research Institute.

7 Geraldine Coster. 1968. *Yoga and Western Psychology*, 209–218. Delhi: Motilal Banarasidass.

8 Hammer & Tongs is the creative team behind the Fatboy Slim video. Dominic Leung, Garth Jennings and Nick Goldsmith form the Hammer & Tongs video production company. Hammer & Tongs. *Features*. Copyright © Netribution Ltd 1999–2002. Available at: http://www.netribution.co.uk/features/interviews/2000/hammer_and_tongs/1.html (accessed on 15 September 2012).

9 According to Wikipedia:

Big beat is a term employed since the mid-1990s by the British music press to describe much of the music by artists such as The Prodigy, Cut La Roc, Fatboy Slim, The Chemical Brothers, The Crystal Method and Propellerheads typically driven by heavy breakbeats and synthesizer-generated loops and patterns in common with established forms of electronic dance music such as techno and acid house.

For more information about the history and style for Big Beat, see Big Beat on Wikipedia: The Free Encyclopedia. Available at: http://en.wikipedia.org/wiki/Big_beat (accessed on 15 September 2012).

10 The description of the video has been taken from *Wikipedia* material on 'Right Here, Right Now'. Available at: https://en.wikipedia.org/wiki/Right_Here,_Right_Now_(Fatboy_Slim_song) (accessed on 17 February 2020).

11 See (https://www.coursehero.com/file/6128273/geography/.

12 All the Dalai Lama quotes are taken from His Holiness Dalai Lama's 'A Human Approach to World Peace'. This practice remains throughout the chapter, unless specified otherwise. His Holiness Dalai Lama. October 2012. 'A Human Approach to World Peace'. *Journal of Human Values*, 18(2), 91–100.

13 W.H. Auden. 1968/1989. 'Musée des Beaux Arts'. In *The Muses' Bower: An Anthology of Verse*, 173–174. Hyderabad: Orient Longman.

14 We have not taken into account the various possibilities of other translations and hence admit that we have overridden the associated probable fallacy. But intuitively, we accept our analysis as worthwhile.

15 The Dalai Lama explains deforestation. Ashoka talks about saving animals and nature. We will take up the environment in detail in chapter 5.

16 Auden. 'Musée des Beaux Arts'.

17 Oprah Winfrey's speech at the 54th Emmy Awards (Copyright © 2008) Famous-speeches-and-speech-topics.info. Available at: http://www.famous-speeches-and-speech-topics.info/famous-speeches-by-women/oprah-winfrey-speech.htm (accessed on 15 September 2012).

18 Unless stated otherwise, for all Gandhi quotes in this chapter, see: M.K. Gandhi. 1960. 'Ahimsa or the Way of Non-violence'. In *All Men are Brothers (Life & Thoughts of Mahatma Gandhi as Told in His Own Words)*, edited by Krishna Kripalani. Ahmedabad: Jitendra T. Desai, © Navajivan Trust. (Site developed by Bombay Sarvodaya Mandal and Gandhi Research Foundation, Jalgaon).

Available at: http://www.mkgandhi.org/amabrothers/chap04.htm (accessed on 15 September 2012).

19 Speech by Aamir Khan. Available at: http://www.youtube.com/watch?v=kycvP6QRXXM (accessed on 26 April 2013).

CHAPTER 4

1 Ronald Duncan (ed). 2005. *Gandhi: Selected Writings*, 105. Mineola: Dover.

2 Jean-Jacques Rousseau. 1754. 'The Second Part'. In *A Discourse*. Maintained by John Roland of the *Constitution Society*. Available at: http://www.constitution.org/jjr/ineq_04.htm (accessed on 18 September 2012).

3 Purandara Dasa (1484–1564) is one of the most prominent composers of Carnatic music and he addressed social issues in addition to worship in his compositions, which are mostly in the Kannada language. This song composed in the Kannada language is freely available on the internet. Shobha Bhatta has done the simple English translation.

4 Thomas Hobbes. 'Chapter XIII Of the Natural Condition of Mankind as Concerning Their Felicity and Misery'. *The Leviathan*. Quotes from Hobbes taken from 'Chapter XIII' of *The Leviathan*, unless specified otherwise.
See also Bill Uzgalis. 'The History of Western Philosophy'. Phl 302, Philosophy Department, Oregon State University. Available at: http://oregonstate.edu/instruct/phl302/texts/hobbes/leviathan-c.html#CHAPTERXIII (last updated in September 1996; accessed on 16 September 2012).
John Forrer, Timothy L. Fort and Raymond Gilpin. 2012. 'How Business Can Foster Peace'. United States Institute of Peace. Available at: https://www.usip.org/publications/2012/09/how-business-can-foster-peace (accessed on 22 March 2013).

5 Jonathan Nolan and Christopher Nolan. *The Dark Knight*. Available at: http://www.joblo.com/scripts/The_Dark_Knight.pdf (accessed on 8 October 2012).

6 Lyrics from Michael Jackson's 'Heal the World'. ©copyright 2012, lyrics007.com. Available at: http://www.lyrics007.com/Michael%20Jackson%20Lyrics/Heal%20The%20World%20Lyrics.html (accessed o 16 September 2012).

7 Lyrics from John Lennon's 'Imagine'. ©copyright 2012, lyrics007.com. Available at: http://www.lyrics007.com/John%20

Lennon%20Lyrics/Imagine%20Lyrics.html (accessed on 19 September 2012).
8 'Arun Gandhi (1): Nonviolence in the Age of Terrorism'. Available at: http://www.youtube.com/watch?v=PCUWr-ekGyk (accessed on 15 October 2013).
9 The Dalai Lama. 2019. 'A Human Approach to World Peace'. His Holiness: The 14th Dalai Lama of Tibet. Available at: https://www.dalailama.com/messages/world-peace/a-human-approach-to-world-peace (accessed on 10 July 2019).
10 'Arun Gandhi (2): Nonviolence in the Age of Terrorism'. Available at: http://www.youtube.com/watch?v=054N28W9lwk (accessed on 15 October 2013).
11 Ibid.
12 The Dalai Lama. 2019. 'A Human Approach to World Peace'. His Holiness: The 14th Dalai Lama of Tibet. Available at: https://www.dalailama.com/messages/world-peace/a-human-approach-to-world-peace (accessed on 10 July 2019).
13 'Arun Gandhi (3): Nonviolence in the Age of Terrorism'. Available at: http://www.youtube.com/watch?v=Dj3d66whhuA (accessed on 15 October 2013).
14 The Mahabharata. Parva XII, Chapter 7, Verse 5 as quoted in B.K. Bhattacharya. *The Mahabharata—An Epic of Santa Rasa*. See also R.N. Dandekar. 1990. *The Mahabharata Revisited*, 95–100. New Delhi: Sahitya Akademi.
15 The Mahabharata. Parva X, Chapter 10, Verses 10–13 as quoted in Bhattacharya. *The Mahabharata—An Epic of Santa Rasa*.
16 The Mahabharata. Parva XII, Chapter 7, Verse 33 as quoted in Bhattacharya. *The Mahabharata—An Epic of Santa Rasa*.
17 The Mahabharata. Parva XIII Chapter 1, Verses 1–2 as quoted in Bhattacharya. *The Mahabharata—An Epic of Santa Rasa*.
18 Indra. 1957. *Ideologies of War and Peace in ancient India*, 157–169. Hoshiarpur: Vishveshvaranand Institute Publications.
19 Timothy Fort and Cindy Schipani. 2004. *The Role of Business in Fostering Peaceful Societies*. Cambridge: Cambridge University Press.
20 Timothy Fort. 2007. *Business Integrity and Peace: Beyond Geopolitical and Disciplinary Boundaries*, 17. New York: Cambridge University Press.
21 Ibid.
22 Ibid., 18.

23 Fort. 2007. *Business Integrity and Peace: Beyond Geopolitical and Disciplinary Boundaries*, 20.
24 International Alert. 2006. 'Local Business, Local Peace: The Peacebuilding Potential of the Domestic Private Sector (Executive Summary)'. Available at: http://www.international-alert.org (accessed on 10 February 2013). See also Fort. 2007. *Business Integrity and Peace: Beyond Geopolitical and Disciplinary Boundaries*, 20.
25 Melissa Powell and Donna Chung. 2010. *Doing Business While Advancing Peace and Development*, 6. New York: United Nations Global Compact.
26 Ibid.
27 Fort and Schipani. 2004. *The Role of Business in Fostering Peaceful Societies*.
28 This example was developed by Ryan Walther when working for the United States Agency for International Development and the full text is available in Powell and Chung. 2010. *Doing Business While Advancing Peace and Development*, 56–57.
29 This example was developed by Brian McFarland and the full text is available in Powell and Chung. 2010. *Doing Business While Advancing Peace and Development*, 54.
30 Powell and Chung. 2010. *Doing Business While Advancing Peace and Development*.
31 Eknath Easwaran, 2006. *Gandhi, the Man*, 49–50. Mumbai: Jaico Publishing House, Seventh Jaico Impression.
32 George Bernard Shaw. *Back to Methuselah*.

CHAPTER 5

1 Kalidasa. *Vikramorvashiya*. V. 25.
2 We refer to the Dalai Lama's speech on 'A Human Approach to World Peace', discussed profusely in the chapter 'Violent Leaders to Non-violent Leaders'. For all the Dalai Lama quotes henceforth, see the Dalai Lama. October 2012. 'A Human Approach to World Peace'. *Journal of Human Values*, 18(2), 91–100.
3 'Arun Gandhi (1): Nonviolence in the Age of Terrorism'. Available at: http://www.youtube.com/watch?v=PCUWr-ekGyk (accessed on 10 October 2013).
4 'Arun Gandhi (3): Nonviolence in the Age of Terrorism'. Available at: http://www.youtube.com/watch?v=Dj3d66whhuA (accessed on 15 October 2013).

5 The ancient Indian scriptures, the Indian classical literature and Ashoka and their relation with nature have been compiled into a journal paper by Bhatta, some portions of which have been reproduced here, but in an edited capacity. See C. Panduranga Bhatta. 2010. 'Environment Friendly Lifestyles: A Dialogue with ancient India'. *Decision*, 36(3), 103–120.
6 Vidya Niwas Misra. 1992. 'Man, Nature and the Poet'. In *Creativity and Environment*, 57. New Delhi: Sahitya Akademi.
7 'Deep Ecology'. 1 April 2013. Available at: www.heureka.clara.net/gaia/deep-eco.htm (accessed on 1 April 2013).
8 Ibid.
9 *Atharva Veda*. V.19–9. All quotes from ancient sources have been reproduced here in English.
10 *Ishavasya Upanishad*. I.1.
11 *Rig Veda*. I.90, 6–8.
12 *Yajur Veda*. 13. 47.
13 *Atharva Veda*. XII, 1, 1–63.
14 C. Panduranga Bhatta. 2017. 'Role of Religion in Conflict Prevention for Social and Environmental Sustainability: Experiential Insights from India'. In *Essays on Sustainability and Management: Emerging Perspectives*, edited by Runa Sarkar and Annapurna Shaw, 33–52. Singapore: Springer.
15 C. Panduranga Bhatta. 'Environment Friendly Lifestyles a Dialogue With ancient India'.
16 C. Panduranga Bhatta. 2000. 'Personality Development through Pancha Yajna'. *Yoga Life*, 31(1), 29–32.
17 G. Naganathan. 2004. *Ecological Spirituality: Hindu Scriptural Perspectives*, 25–27. New Delhi: New Age Books.
18 'Einstein's Big Idea'. NOVA. 5 May 2013. Available at: https://www.pbs.org/wgbh/nova/einstein/lrk-hand-emc2expl.html (accessed on 4 April 2013).
19 *Complete Works of Swami Vivekananda*, Vol. III, 241. 2006. Kolkata: Advaita Ashrama. See also Swami Jitatmananda. 1991. *Holistic Science and Vedanta*, 66–67. Bombay: Bharatiya Vidya Bhavan.
20 *Bhagavad Gita*. X. 20–41.
21 *Vishnupurana*. I. 17. 82–85.
22 W.H. Auden. 1968/1989. 'Musée des Beaux Arts'. In *The Muses' Bower: An Anthology of Verse*, 173–174. Hyderabad: Orient Longman.

23 R.N. Dandekar. 1979. *Insights Into Hinduism*, 195. New Delhi: Ajanta Publications.
24 Martin Heidegger. 1993. 'The Question Concerning Technology'. In *Basic Writings*, edited by David Krell, 321. New York: HarperCollins.
25 The quotes on Taoism and the explanation have been taken from the article 'Notes on Taoism and Nature'.
26 'Notes on Taoism and Nature'. *Haley Stern: PhD Project*. 26 March 2015. Available at: https://haleyphdproject.weebly.com/haley/notes-on-taoism-and-nature (accessed on 10 December 2018).
27 'Serenade of the Woods'. *Research*. Available at: https://sites.google.com/view/serenade-of-the-woods/home/background-research (accessed on 09 Oct 2018).
28 Claude Lévi-Strauss. 1955. 'The Structural Study of Myth'. *The Journal of American Folklore*, 68(270), 428–444.
29 'Native American Buffalo Mythology'. Available at: http://www.native-languages.org/legends-buffalo.htm (accessed on 17 May 2013).
30 *Charakasamhita*. 3. II.
31 *Sushrutasamhita*. II.5.
32 *Vasisthasmriti*. XIX, 11–12.
33 *Arthashastra*. III, 19.
34 *Mastyapurana*. Chapter 154, Verses 511–512; Chapter 59, Verses 17–20. See also *Agnipurana*. Chapter 70, Verses 1–9.
35 B.K.S. Iyengar. 2005. *The Tree of Yoga*, 44. New Delhi: HarperCollins.
36 T.N. Khoshoo. 1995. *Mahatma Gandhi: An Apostle of Applied Human Ecology*, 21–23. New Delhi: Tata Energy Research Institute.
37 C. Panduranga Bhatta. 2000. 'Contribution of Buddhism to Environmental Awareness'. In *Facets of Indian Culture*, edited by P.C. Muralimadhavan, 184–188. New Delhi: New Bharatiya Book Corporation.
38 C. Panduranga Bhatta. 2010. 'Environmental Friendly Lifestyles: A Dialogue with ancient India'. *Decision*, 36(3), 103–120.
39 The edict quotes have been taken from Dhammika. This practice remains throughout the chapter, unless specified otherwise.
40 C. Panduranga Bhatta. 2010. 'Environmental Friendly Life Styles: A Dialogue with ancient India'. In the Special Issue of *Decision*,

Environmental Governance: Ecology, Economics & Policy, edited by Prof. Jayanta Bandyopadhyay, 36(3), 130–120. Kolkata: Indian Institute of Management Calcutta.

41 *Abhijnana Shakuntala*. Act V.9.

42 Ibid., Act I.

43 A.B. Gajendragadkar. 1962. *The Abhijnana Shakuntala, 30*. Surat: The Popular Publishing House.

44 *Abhijnana Shakuntala*. IV.14.

45 Ibid., IV.9.

46 Ibid., IV.13.

47 Ibid., IV.14.

48 Ibid., IV.16.

49 Ibid., IV after Verse 16.

50 Ibid., Act V after Verse 21 in the dialogue between King Dushyanta and Shakuntala.

51 *Vikramorvashiya*, Act V after Verse 10.

52 M.R. Kale. 1968. *Bana's Kadambari (Purvabhaga)*, 61–63. Delhi: Motilal Banarsidass.

53 *Subhashitaratnabhandagara*, 47, 236.

54 *Panchatantra*. II.2.

55 Ranchor Prime. 1994. *Hinduism and Ecology: Seeds of Truth*, 31. New Delhi: Motilal Banarsidass.

56 *Varahapurana*. 162. 41–42.

57 *Nitishataka*. Verse 73.

58 *Subhashitaratnabhandagara*.170.

59 Ibid., 175.

60 'Chinese Symbols and Art Motifs', mostly used verbatim with some punctuation changes and word deletions here and there. See 'Chinese Symbols and Art Motifs'. Chinese Buddhist Encyclopedia. Available at: http://chinabuddhismencyclopedia.com/en/index.php/Chinese_Symbols_and_Art_Motifs (accessed on 20 June 2019).

61 William Henry Davies. 2013. 'Leisure'. Available at: http://www.davidpbrown.co.uk/poetry/william-henry-davies.html (accessed on 4 May 2013).

62 The scene is depicted in the 1994 movie on Vivekananda, named *Vivekananda*. Directed by G.V. Iyer.

63 William Wordsworth. 'Daffodils'. Available at: https://www.poetryfoundation.org/poems/45521/i-wandered-lonely-as-a-cloud (accessed on 15 March 2020).

64 John Keats. 'To Autumn'. Available at: http://www.potw.org/archive/potw279.html (accessed on 4 May 2013).
65 John Keats. 'Ode to a Nightingale'. Available at: http://www.bartleby.com/126/40.html (accessed on 4 May 2013).
66 Percy Bysshe Shelley. 'Ode to the West Wind'. Available at: http://www.bartleby.com/106/275.html (accessed on 4 May 2013).
67 Oscar Wilde. 'The Nightingale and The Rose'. Available at: https://www.math.uh.edu/~tomforde/story.html (accessed on 12 February 2020).
68 Summary of 'The Nightingale and The Rose'. Available at: http://www.enotes.com/homework-help/what-summary-nightingale-rose-by-oscar-wilde-64507 (accessed on 4 May 2013) .
69 Ismael M. Saeed, et al. 2013. 'The Bird Symbol in English Romantic and Post-Romantic Poetry'. Available at: http://www.ircoedu.uobaghdad.edu.iq/uploads/42/The%20Bird%20Symbol-Amended-%20Final.pdf (accessed on 5 May 2013).
70 Ibid.
71 Ibid.

CHAPTER 6

1 All the Dalai Lama quotes are taken from His Holiness Dalai Lama's 'A Human Approach to World Peace'. This practice remains throughout the chapter, unless specified otherwise.
His Holiness Dalai Lama. October 2012. 'A Human Approach to World Peace'. *Journal of Human Values*, 18(2), 91–100.
2 C. Panduranga Bhatta. 2007. 'In Search of Ethical Leadership: Classical and Contemporary Insights'. *Perspectives on Management*, 1(1), 10–20.
This section has been moduled on C. Panduranga Bhatta. 2011. 'Religious Pluralism: Managing Diversity in a Globalised Corporate World'. Paper presented at the International Conference on 'Religion, Ethics and Corporate Culture', organised by the Department of Christian Studies, Madras University, 29 September.
3 Bhatta. 2011. 'Religious Pluralism'.
4 Ibid. See also *Rigveda*. I. 164.46.
5 The Mahabharata. Aranya Parva, 311–312, Verse 33 (Popularly known as Yaksha Prashna).
6 Quoted in Mark Tully. 2007. *India's Unending Journey: Finding*

Balance in a Time of Change, 16. London: Rider.

7 *Naradabhakti Sutra*. 74, 75.

8 Pushpadanta's *Shiva Mahimna Stotra*. 7.

9 Swami Vivekananda. 2016 (Second enlarged edition, 12th reprint). *On Himself*, 128–129 Kolkata: Advaita Ashrama.

10 Anuradha Bhattacharjee's doctoral thesis, submitted to the University of Pune in 2006, documents the comprehensive history of Polish refugees in India. A film directed by Anuradha and Sumit Osmand Shaw and co-produced by India and Poland titled *Children of Jamnagar* to acknowledge the contribution made by Maharaja Digvijay Sinhji Ranjit Sinhji Jadeja of Nawanagar has been shown on Polish TV channels multiple times. See also Anuradha Bhattacharjee. 2012. *The Second Homeland: Polish Refugees In India*. New Delhi: Sage Publications, 235–277.
In reconstructing this case we have used the following online sources: https://defenceforumindia.com/forum/threads/how-one-maharaja-helped-save-the-lives-of-640-polish-children-and-women-during-world-war-ii.79432/ (accessed on 3 February 2020); http://culturama.in/2018/07/31/an-indian-maharajas-polish-legacy/ (accessed on 5 August 2019); https://www.speakingtree.in/blog/great-gesture-of-maharaja-jam-saheb-dihvijay-singh/ (accessed on 5 August 2019); https://defenceforumindia.com/forum/threads/how-one-maharaja-helped-save-the-lives-of-640-polish-children-and-women-during-world-war-ii.79432/ (accessed on 5 August 2019); https://economictimes.indiatimes.com/articleshow/23552730.cms?from=mdr&utm_source=contentofinterest&utm_medium=text&utm_campaign=cppst/ (accessed on 5 August 2019).

11 Harold Coward. 1996. *Pluralism: Challenge to World Religions*, 70. New Delhi: Indian Book Centre.

12 Ibid., Chapter 2.

13 Franklin Watson. 2013. *Let me Finish People: Thoughts and Opinion*. US: Watson.

14 'Prince Shōtoku's Seventeen Article Constitution', Article X. Available at: http://www.koreanhistoryproject.org/Ket/C03/tp/TP0301c.htm (accessed on 6 June 2013).

15 C. Panduranga Bhatta. 1997. *Contribution of Karnataka to Sanskrit*, 269 . Chennai: Institute of Asian Studies.

16 Ibid., p. 272.

17 Ibid.
18 'Muslim-majority Indonesia Gifts Saraswati statue to US'. *Deccan Chronicle*. 10 June 2013.
19 N.R. Narayana Murthy. 2009. *A Better India: A Better World*, 42–43. New Delhi: Penguin.
20 Ibid., 74–75.
21 'Indian Woman Dies After Being Refused Abortion'. Available at: https://www.thehindu.com/news/international/Indian-woman-dies-after-being-refused-abortion/article12508292.ece (accessed on 9 November 2012).
22 Swami Vivekananda. 2016. *On Himself*, 58.
23 Ibid., 45–46.
24 Ibid., 47.
25 Ibid., 54.
26 Ibid., 46.
27 Ibid.
28 Ibid., 53–54.
29 Ibid., 10.
30 Ibid., 50.
31 Ibid., 124.
32 Ibid., 125.
33 Ibid.
34 Ibid., 38.
35 Ibid., 93.
36 Ibid.
37 Ibid.
38 Ibid., 21.
39 Ibid., 75.
40 Ibid., 76.
41 Ibid., 77
42 Ibid., 130–131.
43 Ibid., 131.
44 Ibid.
45 Ibid., 112.
46 Ibid., 129.
47 Ibid., 331.
48 Ibid., 273.
49 Ibid., 132.
50 'Barack Obama's speech at the Parliament'. *The Indian Express*. 8 November 2010. Available at: http://www.indianexpress.

com/news/barack-obamas-speech-at-the-Parliament/708277/ (accessed on 1 April 2013).

CHAPTER 7

1 The Mahabharata. 'Shanti Parva', 66.44–46.
2 Vikramorvashiya, V.25.
3 Eguchi Katsuhiko. 1994. 'The Secret Strength in Weakness'. In *Matsushita Konosuke: His Life & His Legacy*. Tokyo: PHP Institute, Inc.
4 See 'Sir Dorabji Tata Trust and the Allied Trusts'. Annual report 2012–2013. Available at: https://www.tatatrusts.org/ (accessed on 12 December 2019).
5 R.M. Lala. 2011. *The Art of Effective Giving*, Foreword. Noida: HarperCollins.
6 Ibid., XX.
7 See 'Sir Dorabji Tata Trust and the Allied Trusts'. Annual report 2012–2013.
See also R.M. Lala. 2001. *A Touch of Greatness*, 43. New Delhi: Penguin Books.
8 'My Firm and My Journey'. 2004. CD released by All India Management Association and Excel Books, Ahmedabad, India at 31st National Management Convention of All India Management Association.
9 See 'About Us'. https://www.infosys.com/infosys-foundation/about.html (accessed on 10 December 2019).
10 'Talk on Corporate Social Responsibility' by N.R. Narayana Murthy, chairman emeritus, Infosys, on the occasion of award by Chirmule Pratishthan at Pune on 29 March 2013. Available at: http://csrworld.net/Talk-on-Corporate-Social-Responsibility-by-n-r-narayana-murthy.asp.
11 Ibid.
12 N.R. Narayana Murthy. 2009. *A Better India: A Better World* , 215–218. New Delhi: Penguin.
13 R.M. Lala. 2001. *A Touch of Greatness*, 7. New Delhi: Penguin Books.
14 R.M. Lala. 2011. *The Art of Effective Giving*, 88. Noida: HarperCollins.
15 Ibid., 88–89.
16 Letter written by Dr Devi Prasad Shetty to children in 1997. A copy of it was handed over to C. Panduranga Bhatta by Dr Shetty in a personal meeting.

17 Deepti Chaudhary. 'Narayana Hrudayalaya: Striking a Healthy Balance'. Available at: https://www.fortuneindia.com/venture/striking-a-healthy-balance/103036 (accessed on 5 March 2020).
18 Chaudhary. 'Narayana Hrudayalaya: Striking a Healthy Balance'.
19 Visit https://www.narayanahealth.org/about-us
20 'Dr. Devi Shetty—The Power of Touch'. Available at www.youtube.com/watch?v=e2Cg3_OnCPs
21 Pavithra K. Mehta and Suchitra Shenoy. 2012. *Infinite Vision: How Aravind became the World's Greatest Business Case for Compassion*, 179–190. New Delhi: HarperCollins.
22 Ibid.
23 Ibid.
24 Narayan Ram Acharya. 1990 (Reprinted). *Subhashita Ratna Bhandagara*, 29. New Delhi: Motilal Banarsidass.
25 Kumar Managalam Birla. 2007. 'Values, the driving force'. Available at: https://www.adityabirla.com/media/press-reports/values-the-driving-force.
26 'Microsoft's Bill Gates: Harvard Commencement Speech Transcript'. 8 June 2007. Available at: http://www.networkworld.com/news/2007/060807-gates-commencement.html (accessed on 7 June 2013).
27 Rao Bahadur Col S. Paul Memorial Lecture delivered by E. Sreedharan, CMD of Delhi Metro Rail Corporation on 28 February 2013.
28 Visit https://www.ashoka.org
29 Visit https://www.alokanandaroy.com
Mokshagati is an experimental presentation of a film that is projected as a parallel, on the backdrop to a stage performance on the foreground. Fist performance was staged on 24 March 2013 at Rabindra Sadan, Kolkata and the Indian Institute of Management Calcutta hosted a show of this dance-drama on 2 August 2013.
30 Email received from Alokananda Roy on 29 December 2019.
31 R.P. Masani. 1956. *Role of Wealth in Society*, 6. Bombay: Popular Book Depot.
32 Roger Trapp. 1998. 'Punishments Awaits the Companies of Ill Repute'. *Independent*, 26 July.
33 We reproduce for the benefit of our readers an epilogue by Samir Ranjan Chatterjee, professor at International Management, Curtin University, who had chaired a panel discussion on social issues as business issues in the 2010 seminar on CSR or *Lattice*,

as the seminar is popularly called. The *Lattice* was organised by the participants of the Post-Graduate Program for Executives (PGPEX) of the Indian Institute of Management Calcutta (IIMC 2010–2011) along with the Oil and Natural Gas Corporation Limited (ONGC) and the Management Centre of Human Values (MCHV) in IIMC.
See Pragyan Rath. 2011. 'Social Issue is Business Issue: The New Agenda of Lattice 2010'. *Journal of Human Values*, 17(2), 178–183.

34 C.K. Prahlad. 2005. *The Fortune at the Bottom of the Pyramid: Eradicating Poverty through Profits*. Upper Saddle River, NJ: Wharton School Publishing.

35 Jim Powell. 2003. *Derrida: For Beginners*, 145. Hyderabad: Orient Longman.

36 Ibid., 145.

37 Hart. 1997. 'Beyond Greening: Strategies for a Sustainable World'. *Harvard Business Review*, 75(1), 66–76.

BIBLIOGRAPHY

Aamir Khan's speech. Available at: http://www.youtube.com/watch?v=kycvP6QRXXM (accessed on 13 December 2019).

Altekar, A.S. 1992 (Reprint). *State and Government in ancient India*. New Delhi: Motilal Banarsidass Publishers.

Ananthamurthy, U.R. 2016. *Hindutva or Hind Swaraj*. Translated from Kannada by Keerti Ramachandra with Vivek Shanbhag. Noida: Harper Perennial.

Anderson, Max and Peter Escher. 2010. *The MBA Oath*. USA: Portfolio Penguin.

'Arun Gandhi (1): Nonviolence in the Age of Terrorism.' Available at: http://www.youtube.com/watch?v=PCUWr-ekGyk (accessed on 26 March 2013).

'Arun Gandhi (2): Nonviolence in the Age of Terrorism.' Available at: http://www.youtube.com/watch?v=054N28W9lwk (accessed on 27 March 2013).

'Arun Gandhi (3): Nonviolence in the Age of Terrorism.' Available at: http://www.youtube.com/watch?v=Dj3d66whhuA (accessed on 27 March 2013).

Auden, W.H. 1968/1989. 'Musée des Beaux Arts'. *The Muses' Bower: An Anthology of Verse*. Hyderabad: Orient Longman.

Bajaj, Jitendra and M.D. Srinivas. 1996. *Annam Bahukurvita*. Madras: Centre for Policy Studies.

Basham A.L. 2004. *The Wonder That Was India*. New Delhi: Picador.

Bashir, Ahmad. 2009. *Akbar: The Great Mughul: His New Policy and His New Religion*. New Delhi: Aakar Books.

Bhat, G.K. 1982. *Appointment With Kalidasa*. Ahmedabad: L.D. Institute of Indology, L.D. Series 83.

Bhatta, C. Panduranga. 1997. *Contribution of Karnataka to Sanskrit*. Madras: Institute of Asian Studies.

Bhatta, C. Panduranga. 2001. 'Management of Power: Lessons from the Ramayana'. In *Leadership and Power Ethical Explorations*, edited by S.K. Chakraborty and Pradip Bhattacharya. New Delhi: Oxford University Press.

Bhatta, C. Panduranga. 2002. 'Inclusivism in Religio-Philosophical Systems of India'. *Prajna Vihara: The Journal of Philosophy and Religion*, 2(2).

Bhatta, C. Panduranga. 2003. 'Exploring Eternal Leadership Values and Practices for Organisational Excellence'. *Review of Business Research*, 1(2).

Bhatta, C. Panduranga. 2007. 'The Role of Educational Systems in Shaping Culture: ancient Indian Insights for Contemporary Application'. In *Learning, Teaching and Research in a Borderless World*, edited by Sankaran Manikutty. Macmillan.

Bhatta, C. Panduranga. 2010. 'Environment Friendly Life Styles: A Dialogue with ancient India'. *Decision, Environmental Governance: Ecology, Economics & Policy*, 36(3). Special issue edited by Professor Jayanta Bandyopadhyay.

Bhatta, C. Panduranga. 2015. 'Origin and Evolution of Kingship: An ancient Indian Perspective'. In *Souvenir Book 16th World Sanskrit Conference*, edited by Mangameesukhsiri Sombat. Bangkok: Sanskrit Studies Centre, Sipakorn University.

Bhatta, C. Panduranga. 2017. 'Role of Religion in Conflict Prevention for Social and Environmental Sustainability: Experiential Insights from India'. In *Essays on Sustainability and Management Emerging Perspectives*, edited by Runa Sarkar and Annapurna Shaw. Singapore: Springer Nature.

Bhatta, C. Panduranga. 2018. 'Inclusive Communication for Promoting Peace, Harmony and Religious Pluralism: Insights from Exemplary Political Leaders of ancient, Medieval and Modern India'. *Australia and New Zealand Journal of Social Business, Environment and Sustainability* (ANJSBES), 4(2).

Bhatta, C. Panduranga. 2019. 'Revolutionary Political Ideas of Kauṭilya'. *Felicitation Volume of Prof. C. S. Radhakrishnan, Vishvabharati*, V.

Bhatta, C. Panduranga and Pragyan Rath. 2017. 'Management Centre for Human Values in Indian Institute of Management Calcutta: Human Value Education in Management Institutes'. *AIMS International Journal of Management*.

Bhatta, Vinayaka. 1999. 'Vrddhasamyoga in the Education of the King'. In *Kauitilya's Arthashastra and Social Welfare*, edited by V.N. Jha. New Delhi: Sahitya Akademi.

Bhattacharya, B.K. 1990. 'The Mahabharata – An Epic of Santa Rasa'. In *The Mahabharata Revisited*, edited by R.N. Dandekar. New Delhi: Sahitya Akademi.

Bhatti, J.R. 2007. *Total Quality Leadership*. New Delhi: New Age International Publishers.

Bodhananda, Swami. 2007. *Indian Management and Leadership*. New Delhi: Bluejay Books.

Centre for Bhutan Studies. 2007. *Rethinking Development*. Proceedings of Second International Conference on Gross National Happiness, Thimpu.

Chakraborty, S.K. 1997. *Ethics in Management: Vedantic Perspectives*. Delhi: Oxford University Press.

Chatterjee, Margaret. 2005. *Gandhi and the Challenge of Religious Diversity, Religious Pluralism Revisited*. New Delhi: Promilla & Co.

Chaturvedi, Badrinath. 2006. *The Mahabharata: An Inquiry in the Human Condition*. New Delhi: Orient Longman.

Chaturvedi, Badrinath. 2019. *Dharma: Hinduism and Religions in India*. India: Penguin Viking.

Chaudhary, Deepti. 2019. 'Narayana Hrudayalaya: Striking a Healthy Balance'. Available at: https://www.fortuneindia.com/venture/striking-a-healthy-balance/103036 (accessed on 7 January 2020).

Chowdhury, Hemendu Bikash (Ed). 1997. *Ashoka 2300*. Calcutta: Bauddha Dharmankur Sabha.

Chundar, P.C. (Tr). 1995. *Kautilya's Arthashastra*. Calcutta: The M.P. Birla Foundation.

Cicovcki, Predrag and Kendy Hess (Eds). 2017. *Nonviolence As A Way of Life: History, Theory and Practice*. Volume I and II. New Delhi: Motilal Banarsidass Publishers.

Collier, Dirk. 2011. *The Emperor's Writings: Memories of Akbar the Great*. Delhi: Amaryllis.

Collins, Jim. 2001. *Good to Great: Why Some Companies Make the Leap... and others Don't*. New York: Harper Business.

Coster, Geraldine. 1968. *Yoga and Western Psychology*. New Delhi: Motilal Banarsidass Publishers.

Cotterell, Arthur, Roger Lowe and Ian Shaw. 2009. *Leadership: Lessons from the ancient World*. New Delhi: Wiley.

Coward, Harold. 1996. *Pluralism: Challenge to World Religions*. New Delhi: Indian Book.

Dandekar, R.N. 1979. *Insights Into Hinduism*. New Delhi: Ajanta Publications.

Dandekar, R.N. (Ed). 1990. *The Mahabharata Revisited*. New Delhi: Sahitya Akademi.

Das, Bhagvan. 1990 (Seventh Edition). *Essential Unity of All Religions*. Bombay: Bharatiya Vidya Bhavan.

Das Gupta, Anand (Ed). 2004. *Human Values in Management*. Burlington: Ashgate Publishing Company.

Davies, William Henry. 2013. 'Leisure'. Available at: http://www.davidpbrown.co.uk/poetry/william-henry-davies.html (accessed on 4 May 2013).

'Deep Ecology'. Available at: www.heureka.clara.net/gaia/deep-eco.htm (accessed on 1 April 2013).

Dhammika, S. 1993. *Edicts of King Asoka: An English Rendering*. Kandy, Sri Lanka: The Wheel Publication (Buddhist Publication Society).

'Dr Devi Shetty: The Power of Touch'. Available at: www.youtube.com/watch?v=e2Cg3_OnCPs (accessed on 12 November 2019).

Drekmeier, Charles. 1962. *Kingship and Community in Early India*. USA: Stanford University Press.

Duncan, Ronald (Ed). 2005. *Gandhi: Selected Writings*. Mineola: Dover.

Dwivedi, R.C. (Ed). 1975. *Contribution of Jainism to Indian Culture*. New Delhi: Motilal Banarsidass.

Easwaran, Eknath. 2006. *Gandhi the Man*. Mumbai: Jaico Publishing House.

Engineer, A.A., et al. 2011. *Making Sense of Ayodhya Verdict: Towards Efforts for Peaceful Solution*. New Delhi: Vitasta.

Filliozat, P., S.P. Narang and C. Panduranga Bhatta (Eds). 1994. *Pandit N.R. Bhatt Vol.* New Delhi: Motilal Banarsidass Publishers.

Fort, Timothy L. 2007. *Business Integrity and Peace: Beyond Geopolitical and Disciplinary Boundaries*. Cambridge: Cambridge University Press.

Fort, Timothy L. and Cindy A. Schipani. 2004. *The Role of Business in Fostering Peaceful Societies*. Cambridge: Cambridge University Press.

Gajendragadkar, A.B. 1962. *The Abhijnana Shakuntala*. Surat: The Popular Publishing House.

Gandhi, M.K. 1958–1994. *Collected Works of Mahatma Gandhi*. New Delhi: Publications Division, Government of India, XXIX.

Gandhi, M.K. 1994 (First reprint). *Eprigrams from Gandhiji*. New Delhi: Publications Division, Ministry of Information and Broadcasting, Government of India.

Garde, Ashok R. 2006. *Canakya on Management*. Mumbai: Jaico Publishing House.

Garde, Ashok R. 2013. *Groom Thyself: The Chanakya Way*. Ahmedabad: Ahmedabad Management Association.

Gates, Bill. Transcript of Harvard Commencement Speech, 8 June 2007. Available at: http://www.networkworld.com/news/2007/060807-gates-commencement.html (accessed on 7 June 2013).

Ghosal, U. 1923. *A History of Hindu Political Theories*. London: Oxford University Press.

Gupta, G.P. 2009. *Management by Consciousness*. Pondicherry: Sri Aurobindo Institute of Research in Social Sciences.

Hart, S. 1997. 'Beyond Greening: Strategies for a Sustainable World'. *Harvard Business Review*, 75(1).

Hawley, Jack. 1993. *Reawakening The Spirit In Work: The Power of Dharmic Management*. San Francisco: Berrett-Koehler Publishers.

Hazra, Kanai Lal. 2007. *Asoka as Depicted in His Edicts*. New Delhi: Munshiram Manoharlal Publishers.

Hegde, Suryanarayana. 2005. '*Raja Kalasya Karanam*: In Modern Perspective'. In *The Concept of Rajadharma*, edited by Dr Michael. New Delhi: Sundeep Prakashan.

Heidegger, Martin. 1993. 'The Question Concerning Technology'. In *Basic Writings*, edited by David Krell. New York: HarperCollins.

Heider, John. 1985. *Tao of Leadership*. Aldershoot, England: Hant Wildwood House.

Indra. 1957. *Ideologies of War and Peace in ancient India*. Hoshiarpur: Vishveshvaranand Institute Publications.

Interview with Hammer & Tongs. Available at: http://www.netribution.co.uk/features/interviews/2000/hammer_and_tongs/1.html (accessed on 15 September 2012).

Iyengar, B.K.S. 2005. *The Tree of Yoga*. New Delhi: HarperCollins.

Jackson, Michael. Lyrics to 'Heal the World'. Available at: http://www.lyrics007.com/Michael%20Jackson%20Lyrics/Heal%20The%20World%20Lyrics.html (accessed on 16 September 2012).

Jayaswal, K.P. 2005. *Hindu Polity*. New Delhi: Chaukhamba Sanskrit Pratishthan.

Jha, V.N. (Ed). 1999. *Arthashastra and Social Welfare*. New Delhi: Sahitya Akademi.

Jitatmananda, Swami. 1991. *Holistic Science and Vedanta*. Bombay: Bharatiya Vidya Bhavan.

Joish, Rama M. 1996. *Dharma*. Mumbai: Bharatiya Vidya Bhavan.

Kalam, A.P.J. Abdul. 2002. *Ignited Minds*. New Delhi: Penguin Viking.

Kalam, A.P.J. Abdul. 2012. *Indomitable Spirit*. New Delhi: Rajpal & Sons.

Kamath, M.V. 2007. *Gandhi: A Spiritual Journey*. Mumbai: Indus Source Books.

Katsuhiko, Eguchi. 1994. 'The Secret Strength in Weakness'. In *Matsushita Kanosuke: His Life & His Legacy*. Tokyo: PHP Institute.

Keats, John. 'Ode to a Nightingale'. Available at: http://www.bartleby.com/126/40.html (accessed on 4 May 2013).

Keats, John. 'To Autumn'. Available at: http://www.potw.org/archive/potw279.html (accessed on 4 May 2013).

Kennedy, Vans. 1820. 'Some Notices Respecting the Religion Introduced by Akbar'. *Transactions of the Literary Society of Bombay*, II, Chapter XI.

Khan, Iqtidar Alam. 2011. 'Akbar's Personality Traits and World Outlook: A Critical Reappraisal'. In *Akbar and His India*, edited by Habib Irfan. New Delhi: Oxford India Paperbacks.

Khan, S.M. 2016. *The People's President, APJ Abdul Kalam*. New Delhi: Bloomsbury India.

Khoshoo, T.N. 1995 *Mahatma Gandhi: An Apostle of Applied Human Ecology*. New Delhi: Tata Energy Research Institute.

Kim, Min-Sun. 2002. *Non-Western Perspectives on Human Communication*. New Delhi: Sage Publications.

Kouzes, James M. and Barry Z. Posner. 2017 (Reprint). *Leadership Challenge: How to Make Extraordinary Things Happen in Organisations*. New Delhi: Wiley India.

Kripalani, Krishna (Ed). 1960. *All Men are Brothers* (Life & Thoughts of Mahatma Gandhi as Told in His Own Words). Ahmedabad: Navajivan Trust. Available at: http://www.mkgandhi.org/amabrothers/chap04.htm.

Krishna, G.R. 1999. *Indian Ethos for Modern Management*. New Delhi: UBS Publishers Distributors Ltd.

Krishnamurti, J. 2000. *Reflections on the Self*. New Delhi: Bluejay Books.

Lahiri, Nayanjot. 2018. *Ashoka in ancient India*. Ranikhet: Permanent Black.

Lala, R.M. 2001. *A Touch of Greatness: Encountering the Eminent*. New Delhi: Penguin Books.

Lala, R.M. 2011. *The Art of Effective Giving*. Noida: HarperCollins.

Lennon, John. Lyrics to 'Imagine'. Available at: http://www.lyrics007.com/John%20Lennon%20Lyrics/Imagine%20Lyrics.html (accessed on 19 September 2012).

Lévi-Strauss, Claude. 1955. 'The Structural Study of Myth'. *The Journal of American Folklore*. 68(270).

Lionel, Giles. 1910. *The Saying of Confucius: A New Translation of the Greater Part of the Confucian Analects*. London: E.P. Dutton And Company.

Mahabubani, Kishore. 2004. *Can Asians Think? Understanding the Divide between East and West*. New Delhi: Penguin Books.

Mahadevan, B. 2015. *Pearls of Wisdom from Bhagavad Gita*. Bangalore: Sumati Samskriti Trust.

Manikutty, S. and Sampat P. Singh. 2015. *The Essence of Leadership: Explorations from Literature*. India: Bloomsbury.

Masani, R.P. 1956. *Role of Wealth in Society*. Bombay: Popular Book Depot.

Mashelkar, Raghunath (Ed). 2010. *Timeless Inspirator: Reliving Gandhi*. Pune: Sakal Papers.

Mehta, Pavithra K. and Suchitra Shenoy. 2012. *Infinite Vision: How Aravind became the World's Greatest Business Case for Compassion*. New Delhi: HarperCollins.

Misra, Vidya Niwas. 1992. 'Man, Nature and the Poet'. *Creativity and Environment*. New Delhi: Sahitya Akademi.

Mookerji, Radhakumud. 1995. *Asoka*. New Delhi: Motilal Banarsidass Publishers.

Moosvi, Shireen. 1994. *Episodes in the Life of Akbar: Contemporary Records and Reminiscences*. Delhi: National Book Trust.

Mukherjee, Tarapada and Irfan Habib. 1987. 'Akbar and the Temples of Mathura and its Environs'. Proceedings of Indian Historical Congress, 48th Session, Goa.

Muller, F. Max. 1991. *India: What can it Teach Us?* New Delhi: Munshiram Manoharlal Publishers.

Murthy, H.V. Narasimha. 2005. 'Concept of Ramarajya and its Relevance'. In *The Concept of Rajadharama*, edited by Dr Michael. New Delhi: Sundeep Prakashan.

Murthy, N.R. Narayana. 2009. *A Better India: A Better World*. New Delhi: Penguin.

Naganathan, G. 2004. *Ecological Spirituality: Hindu Scriptural Perspectives*. New Delhi: New Age Books.

Nair, Keshavan. 1997. *A Higher Standard of Leadership: Lessons from the Life of Gandhi*. San Francico: Berrett-Koehler Publishers.

Nakamura, Hajime. 1991. *Ways of Thinking of Eastern Peoples*. New Delhi: Motilal Banarsidass Publishers.

Nakamura, Hajime. 1992. *A Comparative History of Ideas*. New Delhi: Motilal Banarsidass Publishers.

'Native American Buffalo Mythology'. Available at: http://www.native-languages.org/legends-buffalo.htm (accessed on 17 May 2013).

Nelson, Jane. 2000. *The Business of Peace: The Private Sector as a Partner in Conflict Prevention and Resolution*. Prince of Wales Business Leaders Forum.

Nolan, Jonathan and Christopher Nolan. Script of *The Dark Knight*. Available at: http://www.joblo.com/scripts/The_Dark_Knight.pdf (accessed on 8 October 2012).

Plato. 1976. *Republic*. Translated by A.D. Lindsay. London: J.M. Dent & Sons.

Powell, Jim. 2003. *Derrida: For Beginners*. Hyderabad: Orient Longman.

Powell, Melissa and Donna Chung. 2010. *Doing Business While Advancing Peace and Development*. New York: United Nations Global Compact.

Prahlad, C.K. 2005. *The Fortune at the Bottom of the Pyramid: Eradicating Poverty through Profits*. Upper Saddle River, NJ: Wharton School Publishing.

Prasad, Pushpa. 2011. 'Akbar and the Jains'. In *Akbar and his India*, edited by Habib Irfan. New Delhi: Oxford University Press.

Prime, Ranchor. 1994. *Hinduism and Ecology: Seeds of Truth*. New Delhi: Motilal Banarsidass Publishers.

Raghavan, V. 1976. *Two Brothers, Rama and Lakshmana*. Madras: Ramayana Printing Works.

Rajendran, C. 2005. 'Rajadharma According to the Mahabharata'. In *The Concept of Rajadharma*, edited by Dr Michael. New Delhi: Sundeep Prakashan.

Rangarajan, L.N. 1992. *Kauṭilya's Arthaśāstra*. New Delhi: Penguin Books.

Rath, Pragyan. 2011. '"Social Issue is Business Issue": The New Agenda of Lattice 2010'. *Journal of Human Values*, 17(2).

Rath, Pragyan. 2011. *The 'I' and the 'Eye': The Verbal and the Visual in Post-Renaissance Western Aesthetics*. Newcastle, UK: Cambridge Scholars Publishing.

Rich, Bruce. 2010. *To Uphold the World: A Call for a New Global Ethic from ancient India*. Boston: Beacon.

Rousseau, Jean-Jacques. 1754. 'The Second Part'. *A Discourse*. Maintained by John Roland of the Constitution Society. Available at: http://www.constitution.org/jjr/ineq_04.htm (accessed on 28 November 2011/18 September 2012).

Roychoudhury, M.L. 1941. *The Din-i-llahi*. Calcutta: University of Calcutta.

Saeed, Ismael M., et al. 2013. 'The Bird Symbol in English Romantic and Post-Romantic Poetry'. Available at: http://www.ircoedu.uobaghdad.edu.iq/uploads/42/The%20Bird%20Symbol-Amended-%20Final.pdf (accessed on 23 June 2014).

Saiyidain, K.G. 1994. *Significance of Gandhi As a Man and Thinker*. New Delhi: Publications Division, Ministry of Information and Broadcasting, Government of India.

Sen, Shekhar. 2001. 'Management of Power in ancient Indian Literature'. In *Leadership and Power Ethical Explorations*, edited by Chakraborty, S.K, and Pradip Bhattacharya, New Delhi: Oxford University Press

Singh, G.P, and Premananda Sigh, 2008, *Kingship in ancient India: Genesis and Growth*.New Delhi: Akansha Publishing House.

Sharma, G.D. 2008. *Excellence in Management*. New Delhi: Rupa & Co.

Sharma, Subhash. 1996. *Management In New Age: Western Windows Eastern Doors* . New Delhi: New Age International.

Shelley, P. B. 'Ode to the West Wind'. Available at: http://www.bartleby.com/106/275.html (accessed on 4 May 2013).

Shelley, P.B. 'Ozymandias'. Available at: http://www.online-literature.com/shelley_percy/672/ (accessed on 15 September 2012).

Shōtoku, Prince. 'Seventeen-Article Constitution'. Article X. Available at: http://www.koreanhistoryproject.org/Ket/C03/tp/TP0301c.htm (accessed on 6 June 2013).

Shourie, Arun. 2017. *Two Saints: Speculations Around and About Ramakrishna Paramahamsa and Ramana Maharishi*. Noida: HarperCollins.

Shukla, A. 2013. 'Impact of Terrorism on Social, Economic and Legal Structure of the Countries Obstacle to Global Peace [*sic*]'. Institute of Management Studies, Bareilly, 25 March. Available at: http://www.upscportal.com/civilservices/mag/vol-3/article/Imapct-Of-Terrorism (accessed on 8 September 2019).

Sircar, D.C. 1976 *Inscriptions of Ashoka*. New Delhi: Publications Division, Government of India.

Sorokin, P.A. and Lunden, W.A. 1994. *Power and Morality*. Bombay: Bharatiya Vidya Bhavan.

Sreedharan, E. 2013. Col S. Paul Memorial Lecture delivered on 28 February.

Sri Aurobindo. 1927. *The Mother*. Available at: https://www.aurobindo.ru/workings/sa/37_32/0010_e.htm (accessed on 7 March 2020).

Summary of Oscar Wilde's 'The Nightingale And The Rose'. Available at: http://www.enotes.com/homework-help/what-summary-nightingale-rose-by-oscar-wilde-64507 (accessed on 4 May 2013).

Suu Kyi, Aung San. 1995. *Freedom From Fear*. London: Penguin Books.

Swami Vivekananda. 2006. *Complete Works of Swami Vivekananda*. Kolkata: Advaita Ashrama.

Swami Vivekananda. 2016. *Swami Vivekananda: On Himself*. Kolkata: Advaita Ashrama.

The Deccan Chronicle. 2013. 'Muslim-majority Indonesia gifts Saraswati statue to US'. Available at: http://www.deccanchronicle.com/130609/news-world/article/muslim-majority-indonesia-gifts-saraswati-statue-us (accessed on 10 June 2013).

The Dalai Lama. 2012. 'A Human Approach to World Peace'. *Journal of Human Values*, 18(2).

The Dalai Lama. 2012. *Beyond Religion: Ethics for a Whole World*. New Delhi: HarperCollins.

The Indian Express. 2010. 'Barack Obama's speech at the Parliament'. *The Indian Express*, 8 November. Available at: http://www.indianexpress.com/news/barack-obamas-speech-at-the-parliament/708277/ (accessed on 1 April 2013).

Trapp, Roger. 1998. 'Punishments awaits the Companies of Ill Repute'. *Independent*, 26 July.

Tully, Mark. 2007. *India's Unending Journey: Finding Balance in a Time of Change*. London: Rider.

Vajpeyi, Ananya. 2012. *Righteous Republic: The Political Foundations of Modern India*. London: Harvard University Press.

Varma, Pavan K. 2018. *Adi Shankaracharya: Hinduism's Greatest Thinker*. Chennai: Tranquebar Press.

Varma, Ravindra. 2006. *The Spiritual Perceptions of Mahatma Gandhi*. New Delhi: Rupa & Co.

Watson, Franklin. 2013. *Let Me Finish People: Thoughts and Opinion*. US: Watson.

Wilson, H.H. 1824. 'Account of the Religious Innovations attempted by Akbar'. *Quarterly Oriental Magazine*, I.

Winfrey, Oprah. Speech at the 54th Emmy Awards. Available at: http://www.famous-speeches-and-speech-topics.info/famous-speeches-by-women/oprah-winfrey-speech.htm (accessed on 15 September 2012).

Wordsworth, William. 'Daffodils'. Available at: http://www.poemhunter.com/poem/daffodils/ (accessed on 4 May 2013).

Yardi, M.R. 1996. *The Yoga of Patanjali*. Poona: Bhandarkar Oriental Research Institute.

INDEX

ABOUT THE AUTHORS

Dr C. Panduranga Bhatta, former professor at the Indian Institute of Management (IIM) Calcutta, has been a prolific Indologist with a career spanning over four decades. He has taught at postgraduate and doctoral levels at IIM Calcutta for two decades in the area of leadership, creativity and ethics. He was the founder coordinator of Business Ethics and Communication Group, coordinator of Management Centre for Human Values and the editor of the *Journal of Human Values* published by Sage Publications. He is also the founder coordinator of Samanvaya Academy for Excellence (samanvaya.net).

He has been a leading consultant and contributor to several research projects undertaken by prestigious institutions in India and abroad. Books authored by him include *Dice-Play in Sanskrit Literature* (1985), *Origin and Genesis of Chess* (1994), *Contribution of Karnataka to Sanskrit* (1997) and *Introduction to Sanskrit Poetics* (2020). He has also published many research articles related to leadership, Indology, human values, creativity and innovation, and organisational excellence through leadership in reputed journals in India and abroad.

He has been honoured with a gold medal by the Association of Indian Management Schools for securing the prestigious AIMS-ICFAI Best Teacher Award, 2011. He was deputed to ICCR Chair Professor at Silpakorn University, Bangkok, for two academic years by the Ministry of External Affairs, Government of India. His vast experience of research and teaching and knowledge of Indian ethos and theories of global leadership, needs and desires provide a whole new experience on leadership.

Dr Pragyan Rath, currently teaching Communications at IIM Calcutta, has worked in a more niche discipline (a virgin area for management studies in particular) called ekphrasis (verbal description of graphic designs) that has been emerging as a major academic concern in literary studies in the Western academia for critical humanities and word-image academia. She has been studying critical theory for more than a decade and has an immediate interest in deconstruction as a critical tool of analysis. She completed her master's in English (MA) and master's in Philosophy [MPhil (English)] from the Central Institute of English and Foreign Languages (CIEFL), Hyderabad, and her doctoral in English (PhD) from the Department of Humanities and Social Sciences of IIT Bombay. She is working on developing a corporate concept called the narrative of things. She is a prolific writer and along with contributing to journals, she has been a part of several book projects, including *Communication Strategies for Corporate Leaders: Implications for the Global World* (Routledge 2018); *Corporate Communication* (Cengage 2018), *New Insights into Prognostic Data Analytics in Corporate Communication* (Business Expert Press 2020).